THE UNKNOWN ERIC

A SELECTION OF DOCUMENTS FOR THE GENERAL LIBRARY

Joseph Gerald Drazan

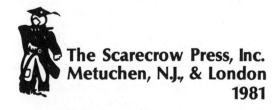

The Scarecrow Press, Inc.
Metuchen, N.J., & London
1981

Library of Congress Cataloging in Publication Data

Drazan, Joseph Gerald, 1943-
    The unknown ERIC.

    Includes indexes.
    1. United States--Government publications--
Bibliography--Catalogs. 2. Educational Resources
Information Center--Catalogs. I. Educational
Resources Information Center. II. Title.
Z1223.Z7D73 [J83]   015.73   80-25975
ISBN 0-8108-1402-1

Once again
for
Daniel Joseph
and
Jennie Rebecca

PREFACE

This bibliography brings to light over five hundred general-interest publications available from ERIC. This information is virtually lost to most libraries, since it is buried in the great mass of educational literature from which this list is extracted. Heretofore, it generally has been available only to the largest public libraries and academic institutions through their subscriptions to Resources in Education. My intent in this book is to make widely known certain documents that should have a broad appeal.

The Educational Resources Information Center (ERIC) of the National Institute of Education, Department of Health, Education, and Welfare, is a national information system for gathering, abstracting, indexing, storing, and disseminating printed materials, mostly otherwise unavailable, that are associated with the field of education. However, over the years several thousand documents have crept into the system that are only remotely, or seemingly not at all, related to the discipline of education. It is from these few thousands of general-interest reports and papers that I have constructed this bibliography.

Resources in Education (formerly Research in Education, which began in 1966) is the ERIC announcement journal from which this bibliography has been selected. Every title in RIE from January 1974 through December 1979 was scanned; the resulting list was collected according to the following criteria: the document should have a wide appeal outside the area of education; it should be interesting, significant, potentially useful, or timely; it must be available from ERIC in hard copy in addition to microfiche; it should be at least twenty pages in length; and it should not be announced in RIE as available from the Government Printing Office, Washington, DC, or be available from some commercial publisher.

Some comments on these criteria: for the smaller public libraries and for the individual, I wanted a list that could be obtained in paper-copy format for their convenience, since many documents are for sale in microfiche only or not at all from ERIC; I wanted a list of items that are more than sketchy treatments, since many documents announced of the over 175,000 indexed are only five, eight, or twelve pages (a very few in this bibliography are under twenty pages and were included due to their significance); publications that

v

are announced as available from the GPO are excluded since these are well indexed and distributed otherwise, as are most commercial publications that are indexed in RIE.

The 516 items in this book have been grouped in sixteen very general subject categories followed by a large miscellaneous section. Therefore, a most important part of the book is the detailed subject index. It is constructed from ERIC descriptors, modifications of ERIC descriptors, and appropriate title keywords to enhance its usefulness.

How to Order the Documents

The reports cited in this bibliography may be ordered from ERIC Document Reproduction Service, PO Box 190, Arlington, VA 22210. The six-digit "ED" number given for each item must be included in the order. Authorized purchase orders will be accepted. As of January 1980, the price schedule for paper copies can be determined by this chart:

Number of Pages	Price
1 - 25	$1.82
26 - 50	3.32
51 - 75	4.82
76 -100	6.32
Each additional 25 pages	1.50

If a microfiche edition is desired, it costs only $.83 for up to a 480-page document.

Joseph Drazan
Whitman College
Walla Walla, Washington

CONTENTS

1.
CHILDREN
AND
YOUTH

1.   Child welfare in 25 states; an overview.   National Center for
        Child Advocacy, DHEW, 1976.   213p.   ED 144678.
        This overview presents a summary of the major findings
of a 25-state survey of child welfare service delivery systems, as
studied by Peat, Marwick, Mitchell & Co. in association with the
Child Welfare League of America (CWLA) during the period of November 1975 through February 1976.   The initial products of the
survey were 25 state profiles; these were analyzed for the strengths,
weaknesses, and exemplary features of their delivery systems as
well as to identify major issues in state child welfare agencies.   The
findings that grew out of the analysis form the basis of this overview.
Chapter I includes a description of the child welfare delivery systems project, a description of the survey, and a discussion of the
development and analysis of the 25 state profiles by clustered states.
Chapter II is a cross-sectional report of administrative form, demographic and economic environment, philosophy and values, goals and
priorities, organization, needs assessment, planning and decision
making, financing, program resource mobilization, management services, outreach, client reception and referral, diagnosis and service
plan development, service delivery, data collection and reporting,
and evaluation.   An analysis of delivery system characteristics by
clustered states is contained in an appendix.

2.   Child welfare strategy in the coming years, by Alfred Kadushin.
        Washington, DC, Children's Bureau, DHEW, 1978.   460p.
        ED 165896.
        This collection of policy papers by a dozen national ex-
perts in subject areas related to child welfare is designed to assist
public and voluntary agency program directors in their efforts to update current programs or to design new ones.   Sequentially the chapters: (1) set a framework for the following papers, (2) examine the
provision of foster care to children as a decision making system,
(3) provide analytic reference points about institutional care of children and use them for the projection of program goals, (4) examine
change in the roles of the key actors in the adoption system, (5)
analyze problems in the implementation of child welfare services,
(6) develop a perspective on adolescent pregnancy and parenthood,

1

(7) examine the functions and other dimensions of the child welfare field, (8) describe the national problem of adolescent status offenders and advocate a program outside of the juvenile justice system, (9) develop plans for children of divorce, (10) advocate reforms to protect the rights of neglected children and to restrict state regulation of family relationships, (11) provide an overview of problems of the Spanish speaking/surnamed poor and advocate appropriate programs, and (12) present reasons for developing a federal level, comprehensive, cohesive family policy.

3.   Directory of child advocacy programs.   Washington, DC, Administration for Children, Youth, Families, DHEW, 1978. 104p.   ED 165913.
       This directory lists 107 child advocacy programs in 37 states, the District of Columbia and the Virgin Islands.   Each entry includes project title, address, telephone number, contact person, a statement of purpose and a summary of current advocacy activities. Entries are indexed under the following terms: adolescent parenthood, appropriations/funding, child abuse and neglect, child care/day care, child labor, child welfare, coalitions, community involvement, comprehensive coordinated planning, deinstitutionalization, delivery of services, developmental disabilities, developing monitoring and assessment instruments, drugs, early periodic screening diagnosis and treatment, foster care, health care, individual advocacy, juvenile justice, lead poisoning, legislative action, mental health, Native Americans, parent education, public education, recreation, rights of children, state-wide child advocacy structure, training advocates, workshop on data collecting and planning, and youth.

4.   Parent's guide to childhood immunization.   Atlanta, GA, Center for Disease Control, October 1977.   27p.   ED 154923.
       This booklet addressed to parents provides information on seven serious childhood diseases and the vaccines that can provide protection for each.   A description of the causes, symptoms, natural course and possible complications of each of the seven diseases--measles, polio, rubella or German measles, mumps, diptheria, pertussis or whooping cough, and tetanus--is followed by information on appropriate vaccination.   The possible side effects of vaccination for each disease are dealt with in some detail.   A suggested immunization schedule is included.

5.   Research involving children; report and recommendations. Washington, DC, Commission for the Protection of Human Subjects of Biomedical and Behavioral Research, 1977. 168p.   ED 146763.
       Presented are the report and recommendations of the National Commission for the Protection of Human Subjects of Biomedical and Behavioral Research regarding the involvement of children in research, with particular emphasis on P. L. 93-348.   Following an introductory section, containing definitions of terms relevant to the report, are 10 recommendations along with comments which cover such areas as criteria for approving research involving children, parental or guardian permission, and guidelines for children

who are wards of the state. Nine chapters address the following
issues: reasons why children are involved as research subjects
(which include the lack of an alternative population); the nature and
extent of research involving children; survey of review and consent
procedures; views presented at public hearings; a psychological perspective on the issue; legal issues; ethical issues; and statements of
members of the Commission regarding the recommendations.

6.   Nutrient requirements in adolescence, by John McKigney and
         Hamish Munro. Bethesda, MD, National Institutes of
         Health, 1975. 17p. ED 115590.
         It is important to understand the nutrient requirements
and the significance of nutrition both in pubescence and adolescence.
The pubescent growth spurt is characterized by an increase in body
size and a change in proportion of different tissues. Both of these
factors are of great nutritional importance, since there is reason to
believe that the growth spurt is sensitive to nutrient deprivation, although our knowledge of the requirements of adolescents for various
nutrients is incomplete. The Food and Nutrition Board of the U.S.
Academy of Sciences has published successive issues of its "Recommended Dietary Allowances (RDA). "The Ten-State Nutrition Survey
(1968-70)," which measured food intake of lower income families in
the United States, shows deficits among adolescents when compared
with the RDA. The dietary inadequacies of adolescents may sometimes be accentuated by situations causing extra demands for nutrients, such as pregnancy, injuries, and involvement in sports. Excessive intake of nutrients also occurs during adolescence; one of the
most common conditions due to an imbalance between food intake and
expenditure is obesity. Excessive intake of dietary fat, notably sat-
urated fat, has been associated with elevated blood cholesterol levels.
Studies have indicated that the onset of both atherosclerosis and obesity may well occur during childhood, and that the most appropriate
time to apply preventative measures and to provide nutritional education is during adolescence.

7.   The Migrant child, by Manuel C. Reyes. 1977. 25p.
         ED 162803.
         A migrant child is one who has moved with his family
from one school district to another during the preceding 12 months
so that a parent or other immediate family member might secure
employment in agricultural or fishery activity. In California, the
92,000 migrants living in 48 of the state's 58 counties include Chicanos, Mexican Americans, Tejanos, Mejicanos, Blacks, Native
Americans, Filipinos, Anglos, East Indians, Vietnamese, Portuguese,
and others. Educational needs of migrant children are tied to inadequate living conditions; interrupted education; health and nutritional
defects; and lack of appreciation of migrant problems, identification
with successful adult role models from their ethnic background, motivation to complete high school, personal, vocational, and family
guidance, communication, common experiences, relevant opportunities, recognition of potential and creativity, and assistance from
the community at large. Self-image may be improved by cross-
cultural education and teaching about events and contributions made

to society by persons of different ethnic backgrounds, i. e. , American Indian Day, Mexican Independence Day, Vietnamese Day, Dr. Charles R. Drew, Elijah McCoy, and Roy Wilkins.

8.   Evaluation of prekindergarten head start, by Sherran Toll.
        Philadelphia, School District Office of Research and Eval-
        uation, July 1976.   111p.   ED 132170.
        The Philadelphia Prekindergarten Head Start program is
a child development program for three and four-year-old children
from low income families which stresses an interacting and multidisciplinary attempt to improve the child's physical and emotional
health, his family relationships, and his abilities to function better
as a person.   The program was designed from the beginning to implement five different early childhood educational models (Bank Street,
Behavior Analysis, Montessori, Open Classroom, and Responsive
Learning).   The 1975-1976 evaluation activities for Philadelphia's
Prekindergarten Head Start program continued to focus on the major
goals for children.   There was found to be some range in practices
among centers in terms of (1) extent of model implementation, (2)
classroom differences within a model, (3) number of parent volunteers, (4) grouping practices, and (5) provisioning.   Observation data
yielding the above information are summarized according to model
and across the total program.   The Denver Developmental Screening
Test (D. D. S. T.) was administered during October and April to 82%
and 84% of the population respectively.   In April only 1. 8% of the
population was identified as having a developmental delay as defined
by the D. D. S. T. , a decrease of about 40% from the Fall administration.   While Prekindergarten Head Start children are from families
of low socio-economic status, the April D. D. S. T. results confirmed,
as was the case in 1974-1975, that the population screened had improved after a year of program participation so that there were far
fewer children "at risk" than were found in the norming population.

9.   Head Start program performance standards.   Washington, DC,
        Office of Child Development, DHEW, July 1975.   70p.
        ED 122936.
        This manual presents the Project Head Start program
goals and performance standards in the areas of education, health
and nutrition services, social services, and parent involvement.   A
short discussion of general Head Start goals, performance standard
development, implementation, and enforcement is included.   Each
performance standard is accompanied by guidance material which provides further information about the purpose of the standard and the
methods and procedures for implementation.   Appendices provide
statements of policy concerning the development and implementation
of program design variations for local Head Start programs as well
as policy for the involvement of parents of Head Start children.

10.   How can I help my child; an answer for parents of young chil-
        dren.   Jacksonville, FL, Duval County School Board,
        November 1974.   54p.   ED 115013.
        Provided are suggestions and activities to be used by
parents in working with their preschool children.   Ten suggestions

deal with questions such as how much time should be spent, how to praise the child, and what to do if the child misuses the materials. Specific instructions are given for 15 activities such as puppets, puzzles, teaching songs, and playing matching games. Instructions include why the activity is important to the child, what materials are needed and how to make them, and how to use the activity over a period of days. Also included are a list of 24 common household items that can be used to help a child and several songs, rhymes and fingerplays.

11. Success begins in the cradle; a curriculum for infants and toddlers in daycare, by Sylvia Johnson. Atlanta, GA, Georgia Appalachian Child Care Project, 1973. 189p. ED 114161.
A Piagetian day care curriculum for infants and toddlers is presented. Six chapters, divided by developmental stage from birth to 24 months of age, discuss developmental characteristics of the child, suggest tasks for the caregiver to enhance social/emotional growth and language development, and describe appropriate games and activities. Additional color-coded sections provide fine and gross motor activities (including art and music) for groups of children, sample schedules and room arrangements, and checklists of developmental norms for use in evaluation. An appendix contains songs, fingerplays, poems, flannel stories, record lists, and book lists.

12. Redevelopment of disadvantaged youth: the U.S.A. experience, by A. Harvey Passow. August 1978. 36p. ED 160685.
Since the early 1960s, there has been an outpouring of research and a mounting of programs and projects dealing with compensatory education for the disadvantaged. Despite continued debate over what constitutes compensatory education, many programs for the educationally disadvantaged share common characteristics. Three of the largest Federally sponsored programs--Head Start, Follow Through, and the Elementary and Secondary Education Act (ESEA) Title I, focus on early childhood education. Two Federally funded programs, Upward Bound and Job Corps, are specifically aimed at adolescents and young adults. Studies and surveys of these and other compensatory programs are being conducted by the National Institute of Education (NIE) because earlier evaluations, especially of Title I (ESEA), have proven to be unsatisfactory. The NIE study consists of 35 research projects which deal with areas of funds allocation, compensatory services, student development, and administration. Another NIE study is examining the effectiveness of reading and mathematics instruction provided for compensatory education students. The emphases of compensatory programs and the foci and conclusions of their evaluations are reviewed in this paper.

13. What Head Start means to families, by Ann O'Keefe. Washington, DC, Administration for Children Youth and Families, DHEW, August 1978. 72p. ED 161525.

This paper describes Head Start services to parents and families involved in the Head Start program, what the program impact has been on these families, and the goals, services, and accomplishments of other family-focused Head Start programs. There are 14 sections, most of them brief. The sections discuss sources of data information, Project Head Start Performance Standards, and ways parents contribute to the functioning of the program as decision-makers, home educators and employees. Program-community relations, service benefits to handicapped children and their parents, and gains parents receive from participating in the program are noted. Also described briefly are post Head Start parent activities in the school and community. An extensive review of the historical impact of the program on parents and families is also presented and documented with research study results. The last section focuses on 3 special Head Start demonstration programs (Parent Child Centers, Home Start, and the Child and Family Resource Program).

14. Concept paper on the effects of the physical environment on day care, by Elizabeth Prescott and Thomas G. David. July 1976. 159p. ED 156356.

This paper presents a discussion of the effect of the physical environment on children receiving day care services. Various dimensions of the physical environment which may affect the well-being of infants, preschool and school age children in group or family day care settings are examined. The focus is on the overall well-being and development of children rather than on questions of health and safety. Included in the review are current practices in designing and licensing day care settings, recommendations intended to improve the quality of the day care environment, and current research evidence which suggests ways in which the Physical environment affects the behavior and development of children as well as the behavior of the adults involved in their care. Also included is a discussion of the usefulness of the Federal Interagency Day Care Requirements (FIDCR) as a means to control the quality of the physical environment in day care programs. These issues are examined under six major headings: indoor space, outdoor areas, play equipment, questions of organization and program, contextual constraints, and recommendations for changes in the FIDCR as they relate to the physical environment.

15. A Practical guide for day care personnel; let the sun shine in, by John L. DeLorey, Jr., and Marjorie E. Cahn. Washington, DC, Day Care and Child Development Council of America, Inc., 1977. 157p. ED 142315.

This handbook of practical guidelines for daily life in day care is addressed to caregivers, teachers, directors, and students who want to provide high quality care for children. Separate sections are devoted to (1) day care as a daily living experience; (2) the parent-caregiver relationship; (3) priorities for health and safety, staff communication and knowledge of children and their needs; (4) program elements of curriculum, materials, room ar-

rangement, communications and daily schedules; and (5) specific aspects of safety, health and nutrition, as they relate to daily occur-
rences.   Various types of parent-caregiver contact recommended
include: daily, on-going communication; periodic individual-parent
conferences; regularly scheduled group meetings; and occasional
parent participation.   The guidelines on program elements are elabo-
rated in detail.

16.   Choosing a day care home; a parent checklist and resource
         directory.   Chicago, Roosevelt University, October 1978.
         30p. ED 168676.
         This booklet offers guidelines for parents on selecting a
good quality day care home.   Lists of questions are provided to
help parents judge the physical setting, the learning activities, the
caregiver, meals served and the safety of the day care home.   Also
discussed are advantages of family day care, things to consider
when making arrangements for child care, and how to withdraw from
an arrangement if a mistake is made.   A parent directory listing
a variety of resources for parents with young children is provided.

17.   Serving children and their families; the role of the child care
         center, by John W. Hollomon.   Austin, TX, Texas State
         Department of Public Welfare, 1976.   44p.   ED 131950.
         Details the role of the child care center in the provision
of social services to children and their families and argues that the
need for such services is no longer debatable, but rather the need
to communicate and deliver services is the issue.   The essay ex-
plicates the role of the child care center in terms of what it means
to provide comprehensive child care, discusses efforts made to deal
with this role, and the urgency of the need to communicate and deliver services.   A job description is provided delineating the role
of the social services specialist as related to task-performance
criteria and responsibilities, required qualifications, characteristics,
and abilities and strengths, including working with center staff, parents, and social service agencies.   The appendix lists a variety of
human service sources to be found in the local community, with the
intent of motivating child care providers to provide existing services
to children and their families.

18.   Choosing child care; a guide for parents, by Stevanne Auerbach
         and Linda Freedman.   San Francisco, Parents and Child
         Care Resources, 1976.   80p.   ED 125737.
         This booklet, designed for working parents, presents a
step-by-step process for locating and making informed choices concerning child care alternatives.   Included are suggestions for finding babysitters, child care centers, and family day care homes
which satisfy extensive checklists of physical, social, emotional,
and learning environment criteria.   The checklists provide a means
of evaluating the child care environment, staff-child relationships,
and activities offered in each child care situation.   In addition, suggestions are provided for: (1) contacting community child care re-

sources, (2) budgeting for child care, (3) preparing the child for child care center or family day care home, and (4) parent participation in the child care program. A list of additional reading resources for parents is also included.

19. A Good beginning for babies; guidelines for group care, by Anne Willis. Washington, DC, National Association for the Education of Young Children, 1975. 200p. ED 122917.

   This book presents principles, guidelines, and procedures for establishing and maintaining a quality group care environment (either family- or center-based) for infants in the first year of life. The following areas are covered: (1) a general statement of program goals, (2) relationships with families, (3) program and staff organization, (4) a typcial day in the nursery from the perspective of the caregiver, (5) play and learning, (6) management of crying and the relief of distress, (7) routine caregiving, with emphasis on caregiver-infant interaction during feeding, diapering and naptime, (9) physical space and equipment, and (10) health and safety. Included are lists of resources related to infant care and appendices containing sample information sheets and daily records, plus an outline of selected developmental landmarks during an infant's first two years of life.

20. Child maltreatment in the United States; a cry for help and organizational response, by Saad Nagi. Columbus, OH, Mershon Center, Ohio State University, 1976. 231p. ED 126645.

   Reported are the research results from a national child maltreatment study planned around three aspects--intensive interviews with individuals in the field, a survey of organizations and programs related to child abuse and neglect, and the formulation of recommendations for policy and program planning. Covered in Chapter 1 are the background and scope of the work, methodological approaches, attributes of respondents, and the interview situation. Reviewed in Chapter 2 are the rights of children and the role of the state, the status of knowledge and technology in the field, incompatibilities between punitive and therapeutic approaches, conflicts within professional roles, and the protection of organizational and professional domains. The third chapter on the magnitude of the problem and epidemiological patterns provides estimated child abuse incidence statistics. The presentation of findings on the structure and performance of programs concerned with child abuse and neglect is organized in Chapter 4 around the following functional categories: identification and reporting, response to reporting, availability and provision of services, legal intervention and the problems of custody and placement, decision-making, and the coordination of programs. Summarized in the final chapter are goals for child maltreatment programs considered in planning the study, evaluative statements based on study findings, and recommendations for future programming.

21. Child abuse and neglect; a school community resource book,
by I. Lorraine Davis and others. Madison, Wisconsin
State Department of Public Instruction, 1977. 171p.
ED 152041.

The school cummunity resource book on child abuse and
neglect is the result of a 12-month project to aid Wisconsin school
districts in developing community teams who would in turn work with
the schools in setting up a policy and procedure concerned with the
identification, reporting, referral, and prevention of child abuse/
neglect. Sections provide information on the following topics: introductory information (including project goals, rationale for school
involvement, and a list of participants); legal responsibilities (including an outline of the Wisconsin Abused Child Law); task definition and organization of community teams; Parents Anonymous, a
national organization with local chapters to provide supportive help
to parents; formats for workshops and inservice sessions; key regional, state, and national resource people and agencies; audiovisual
materials and publications on child abuse and neglect; and policies
of participating school districts. Appended are sample referral forms,
brief descriptions of reporting procedures, and the texts of federal
(P.L. 93-247) and state (Senate Bill 414) legislation regarding child
abuse and neglect.

22. "I love my child but I need help ...''; how to develop a crisis
nursery, by Joan C. Curtis. Athens, GA, Regional Institute of Social Welfare Research, 1977. 26p. ED
151084.

This booklet presents guidelines for the development of
various types of 24-hour crisis nurseries designed to counter or prevent child abuse by providing parents with emergency relief from
child care. Such centers accommodate small groups of children for
a limited maximum time, ranging from 72 hours to six months.
Topics covered are: types of nurseries, funding, staff, policies
and prodecures, and public awareness. Two model programs (an
emergency shelter and a residential treatment center) are discussed
in terms of goals, functions and logistics (location, number of children and duration of stay). Options for local, state or federal funding and the comparative advantages and disadvantages of each are
discussed. Staff composition and training are discussed, and special
staffing needs relating to care of abused or neglected children are
considered. A section on policies and procedures deals with possible
center misuse by parents, relationships with local social service
agencies, laws relating to child abuse reporting standards, and admission procedures. Involvement of the media in encouraging client
self-referral is discussed.

23. The Supreme Court spanking rule; an issue in debate, by Ralph
S. Welsh. Paper presented at the annual convention of
the American Psychological Association, April 1976. 77p.
ED 151664.
Few issues have polarized the educational community so

completely as the 1975 and 1977 decisions by the U.S. Supreme
Court to allow corporal punishment in the schools. The symposium
reported here was organized and conducted following the 1975 decision but prior to the 1977 one. Three papers in support and three
papers against the ruling were read, after which the participants
debated the matter. Finally, one pro and one con participant sum-
med up the views for each side. The supporters of the ruling view
corporal punishment as an effective deterrent to misbehavior, insist
that it is necessary tool for keeping order in the classroom, and
see it as an alternative to permanent suspension. They admit that
corporal punishment is occasionally misused, but point to the fact
that other useful tools of a civilized society are also subject to misuse. The non-supporters of the ruling view corporal punishment as
a type of legalized child abuse and are convinced that it compounds
the teachers' problems by escalating anger in the child. They bol-
ster their position by pointing out instances of abuse that have occurred in the past. Both groups agree that effective alternatives to
physical discipline, coupled with teachers more adequately trained
to handle disciplinary problems in the classroom, would largely re-
move the need for the continued future use of corporal punishment.

24. Children alone; what can be done about abuse and neglect, edi-
            ted by M. Angele Thomas. Reston, VA, Council for
            Exceptional Children, 1977. 117p. ED 143163.
        Provided are papers resulting from an Invisible College
on Child Abuse and Neglect conducted by the Council for Exceptional
Children which focused on what schools can and should be doing in
the treatment of child abuse and neglect. Entries are included with
the following titles and authors: "The Sensitive Teacher" by D.
Howell; "The Abuse of Adolescents" by I. Lourie; "Family Structure
and Professional Roles" by M. Lauderdale; "When I See an Abused
or Neglected Child, What Do I Do About It?" by D. Broadhurst;
"Policies and Procedures for Reporting" by M. Nicholson; "What
Will It Cost Me if I Report?" by B. Fraser; "The Consequences of
Neglected Cases" by D. Kline; "What Will It Cost the Child if I
Don't Report?" by F. Green; "Program Development in Child Abuse"
by D. Davis; "How Do We Get Started?" by P. Fox; "Therapeutic
Interventions for the Maltreated Child" by E. Brocck; and "Strategies
of Prevention" by J. Kent. A list of key ideas covered in each
paper precedes entries.

25. Child abuse; a national perspective, by H. Philip Hepworth.
            Paper presented at the Child Welfare League of America
            Northwest Region Conference, June 1977. 57p. ED
            144295.
        Discussed are the child abuse reporting laws in Canada
and the operation of child abuse registers. Comments on the recommendations of the House of Commons are quoted in the following
areas of need: preventive services, research, statistics and information, amendment of the Canada Evidence Act and the Criminal
Code, and public and professional education. A task force of vol-

untary organizations concerned with child abuse and neglect, as proposed by the author, is described. The bulk of the document consists of the following appendixes: a statement of the laws concerning child abuse and neglect; statistical documentation from child abuse registers; and legislative provisions and documentation relating
to child abuse in the provinces, presented by province.

26. How to plan and carry out a successful public awareness program on child abuse and neglect. Washington, DC, National Center on Child Abuse and Neglect, 1976. 99p.
ED 144287.
Intended for public and private agencies working in the
field of child abuse and neglect prevention and treatment, the manual is designed to assist those responsible for creating public understanding of the problem of child abuse and neglect. Chapters cover
the following areas: the value of a public relations program; planning and budgeting a public relations program; implementing the program (including dealing with the news media, writing the news release, and enlisting the support of other community agencies and
groups); taking action when a child abuse tragedy occurs in the community; and evaluating the program. Also provided are a list of
resources (books, films/filmstrips, slide presentations, radio/TV
spots, child abuse and neglect organizations, and advertising and
public relations organizations) and a glossary of terms. In addition,
reduced photographs of sample brochures, posters, and newspaper
advertisements are given.

27. Family center; a community based approach to the problems
of abusive families, by Margaret A. Nicholson and Carol
J. Schneider. Commerce City, CO, Adams County
School District 14, 1977. 560p. ED 158454.
Presented is the final report of the Family Center Project, a program designed to increase the number of reported cases
of suspected child abuse and neglect and increase the services for
abused and neglected children and their families in Adams County,
Colorado. Three chapters which address the goal of increasing
child abuse referrals focus on public awareness and professional
education, a school referral program, and the crisis intake process. Eight chapters concern the following treatment topics: the
role of the nurse on a child abuse team, the multidisciplinary review team, treatment of abusive adults, lay therapy, treatment of
abused and neglected children, the crisis nursery, therapeutic nursery care, the therapeutic day care. Three chapters focus on project dissemination and research aspects.

28. Civil liability for failing to report child abuse, by Neil J.
Lehto. 1977. 35p. ED 158442.
The article examines the Landeros decision (which ruled
that a doctor who fails to report a child abuse victim can be held
liable for subsequent injuries inflicted on the child) and discusses
three theories of proving civil liability for the failure to report child

abuse victims. Addressed are the following topics: the problem of child abuse and reporting laws, the fact and issues of the Landeros v. Flood court case, medical malpractice for the failure to report child abuse, defining the statutory duty to report, statutory negligence for failing to report child abuse, liability per se for the violation of mandatory reporting laws, the proximate cause problem and reporting laws and due process. A widespread and continuing public and professional education and training program is suggested instead of approaches which involve toughening civil, criminal, or administrative penalties.

29. Child abuse; where do we go from here? edited by Susan Ar-shack. Washington, DC, Children's Hospital of the District of Columbia, 1977. 153p. ED 159840.

The document presents the proceedings of the conference on "Child Abuse: Where Do We Go From Here?" held at the Children's Hospital National Medical Center in 1977. Six chapters focus on corporal punishment, etiology of child abuse, sex abuse, treatment modalities, court reform, and parental rights and civil liberties. Among the entries are the following titles and authors: "Corporal Punishment and Alternatives in the Schools: An Overview of Theoretical and Practical Issues" (I. Hyman, et al.): "Corporal Punishment in the Schools: The Civil Liberties Objections" (A. Reitman): "The Role of the Co-Mingled Family in the Sexual Abuse of Children" (M. Ramey): "Identification of Infants At-Risk for Child Neglect: Observations and Inferences in the Examination of the Mother-Infant Dyad" (C. Schwarzbeck): "Incest as a Causative Factor in Anti-Social Behavior: An Exploratory Study" (J. Densen-Gerber and J. Benward): "Individual Psychotherapy with Abused Preschool Children" (M. Engel): "Approaches in Adolescent Abuse" (G. Caruso): "Criminal Justice Reform in Handling Child Sex Abuse" (C. Bahn and M. Daly): and "State Intervention and the Termination of Parental Rights."

30. Parents and protectors; a study in child abuse and neglect, by Deborah Shapiro. 1978. 127p. ED 163731.

The report documents a study in which parents identified as abusive or neglectful were interviewed to examine the relationship between the dependent variable of reduction of abusive or neglectful behavior and the independent variables describing the families (N = 171) and the services given. Chapter I provides an overview of the study design. Chapter II covers demographic variables and describes the socioeconomic status of the families at the time of the interview with respect to employment and housing, as well as involvement with the extended family and social relations. Chapter III centers on the abuse and neglect problem that resulted in agency involvement, the families' response to it, and the characteristics of the workers and the services they offered. Focused on in Chapter IV are findings relative to improvement of the parents, factors associated with successful outcomes, dubious outcome variables, and areas in which no differences were found. Chapter V looks at the differences among the types of parents served and at the differences in agency responses to these parents. A final chapter summarizes findings and discusses the implications for research, agency practice, and family policy.

31. Child abuse and neglect in residential institutions; selected
        readings on prevention, investigation, and correction.
        Washington, DC, National Center on Child Abuse and
        Neglect, DHEW, 1978. 216p. ED 163697.
        The document contains five selected readings and a listing of resource materials on the prevention, investigation, and correction of child abuse and neglect in residential institutions. Section I contains an excerpt from the February 1977 issue of Child Abuse and Neglect Reports. Section II covers the final report of the National Conference on the Institutional Maltreatment of Children (June 1977). In section III excerpts from the Human Ecology Forum are given, including, "Viewpoint--Institutions are Abusive", "Our Children's Keepers--Institutions in an Abusive Society", "Wordsworth-Rachel Won't Be Going Home", among others. Section IV contains excerpts from the draft of Federal Standards for Child Abuse and Neglect Prevention and Treatment Programs and Projects, mandated by Public Law 93-247. In section V the Model Child Protection Act with Commentary draft is provided, giving a structures model for the organization and implementation of state services.

32. The Use of psychopharmaceutical stimulants for the control of
        childhood hyperkinesis, by John P. Cronin. 1975. 15p.
        ED 126654.
        Reviewed is literature and research on the use of psychoactive drugs for control of hyperkinesis in children. Briefly discussed are such topics as the prevalence (close to 1.5 million children on medication) of drug therapy, the misuse of stimulant drugs in the schools, the three major drug groups (stimulants, anticonvulsants, and antidepressants) used in treating hyperactivity, problems (including side effects such as loss of appetite) involved with drug therapy, and alternative approaches (which include diet regulation) for treating hyperkinesis.

33. You are not alone; a parent discussion of hyperactive children
        and the group process, by Marilyn Bourcier. Sponsored
        by the Michigan State Department of Education, 1974.
        30p. ED 117924.
        Intended for parents of hyperactive children, the two booklets provide general information on the management of hyperactivity and a summary of a video taped parent discussion group. Sections are on the following topics: what is hyperactivity? what causes hyperactivity? traits of hyperactive children, concerns and feelings of parents, behavior management, selected comments from the video tape group discussion, and how to form a discussion group of your own. Summarized in the second booklet are eight segments of the 30-minute video tape in which individual parents share their concerns.

34. The Role of drugs, diet, and food additives in hyperactivity,
       by Mary E. Harshbarger. Paper presented at the annual
       meeting of the International Reading Association Great
       Lakes Regional Conference, October 1978. 17p. ED
       163439.
       A variety of causes have been suggested for hyperactivity:
anoxia and other adverse birth conditions, genetic factors, delayed
maturation, maternal smoking and drinking during pregnancy, interaction of temperament and environment, lead poisoning, radiation
stress, allergy and food additives, and deprivation of required stimulation. Treatments include drug treatments, especially with Rita-
lin or Dexedrine; the Feingold diet restricting sugars and artificial
colorings; administration of megavitamins; behavior therapy; differential reinforcement procedures; modeling; role-playing; filial therapy (helping parents develop empathy with their children); and brief
therapy (isolating specific complaints and attempting to bring about
an observable behavior change). Possible educational involvement
with the hyperactive includes developing minimal stimulation programs; developing structures, predictable, consistent, and logical
programs; having engineered classrooms; creating insight-oriented
therapy groups to help parents understand their feelings and make
necessary changes at home; behavior modification programs; self-
instructional training; relaxation training; and biofeedback. Cooperation between parents, teachers, and physicians is important in
treating children who are hyperactive.

35. Parentspeak on gifted and talented children. Los Angeles,
       National/State Leadership Training Institute on the Gifted
       and Talented, January 1976. 67p. ED 131616.
       Several subjects of interest to parents are covered in the
collection of six chapters authored by parents of gifted and talented
children. In "The Future Belongs to Those Who Prepare for It" by
D. McCartney, reasons for paying special attention to the education
of the gifted and talented are pointed out. Recounted in a second
chapter--entitled "'Pushy Parents' Working for Gifted and Talented"
by K. Wood--are a father's practical solutions to many of the problems caused by community opposition to the education of gifted and
talented children. Political action in the field of legislation for educational programs is the topic of "How 'Organized Persuasion'
Works for the Gifted in Public Education" by C. Nathan. An outline of guidelines for organizing statewide and local groups is presented in the chapter "Are You an 'Only'? Organize for the Gifted
and Talented!" by K. Coffey. A final chapter--"Practical Hints for
Parents of Gifted Children" by G. Ginsberg--provides a list of 20
suggestions for home life with the gifted child. Appended exhibits
include an outline of the qualities of gifted children in the preschool
and elementary school years, a table of mini-courses sponsored by
the Gifted Children's Association of San Fernando Valley for children
from preschool to senior high school level, a community resource
form for parent organization, and a description of suggested permanent committees for parent organization.

36. An Identification model; gifted and talented, by Cornelia Tongue and Charmian Sperling. Raleigh, North Carolina State Department of Public Instruction, 1976. 65p. ED 125226.

Presented is a model designed to aid school personnel in identifying gifted and talented children. In the chapter on problems and challenges of identification, the inadequacies of standardized group intelligence tests are pointed out and factors contributing to the broadening of the concept of giftedness are outlined. Stressed in chapter 2, on developing a logical plan, is the interrelatedness of three program components: identification, curriculum, and staff development. Listed in chapter 3 are several authors' descriptions of the gifted student. Provided in the final chapter is a matrix for identifying the mainstreamed or culturally different gifted student on the basis of test data, performance data, and developmental data in five talent categories: academic/intellectual, artistic/expressive, leadership/psychosocial, divergent production/processes, and kinesthetic. Appendixes include a list of tests and instruments for identifying gifted and talented students, sample behavior rating scales and checklists, and forms for preparing a composite student evaluation profile.

37. On being gifted; student perspectives. New York, Robert Sterling Clark Foundation, Inc., April 1977. 150p. ED 140559.

Designed by 20 gifted and talented adolescents, the book focuses on ways the gifted student can assume responsibility for his own education. Discussed in Chapter I on being gifted are problems of peer rejection, teacher influences, social values, and age disparities, as well as ways of dealing successfully with these difficulties. Chapter II examines those people--parents, teachers, and adult mentors--who have had the most influence on the students. Covered in Chapter III are the pros and cons of some school experiences, plus some options (such as independent study) which the students would like to see in the schools. Several types of programs regarding career education are explored in Chapter IV. Described in Chapter V are alternative types of educational programs, beginning with a vignette about a special school that includes community resources and activities in a curriculum designed for special talents and interests. A final chapter includes statements on priorities in public education and on the validity of participation in student government. Appended are lists of student participants, symposium consultants, and panel participants.

38. Your gifted child and you. Revised edition by Felice Kaufmann. Reston, VA, Council for Exceptional Children, 1976. 56p. ED 172501.

Intended for parents and teachers of gifted and talented children, the book discusses identification criteria and educational strategies for developing their potential. Case studies of gifted and talented children are cited and a checklist of common characteristics

is provided. Suggestions are given for fostering creativity in the
home; and special problems of the gifted are explained to include
underachievement, cultural differences, and learning difficulties.
Answers are presented to parents' questions about raising a gifted
child and guidelines are given for developing a parent organization.
Among appendixes are a bibliography, resource listing, and directory of state parent organizations for the gifted.

39. Parent handbook. Blue Bell, PA, Montgomery County Inter-
        mediate Unit 23, 1975. 29p. ED 158211.
            This booklet is for the parents of exceptional children.
It explains the process by which an exceptional child is evaluated,
identified and assigned to a program and placement. It also offers
general guidelines for parent participation with local school districts
and other educational agencies in planning the exceptional child's
educational program. These guidelines specifically apply to the
parents and children in the Montgomery County, Pennsylvania school
system and give information regarding Montgomery County community
agencies and resources and Pennsylvania state law. However, this
booklet can also be used by parents whose children are served by
other school systems since it includes information on Individualized
Education Programs (IEP's) and on terminology related to Public
Law 94-142. This booklet can also serve as a model for other
school districts in their efforts to inform parents on the educational
programming of their children.

40. Subsidized adoption in America, by Ursula Gallagher and San-
        ford Katz. Washington, DC, Children's Bureau, August
        1976. 74p. ED 136909.
            The Model State Subsidized Adoption Act, developed to
supplement existing state statutes, is presented in full, with accompanying Model Regulations. The act is designed to help provide a
child in special circumstances with a permanent adoptive home.
When efforts to achieve placement without subsidy have failed, the
Act would provide that the child be certified as eligible for subsidized adoption, under the following conditions: physical or mental
disability, emotional disturbance, recognized high risk of physical
or mental disease, age disadvantage, sibling relationship, racial or
ethnic factors, or any combination of these conditions. It is noted
that certifying the child as eligible for subsidy places emphasis on
the child and his needs, rather than on the financial ability of the
adoptive parents to meet those needs. The text of the Act is accompanied by a discussion of the background of subsidized adoption
in the United States. A supplementary section presents a comparison of the Model Act with existing state laws. Tables are included.

41. Foster care in five states; a synthesis and analysis of studies
        from Arizona, California, Iowa, Massachusetts, and
        Vermont, by Shirley M. Vasaly. Washington, DC, Social
        Research Group, George Washington University, 1976.
        156p. ED 133071.

A synthesis of data and major recommendations from foster care studies undertaken by the states of Arizona, California, Iowa, Massachusetts and Vermont, this report focuses on areas needing improvement. Covered in detail are: (1) the foster care system, its programs and goals; (2) foster children and their natural and foster families; (3) agency staffing and services; (4) fiscal considerations; and (5) community involvement. Emphasis is placed on the need to arouse public concern for action in improving foster care systems, which in the U.S. today involve some 400,000 children. Although differing in geographic location, ethnic composition and economic structure, all five states show similar inadequacies in their foster family service systems. Preventive and preplacement services are seen as particularly inadequate: family problems go unaided until the crisis state, forcing otherwise unnecessary foster care placement. Numbers of children in foster care then become overwhelming and children's needs and problems are neglected and increase in complexity, requiring specialized care facilities which are lacking. It is suggested that other states might find this report useful. Synopses of the major studies are included in the appendix.

42. We care for kids; a handbook for foster parents. Springfield, IL, Illinois State Department of Children and Family Services, 1974. 59p. ED 119821.
    This handbook outlines essential information for foster parents under these basic headings: (1) legal rights and responsibilities of children, parents and foster parents; (2) recruitment, licensing, training, and evaluation of foster homes; (3) placement and removal of foster children; (4) payments and expenses; (5) medical care; (6) confidentiality and family contracts; (7) agency and community resources; (8) education and religion; and (9) complaints and grievances about agency services and foster homes. Appendices include information related to foster home standards, study and evaluation; and lists of the responsibilities and duties of the juvenile court, guardianship administrator, field/casework staff, and foster parent or custodial institution.

43. Foster parents handbook. Bismarck, North Dakota State Board of Social Service, 1978. 56p. ED 162729.
    A wide range of information pertaining to foster care and the role of foster parents is presented in this handbook. The nature of and the need for foster care are discussed briefly. Specific information is presented on the relationship of foster children to their parents, the court, their custodian and their guardian, and the process of becoming a foster parent (recruitment, the application process, screening, and foster parent education) is discussed. The rights and responsibilities of the social worker/agency, foster parents, and natural parents are delineated, with the importance of teamwork highlighted. The placement procedure is described in detail including preparation for placement, suggestions for facilitating successful adjustment to placement, and what happens when a place-

ment proves unsuccessful. Specific financial information is provided
on foster care payment rates, income tax, medical and educational
costs, and foster parents' liability insurance. Several aspects of
providing care for the foster child are discussed, including discipline, religion, confidentiality, subsidized adoption, and complaints.
Foster parent associations are discussed briefly. Appendices include copies of various forms involved in the process of becoming
a foster parent and a book list recommended for use with foster
children.

44. Foster parenting. Washington, DC, Arthur D. Little, Inc.,
1978. 77p. ED 170049.
This manual provides information on the recruitment,
selection and training of foster parents. Part I stresses methods
for effectively recruiting and screening foster parents including: defining foster parent roles and responsibilities; targeting groups of
potential foster parents; developing recruitment strategies; conducting initial and in-depth screening; and using screening information
to assess foster parent training needs. Part II presents a foster
parent training course, and suggests guidelines for working with
adults in groups (role play, visual aids, discussion techniques).
The appendices provide descriptions of five foster parent training
curriculums including availability information and references to books,
tapes and films relevant to selection and training.

45. Gay parents and child custody issues, by Dorothy Riddle. 1977.
22p. ED 147746.
There are difficulties confronting gay parents when they
seek custody of their children in a divorce suit. Court decisions
are running about 50-50 in favor of the gay parent. Homophobia,
the fear of same-sex intimacy or relationships, is rather strong in
our society. The scant research done on gay families shows no
negative effects on the children and that any difficulties with the
parent were typical for any children of divorced parents. The parent's sexual orientation has little to do with whether one wants to
be a parent or can be a good one. Neither does this orientation
have an effect on the child's sexual identity or whether he becomes
heterosexual. The anti-gay campaign of Save Our Children (SOC) has
not only had an effect on child custody battles, but has re-activated
homophobia in this country. In view of this, psychologists called
as expert witnesses should work to offset the inaccurate stereotyped
opinions others have of homosexuals.

46. Developing community acceptance of sex education, by Medora
Bass. Paper presented at the annual conference of the
National Council on Family Relations, October 1977.
34p. ED 153089.
This paper stresses the need for sex education in the
schools, to complement what may be learned in the home or church.
Due to negative community pressure, the youth service field has
often hesitated to introduce such programs. Evidence is presented

that there may be less opposition to sex education programs for the handicapped. An attempt to introduce such a program in one community is described. The importance of setting up a coalition of community leaders and agencies to support the schools and teachers against attack is emphasized. Objections and questions are answered, and excerpts from relevant studies and articles are included in the appendix. Brief descriptions are given of programs in other communities which have contributed to developing community acceptance of sex education in the schools.

47. School-age pregnancy and parenthood in the United States, by
      Lucy Eddinger and Janet Forbush. Washington, DC,
      National Alliance Concerned with School-Age Parents,
      1977. 45p. ED 151652.
      The National Alliance Concerned with School-Age Parents
(NACSAP) is a private, non-profit, multidisciplinary membership
organization specializing in technical assistance to those working
with school-age parents, young families at risk, and sexually active
youth. This publication represents a compilation of information relating to adolescent pregnancy. It views adolescence as a time of
values testing, and brings together data from a number of surveys
and studies. Topics include: needs and opportunities of school-age
parents; evaluation of current programs; staff training needs and the
role of technical assistance.

48. The Influence of contraception on adolescent sexual behavior,
      by Paul A. Reichelt. Paper presented at the annual
      conference of the American Association of Marriage and
      Family Counselors, October 1978. 23p. ED 166567.
      Effective birth control is needed to combat adolescent
pregnancy which is a major health and social problem, the adverse
consequences of which have been well-documented along a variety of
dimensions. A significant obstacle to the provision of birth control
services to teenagers is the belief that such services will encourage
adolescent coital activity. The validity of this belief was studied by
a longitudinal study which assessed teenage sexual behavior prior
to and one year after obtaining oral contraception. Almost all the
young women were coitally experienced when they first came to the
clinic for birth control. During the year the young women used oral
contraception, they showed a very moderate increase in frequency
of coitus which was not accompanied by an increase in their current
number of sex partners. Given the opportunity to obtain prescrip-
tion contraception, these adolescent women demonstrated good con-
tinuity of usage. These results, considered in conjunction with other
research, support the conclusion that providing teenagers with effective birth control will not markedly increase their sexual activity.

49. Choices and careers; free to choose; parenting daughters, by
      Cathaleen Finley and Delores Wolf. Madison, University
      of Wisconsin Extension. 24p. ED 158940.
      Pressure from the mass media, parents, and peers often

causes young girls to concentrate on their most external aspects at
a time when the inner demand for self definition is equally important.   In the struggle to receive attention from boys, many girls
suppress their identities, fearful that if they allowed their true
selves to emerge they would not be attractive as women.   Physical
activities are often abandoned and girls fail to develop strength and
pride in their bodies.   Grades slide as they decide to settle for being clerical workers or teachers instead of scientists or engineers.
Society seems to declare motherhood as the ultimate goal for a girl,
regardless of her abilities or interests, yet often that is completed
by the time a woman is 40.   Her children are grown, the external
beauty is faded, and little else is left for her.   Girls need to be
aware of all that the future may hold; they need to prepare themselves in terms of their own goals, abilities and preferred life
styles.   This document concludes with two sections that suggest discussions and other activities parents can utilize in helping their
daughters develop their own individual talents, independence, and
self confidence.

50.   Adolescent development and teenage fertility, by George
            Cvetkovich and Barbara Grote.   Paper presented at the
            Planned Parenthood Regional Conference on Adolescence,
            Boise, ID, June 1977.   22p.   ED 158196.
            This study considers how adolescent development is re-
lated to teenage fertility.   Findings from two studies indicate that
in some ways teenagers as a group differ from older individuals.
The paper details some of the ways in which sexual experiences
are influenced by social and emotional maturity and outlines some
of the problems which result from the need to coordinate development on the levels of biology, individual differences, and social interactions.   Many of these problems are more pressing during adolescence than they ever appear in later life.   The author points out
that human fertility decisions always demand a blend of emotion and
logic.   The ability to make life decisions which combine both feelings and facts develops during the adolescent years, and this characteristic must be central to all thinking about psychosocial development.

51.   Out-of-wedlock pregnancy and childbearing, by Kristin A.
            Moore and Steven B. Caldwell.   Sponsored by HEW,
            September 1976.   229p.   ED 162202.
            Out-of-wedlock birth rates have not fallen much at all
among teenagers.   New analyses of existing data sets indicate that
becoming an out-of-wedlock parent is a process with three stages:
commencement of sexual activity; conception among the sexually
active; and pregnancy outcome among those who conceive.   Public
policy variables such as AFDC benefits, family planning services
and abortion availability did not increase the likelihood of sexual
intercourse.   Teenagers were found likely to make the transition
as they become older, if their fathers were poorly educated; if
(among non-blacks) they lived on the Pacific Coast; if they were

black; and if they were from a more recent birth cohort or a non-intact family. The examination of data regarding pregnancy among the group who were sexually experienced indicated that AFDC benefits did not serve as an economic incentive to childbearing outside of marriage. On the other hand, the impact of liberal family planning and abortion policies is cited in reducing the incidence of out-of-wedlock childbearing.

52. Early adolescent childbearing; some further notes, by Marie Hoeppner. 1978. 33p. ED 162195.
Current research on adolescent fertility indicates that illegitimacy is becoming concentrated in the teenage and even pre-teen years. Increasing sexual activity, lack of contraceptive information and techniques, and a desired pregnancy are possible explanations. Some of the problems faced by adolescent mothers include more complicated pregnancies, higher maternal mortality, interruption of both education and socialization processes and inability to cope with stressful situations. Because early adolescent childbearing foreshadows far-reaching social consequences three options are considered: (1) education programs to increase communication between parents and children; (2) more organized sex education and contraceptive programs, and (3) more information on adoption possibilities available to pregnant adolescents.

53. Understanding and responding to violence in young children, edited by Lillian Genser. Detroit, Center for Teaching about Peace and War, Wayne State University, 1976. 52p. ED 152007.
Presented are proceedings from a 1976 conference entitled "Understanding and Responding to Violence in Young Children" which was attended by over 600 students, teachers, child care workers, and parents. Following an introduction by L. Genser are entries with the following titles and authors: "The Course of the Development of Violence in Young Children" by E. Callard, "Socialization Processes Affecting Violence in Society--What are the Prospects for Change?" by W. Wattenberg, "Violence and the Social Order" by M. Ravitz, and "Workshop Report--Where Do We Go From Here?" by W. Innerd. Among conclusions offered by each contributor are that the research indicates that the infant is not born violent and there is no innate drive toward hostile aggression and that the reality of violence in our society is the major cause of violence in young children.

54. Guide to alcohol programs for youth, by Susan K. Maloney. Rockville, MD, National Clearinghouse for Alcohol Information, DHEW, 1976. 30p. ED 142900.
This program guide was prepared by the National Clearinghouse for Alcohol Information of the National Institute on Alcohol Abuse and Alcoholism. Its purpose is to assist program planners in the development of strategies to minimize the abuse of alcoholic beverages by youths. It provides information and direction to: (1)

youth-serving organizations wanting to add an alcohol education component to ongoing programs; (2) educational institutions wanting to
examine alcohol use among their students and develop strategies to
minimize its abuse; and (3) any community group interested in di-
recting their resources to reducing alcohol abuse by young people.
It might also be of value to alcohol program planners and community
or private foundations. The booklet is designed to be adapted to the
needs of the individual community. Topics covered include trends
in drinking behavior, strategies for change, implementation considerations, and program development. The guide also includes a list
of programs and contact addresses.

55. Why children misbehave, by Floy C. Pepper. Portland, OR,
    Multnomah County Intermediate Education District, April
    1977. 22p. ED 139181.
    Reviewed are four reasons for misbehavior in children,
and suggested are methods for adults to deal with the misbehavior.
It is explained that motivation can be classified according to the following factors: attention getting mechanism (with passive/active and
constructive/destruction patterns); power seeking; revenge seeking;
and assumed or real disability (a deficiency displayed in order to
be left alone). Adult responses to each of the four types of misbehavior are analyzed.

56. Runaway youth; an annotated bibliography and literature over-
    view, by Deborah K. Walker. Washington, DC, DHEW,
    May 1975. 122p. ED 138907.
    This annotated bibliography and literature review aims
at acquainting the reader with the knowledge base that presently
exists in various literature sources on runaways. Although available knowledge from the literature is limited in reference to certain
policy questions, the bibliography/overview does serve as an important beginning point for future inquiry about runaways. This effort is an attempt to determine the underlying causes, measures
for prevention, methods of coping and rehabilitation. The 156 entries are grouped into sections, and include books, journals (English
and Foreign language), government documents, dissertations, magazine and newspaper articles.

57. Teenagers discuss the generation gap, by Elizabeth Herzog.
    Washington, DC, Children's Bureau, DHEW, 1970. 43p.
    ED 112324.
    This report details the results of a study undertaken to
poll high school student opinion on the "Generation Gap." A panel
was randomly selected from students in college preparatory courses,
in metropolitan areas located in the four main geographical regions
of the United States. Replies to the questions were received from
251 students, in 53 schools, in 12 cities. Two open-ended questions
asked the students to report the views that prevail among their friends
and classmates as to (1) the main things adults do or say or
fail to understand, that bother teenagers, and (2) the main things

young people do or don't do that make things worse. The results
of the study are reported as patterning of opinions rather than as
exact count. The opinion patterns are complemented by numerous
examples of student response.

58. The Daily experience of high school students, by Patrick L.
     Mayers. Chicago, Spencer Foundation, 1978. 31p.
     ED 159583.
     A beginning step in understanding intrinsic motivation in
school can occur through examination of adolescents' subjective experience and the relationship between enjoyment and school learning.
Subjects (85) filled out self-report forms, recording their level of
concentration, moods, feelings and activities at random times during
the waking hours of a normal week in their lives. Hypothesized is
that when students perceive their classes as providing challenges
which match their skills, they experience positive affect and involvement (theory of flow). The results indicate that indeed the students'
energy in classes is related to their perception of the balance of
challenges and skills. Suggestions for future research emerging
from this study are proffered.

59. Children in jail, by Thomas J. Cottle. Hackensack, NJ, New-
     gate Resource Center, 1978. 47p. ED 155821.
     One of 52 theoretical papers on school crime and its
relation to poverty, this chapter presents a series of life studies of
children in jail, along with a brief discussion of prison reform.
The purpose of the life studies is to allow jailed children or children who have been in jail to speak for themselves of the conditions
of jail and the experience of being incarcerated. The studies include children who have been tried and sentenced to jail, as well
as children held in detention centers awaiting trial. One of the
studies is of a girl who was held illegally in an adult prison.
Among the many topics discussed by the children are medical treatment, the lack of educational facilities, the changing nature of their
relationship with their parents, the shame and fright of imprison-
ment, and the physical and psychological effects of being in jail.

60. Little sisters and the law. Sponsored by National Institute for
     Juvenile Justice and Delinquency Prevention, Washington,
     DC. August 1977. 97p. ED 155561.
     At many points within the juvenile justice system, there
is evidence of differential treatment of male and female juveniles.
Nearly 75% of females under 18 who are arrested and incarcerated
are charged with status offenses such as disobeying their parents,
promiscuity, running away and other acts for which adults cannot
be charged and boys infrequently are. Girls are often held in detention for longer periods of time and less fequently placed in community programs than boys. These and other examples of differential treatment are detailed in this report. The first part briefly
describes how decisions are made in the juvenile justice system
and summarizes studies which reveal the differential treatment of

males and females, including results of a national survey of educational and vocational programs in state training schools. The second part provides a profile of the young female offender. The third part focuses on communities and what they can do to prevent girls from becoming involved in the juvenile justice system as well as assist those who have been referred to court. The fourth part, the resource section, offers information on publications and organizations.

61. Punishment; parent rites vs. children's rights, by Norma D. Feshbach. Paper presented at the annual meeting of the American Psychological Association, August 1975. 31p. ED 119829.

This critical review of literature on punishment practices and child rearing examines the question of children's rights in the context of parent practices, values and prerogatives. Society regards the family unit as a sacrosanct system open to inspection and intervention only when there is tangible evidence of physical child abuse. The recent upsurge of interest in the problem of child abuse may be attributed to heightened awareness rather than an increase in abuse occurrence as it was not very long ago that many abusive child rearing practices were accepted procedures for socializing the child. The definition of cruel and unusual punishment should be extended to all forms of punishment which leave negative consequences for the growth and well-being of the child. Literature is reviewed on: (1) patterns of parent punishment practices, (2) effects of physical and psychological punishment practices, (3) alternatives to physical and psychological punishment which serve the functions of socialization while furthering the cause of children's rights and welfare, and (4) implications and implementation of the proposed alternatives. It is suggested that making child rearing practices more open to scrutiny would not only protect children's interests and rights but would encourage parents to discuss their problems, ask for guidance and take advantage of available resources.

62. Youth's rights to be regarded as persons, by Nancy Belbas. Minneapolis, Center for Youth Development and Research, University of Minnesota, August 1975. 54p. ED 111923.

Ideas and information gathered from eight monthly seminars focusing on issues related to rights of youths are presented here. The topics that are covered are as follows: what it means to be regarded as a person, a definitive look at moral and legal rights, adult and youth rights, the rights of youth to be regarded as persons in schools and in families, the right of youth to be regarded as persons having access to confidential services, the right of youth to be regarded as persons in court, due process, right to treatment, implementing the right to treatment, and ways to further youth's right to be regarded as persons. A suggested reading list is provided.

63. Your legal rights and responsibilities; a guide for public school

students. Washington, DC, Administration for Children, Youth, and Families, DHEW, 1978. 29p. ED 162040.

Supreme Court decisions and Acts of Congress relating to students' rights are discussed in this pamphlet. The legal principles outlined by the Supreme Court decisions are presented for various areas, including religion, speech and expression, flag salute and pledge of allegiance, suspension and expulsion, racial discrimination and segregated schools, and enforcement of legal rights. Some background information on respective cases is provided. The rights given through Acts of Congress are described for the areas of student records, discrimination against minority group students, sex discrimination, and the rights of handicapped children and special education. Steps a student should take in the event that his/her rights are violated are suggested. A listing of organizations that offer advocacy and other services to young people in need is appended.

64. The Youngest minority; are they competent to waive their constitutional rights? by Saundra Brewer. Santa Monica, CA, Rand Corporation, March 1978. 25p. ED 163378.

Although juveniles are not considered criminals, it has been only in the last decade that they have been accorded the constitutional rights to fairness and due process of law accorded to adults - - basic rights guaranteed by the United States Supreme Court decision in the Miranda case. However, since a large proportion of youthful arrestees are of low socioeconomic status, intellectual deficiency, poor home background, and low educational attainment, there is great concern as to whether these youth completely understand both what their legal rights are and what it means to waive them. References are made to many legal decisions, and suggestions are provided for re-evaluation of the process by which juvenile confessions are obtained. They include: (1) revision of the wording in the Miranda statement; (2) establishment of stricter criteria for considering a waiver valid; and (3) greater involvement of parents and/or lawyers before questioning occurs.

65. Children bicyclists; should a minimum age be required? Santa Barbara, CA, Department of Public Works, 1975. 91p. ED 152393.

This paper reports on a Santa Barbara, California study to determine the need for establishing a minimum age for bicyclists using the public roadways, examining the proposition that children below a certain age are developmentally unable to perform safely in traffic. Data on the disproportionate incidence of accident involvement among young cyclists include statistics on fatalities, injuries and cyclist behavior. A general description of the cognitive development process in children is presented, with specific discussion of the development of concepts of speed, time and distance, and the concept of rules. Results of a survey of 1,373 parents of 2,764 children, aged 5 to 13, in which parents selected an average minimum age of about 11 years, indicate good-to-enthusiastic parent

support of the minimum age idea. The report concludes: (1) that
the cognitive deficiencies associated with the incompletely developed
child justify a minimum age of 13 years or older for cyclists using
public roadways and (2) that registration of bicycle operators using
public roadways is the best way to enforce this minimum age requirement. An introductory statement by the project director suggests a minimum age requirement of 9 years and presents additional
opinions on licensing and bicycle safety education.

66. A Review of play and its relationship to learning, by Janet
Naumburg. May 1978. 120p. ED 164097.
The value and function of play behavior in young children,
and the process and conditions by which play contributes to learning,
cognition and problem solving, are explored in this literature review. The first section examines early theories of play, the psy-
choanalytic theory of play, and the development stages of play.
Common elements of play are described and criteria for distinguish-
ing play from non-play behavior are examined. The second section
describes different approaches to viewing play: sciencing (which includes testing and rehypothesizing); symbolic (designating some object or activity to replace others); socio-dramatic (using symbolic
play with regard to role playing); creativity (in which something
unique evolves through divergent thinking, problem solving and hypothesis testing); and block play (involving construction). The third
section discusses the relationship between play and learning, cognition, knowledge and knowing. Piaget's theories of child's play and
intellectual development are central to this discussion. The last
section explores the decisive role the child's environment has in the
play and learning process. Parents, other adults and teachers are
seen as having a crucial role in creating an environment for play.
Ways in which parents' actions can foster or discourage play behavior are discussed.

2.
SENIOR CITIZENS
AND
GERONTOLOGY

67. Gerontology; an annotated bibliography, compiled by Robert L.
Plotz. New York, Center for Advanced Study in Education, CUNY, August 1976. 88p. ED 143911.
This annotated bibliography deals with many aspects of
gerontology. In addition to a group of general works, there are
sections on psychological characteristics, intervention, education,
work and retirement, services, and living situations. Annotations
are quite detailed, often listing findings of studies and summarizing
the author's main arguments.

68. A Tarnish on the golden years, by Vicky Bradford. 1978.
23p. ED 150659.
Twenty-two advertisements from "Reader's Digest" and
twenty-two from "Retirement Living" magazine were analyzed in
order to determine the way in which old people are portrayed. The
advertisements were found to support the common societal stereotypes that old people are unproductive, prefer to associate with
other old people rather than with younger people, are uninterested
in sex, and are serene. In addition, the advertisements fostered
the advertising stereotypes that old people have a great deal of
money, have youthful appearances, are grandparents, and have living spouses. However, the advertisements were not found to support the societal stereotypes that the aged are inflexible, senile,
physically deteriorated, and dependent. No great differences were
found between the images in the "Reader's Digest" advertisements
and those in "Retirement Living." The results of the study indicate
that the rhetoric of magazine advertisements conveys incomplete
and inaccurate information about the aged and does not acknowledge
their individual differences. As a result, the needs, preferences,
and abilities of individual old persons are ignored.

69. Senior centers; report of senior group programs in America,
by Joyce Laense and Sara B. Wagner. Washington, DC, National Council on the Aging, Inc., 1975. 263p. ED 134885.

This report presents results of an interview study made by the National Institute of Senior Centers (NISC), a program of The National Council on the Aging, Inc. (NCOA). Thirty Centers were selected for on-site study. The criterion was a program directed to older adults, meeting at least once weekly on a regularly scheduled basis and providing some form of educational, recreational or social activity. Sites included at least one Center within reach of the 10 HEW regions. Selection of 20 other Centers was determined by systematic examination of two mail questionnaires submitted by Senior Centers themselves. From intake data supplied, NISC staff members assigned to the project selected, at random, persons to be interviewed at the Center. Appointments were arranged in advance. Interview time averaged 50 minutes per individual over a period of five man-days. Case studies of the 30 sites visited reveal implications of the findings, policy recommendations made -- and problems, possible solutions and topics in need of further discussion. It is anticipated that the findings reported here may be useful to those responsible for planning and implementing Senior Center and other group programs.

70. Information in social gerontology, by Marta Dosa and Stephanie
      Ardito-Kirkland. Syracuse, NY, ERIC Clearinghouse on
      Information Resources, Syracuse University, 1978. 54p.
      ED 169951.
      The objective of this essay and bibliography is to assist
information and library professionals, as well as individuals from
other disciplines, to gain some insights into the major themes and
issues of social gerontology. The focus is on the role of information and data in gerontological research, public policy, service delivery, and information and library services, with emphasis on individual rather than societal aging. The bibliography is divided into
two parts. Part one discusses background issues in social gerontology; including concepts and development, research, public policy,
human services and advocacy, and education and training. Part
two examines the role of information in social gerontology with emphasis on information for older persons, information for those who
work with the elderly, and international issues. This is not primarily an Educational Resources Information Center (ERIC) bibliography, although almost half of the citations are either ERIC documents announced in Resources in Education (RIE) or journal articles
reviewed in Current Index to Journals in Education (CIJE). A list
of bibliographic sources is included.

71. Testimony on physical fitness for older persons. Washington,
      DC, National Association for Human Development, 1975.
      101p. ED 131023.
      Collected here are fourteen statements on the beneficial
effects of physical fitness programs for older persons presented at
hearings before the Subcommittee on Aging of the Committee on
Labor and Public Welfare, U.S. Senate. Areas discussed include:
What research tells us regarding the contribution of exercise to the

health of older people, exercise and the aging process, activity and older Americans, staying youthful and fit, importance of physical activity for the elderly; physical activity and aging; psychological importance of physical fitness; value of regular exercise programs for senior citizens; and a fitness program for senior citizens developed by the National Association for Human Development with quotes from various leaders of physical fitness. A statement by C. Carson Conrad, Executive Director, President's Council on Physical Fitness and Sports, is representative of much of the testimony: Regular exercise can significantly delay the aging process by inhibiting the losses of vital capacity, muscular strength, and joint flexibility, which are characteristic of the middle and later years. It is a fundamental law of physiology that the functional efficiency of an organ or system improves with use and regresses with disease. Regular exercise may deter the onset of degenerative diseases, which are among today's major killers, and it may improve the ability to survive and recover from heart attack by promoting the development of collateral circulation in the heart muscle. A state of physical fitness enhances the quality of life for the elderly by increasing their independence. The ability to go places and do things without being dependent on others provides a strong psychological lift that is conducive to good mental health.

72.   Releasing the potential of the older volunteer, by Mary M.
         Seguin and Beatrice O'Brien. Los Angeles, Ethel Percy
         Andrus Gerontology Center, USC, 1976. 97p. ED
         123367.
         Aimed at retired persons, employers and potential employers of senior volunteers, and students of gerontology, the book examines the Older Volunteer Project of the Ethel Percy Andrus Gerontology Center, University of Southern California, 1973-75. The 40 Andrus volunteers were between 49 and 78 years old, generally highly educated, with 66% having held professional jobs. The project demonstrated how retired adults can enter an organization that employs mostly paid, non-retired personnel, generate work, and gain acceptance in that work setting. Offering historical flashbacks, and discussing principles, procedures, and participant reactions, chapters include: (1) "Here We Are Now", describing the project's progress, with volunteer comments; (2) the Worker/Volunteer, giving a profile; (3) The Setting, discussing the volunteers' adjustment to them, with volunteer comments; (4) The Work (Tasks), tracing task development, with volunteer comments; (5) New Roles for Senior Volunteers in Organizations, presenting an adaptable model for older volunteer program organization; and (6) Utilization of Older Volunteers in Organizations: Issues and Potentials, reviewing key issues. Appended materials includes: 12 tables and 7 figures presenting data on volunteers and the project; 2 reference lists; and, a subject index.

73.   A Look at senior citizens programs in the United States, by
         Benjamin C. Hughes and Linda S. Barnard. Paper pre-
         sented at the annual convention of the American Personnel

and Guidance Association, March 1978. 23p. ED
163356.

The problems of the aged include: inadequate health
care, insufficient income, transportation, substandard housing, crime
victimization, poor nutrition, loss of home, sense of being valueless,
forced retirement and apathy from the police. Survey objectives
were: determination of the extent to which cities were serving senior populations and how they were easing the problems as well as
identifying local civic groups in providing help to the aged. Addition-
ally, the survey identified other pervasive problems for the service
providers: lack of central direction and guidance, no central location from which to disseminate information, and complex funding
problems. Recommendations included city-wide organizational planning changes in counselor training to include programs for practicing
gerontology counselors. A program involving church facilities on
a rotating day of the week basis was suggested. Training of seniors
themselves as first-line listeners was included as a part of the program.

74. Advocacy and age; issues, experiences, strategies, edited by
Paul A. Kerschner. Los Angeles, Ethel Percy Andrus
Gerontology Center, USC, June 1976. 165p. ED 159359.

This monograph seeks to bring understanding to one component of the advocacy field, that of advocacy and the aged, by over-
viewing this component through a series of articles. (Advocacy is
an activity by which changes can be effected in a power structure
to improve a subgroup's situation.) There are four parts to the
document: part 1, entitled "Issues," contains an overview of advocacy as a social movement. In this part, Mark Berger views
major philosophical approaches to the advocacy issue. Paul A.
Kerschner explores the theory of pluralism as it applies to the aged.
Neal E. Cutler examines common misconceptions regarding partisan
political behavior on the part of older adults. Stephen McConnell,
Dorothy Fleisher, Mel Spear, and Jodi Cohn discuss major organizational and policy problems which constitute the aging/advocacy
issue. In part 2, entitled "Experiences," Margaret E. Kuhn, Ho-
bart C. Jackson, and Barbara Kaplan provide case studies on advocacy by and for the elderly. In part 3, "Strategies," students of
administration, planning, and community organizations are provided
with a discussion of requisite tools for implementing advocacy efforts. Paul Nathanson and John L. Lamb focus on advocacy and
the necessity of legal services. James A. Danowski emphasizes
the use of media as a strategy for elderly advocate organizations.
A selected bibliography is included in the final section.

75. The Social-psychological aspects of aging, by Charles B. White
and David Larson. Albany, NY, State Office for the
Aging, June 1976. 25p. ED 160908.

This monograph is written to convey the point that the
aged are ill-served by people's negative attitudes and by youth-
centered social systems. It is designed for individuals who are

aged as well as those who work with aged relatives or friends.   It
will also be useful as preparation for training programs or discussion groups, as well as those who desire a relatively brief summary
of current thought in gerontology.

76. Communication with the elderly; shattering stereotypes, by
Vicki S. Freimuth and Kathleen Jamieson.   Falls Church,
VA, Speech Communication Association, 1979.   43p.   ED
172285.

Designed to present communications problems faced by
the elderly and to assist classroom teachers to develop activities
for dealing with them, this booklet begins by examining stereotypes
of older persons which minimize and distort communication with
them.   It outlines common misconceptions about the elderly, center-
ing on their state of mind, health, capacity for work, interest in
life and sexual activity, and financial condition, and it notes that
despite television's capacity to serve a number of functions for the
elderly, it reinforces such stereotypes in advertising and programing.   The second part of the booklet provides exercises for use in
a unit on communication and the elderly, designed to restructure
patterns of communication that manifest or reinforce negative stereotypes about older persons and the aging process.   Exercises are
grouped in the following four sections: diagnosing attitudes toward
the elderly; examining the various media (television, magazines,
and children's books) for positive and negative stereotypes toward
the aging; encouraging empathy with the elderly regarding their communication difficulties; and encouraging intergenerational communication.   A list of classroom film, musical, and literary resources is
included.

77. Old and alone, by Tora K. Bikson and Jacqueline Goodchilds.
Santa Monica, CA, Rand Corporation, November 1978.
21p.   ED 172120.

A common assumption, reflective of data obtained from
older males, often in institutional or outpatient settings, is that being old and alone is a severely negative condition.   A sample of
300 older men and women in community settings provides an alternative perspective.   For a number of daily living activities as well
as personal and interpersonal attitudes and orientations, comparisons
between older adults currently living with spouse and those alone
make it apparent that sex of the subject importantly affects outcome.
For older women in the lone status, life is far from unpleasant; in
fact, they fare better not only than their single male counterparts
but also than still-coupled women of comparable age.   For men, on
the other hand, the stereotypic views seem to have more substance.
Results are interpreted in the light of previous history of traditional
role enactment and its differential impact during aging for men and
women.

78. The Older worker; a case study, by Ilene Changar-Shaw.   1979.
77p.   ED 173593.

The number of Americans between the ages fifty-five and seventy-four will significantly increase during the next few decades. Within this group is the fastest growing poverty group in the country. For them the right to work is basic to the right to survive. Studies have shown that older workers are able to produce work which is, in quality and quantity, equal to that of younger workers, thus dispelling some of the myths associated with aging. One important study was conducted by Lou Harris and is entitled "The Myth and Reality of Aging in America." Various titles of CETA (Comprehensive Employment and Training Act) could conceivably encompass older adult employment programs. At present funds for such programs are supplied by Title IX of the Older Americans Act, which provides for and promotes part-time employment in community service jobs for economically disadvantaged persons fifty-five years old or older. To protect persons up to age sixty-five from widespread age discrimination in the job market, the federal government enacted the Age Discrimination in Employment Act. Another option for providing employment to the older worker is career retraining. Since age is not an accurate indicator of ability, the policy of mandatory retirement should be re-examined by employers. Likewise, the federal government should re-examine the Social Security system which limits the earnings of older workers.

3.
WOMEN

79. <u>World plan of action; decade for women.</u> Washington, DC,
       Women's Equity Action League, 1975. 18p. ED 123173.
       The World Plan of Action adopted by the United Nations
World Conference of the International Women's Year in Mexico City
in July 1975 is presented in condensed form. The major purpose
is to provide guidelines for national action over the ten-year period
1975-1985 as part of a sustained, long-term effort to achieve the
objectives of International Women's Year. The report is addressed
primarily to governments and to public and private institutions, women's and youth organizations, employers, trade unions, mass communications media, nongovernmental organizations, political parties,
and other groups. The report calls for a clear commitment at all
levels of government to take the action necessary to implement the
plan and for governmental review of legislation affecting the status
of women in the light of human rights and principles and internation-
ally accepted standards. The guidelines treat the following topics:
peace, political action, education, employment, health, the family,
population, housing, social problems, social services, research,
the media, and international action.

80. <u>Changing roles of women in industrial societies; a Bellagio</u>
       <u>Conference,</u> March 1976. New York, Rockefeller Foun-
       dation, December 1977. 175p. ED 164626.
       In this report, the proceedings of a 1976 conference on
the changing role of women are outlined. Topics discussed focus
around the four papers presented: "Social Trends and Women's Lives,
1965-1985," by Alice Rossi; "Evolving Relationships Between Women
and Men," by Joseph Katz; "Educating Women for Leadership," by
Margherita Rendel, and "Projected Future Employment and Leadership Needs and Areas," by Andree Michel. Major areas of interest
included changing sexual trends, women's economic status and attitudes towards finances, continuing male domination of institutions,
male-female development, and coresidential living. Comments of
participants from the United States, Sweden, Italy, England, France,
and Finland about the role of women in those countries are summarized.

81. <u>California women; report of the California Commission on the
    Status of Women.</u> Sacramento, The Commission, De-
    cember 1975. 118p. ED 156581.
    Major activities of the California Commission on the
Status of Women during 1974-75 are described, and summaries are
presented which characterize the status of women in California in
areas of social, political, and economic life. Established by the
state legislature in 1965, the Commission has among its goals the
study of changing roles and responsibilities of women, elimination
of inequities in law, operation as an information center for government and the public, and provision of technical and consultive advice to groups working toward women's equity. During 1974-75,
the Commission conducted public awareness activities, developed
publications, and supported legislative changes for women in areas
of legal equity, credit, government participation, insurance, child
care, education, counseling, employment, and the media. Seven
chapters explore these areas in detail, giving statistical information
and explanations of women's changing status. Each chapter reviews
recent legislation which promotes equity for women. Also presented
are lists of resources and some Commission publications on the
topics covered. Appendices identify California city, county, and
community commissions on the status of women; regulatory agencies;
member groups of the California Coalition for the Equal Rights
Amendment; and resource organizations concerned with women's
equity.

82. <u>Sex roles in sexual behavior; an historical perspective,</u> by
    Donna Iven. 1973. 26p. ED 092857.
    This paper attempts to trace the historical and societal
development of sex roles as related to women in today's society.
Discussions include the role of the female in tribal societies, the
development of monogamous marriage, and the societal influences
which identify a woman primarily as a housewife and mother from
the 16th-20th centuries. Careful consideration is given to the socialization of sex roles in children and how this relates to marriage
expectations. The feminist movement is viewed as an attempt to
equalize sex roles in education, sexuality, and the world of work.

83. <u>Freeing our lives; a feminist analysis of rape prevention,</u> by
    Sunny Graff.⁻ Sponsored by the National Institute of Men-
    tal Health, DHEW. 1978. 30p. ED 163302.
    The factors which contribute to women's vulnerability to
rape are a lack of information about and understanding of rape; women's subordinate relationship to men; socially reinforced physical
weakness and passivity; isolation from other women; isolation in the
community. Prevention means more than just reducing the incidence
of rape or providing security for some women. Prevention means
eliminating rape so that all women will be free from the threat of
assault. Some strategies which all women can implement to reduce
our vulnerability include: (1) redefining rape in terms of shared
knowledge and experience, thus making rape a public issue; (2)

changing the power-dependence relationship between men and women
in a patriarchal culture; (3) developing physical strength and skills,
and gaining confidence in women's ability to assert their rights; (4)
learning to recognize their power as a group; (5) organizing for common defense in neighborhoods and making women's safety a community priority. Women need to continue the work of developing
strategies which will increase their strength, mobility, independence
and freedom.

84. Women as victims of violence; battered wives / rape; a se-
    lected annotated bibliography, by Marilyn Gehr. Albany,
    New York State Education Department, January 1978.
    26p. ED 163341.
    This selected annotated bibliography focuses on women
as victims of violence, specifically battered wives and rape victims.
Areas of concern include the history of violence, causes, statistics,
legal remedies, and suggestions for reform. Case studies highlight
the involvement of police, social agencies, hospitals, and the community. Summaries of research are also included.

85. How to start a rape crisis center. Washington, DC, Rape
    Crisis Center, 1972. 47p. ED 108060.
    This booklet, written in response to requests from
throughout the nation about how a rape crisis center can be started,
presents the history of the founding of the Washington, D.C. center.
The booklet offers sections dealing with specific issues. A section
discusses, for the rape victim, pros and cons of working with the
police, together with the various legal implications. The medical
and hospital information section describes hospital procedures and
the problems of venereal disease and pregnancy. Additional sections
discuss the emergency phone service of the crisis center, transportation and counseling, conducting rape conferences, and publicity.
The final section, called "Putting it All Together", covers other
important issues not mentioned in previous parts of the booklet.
Appendices containing sample forms, bylaws of the rape crisis center, and a mock phone conversation are attached.

86. Rape and its victims; a report for citizens, health facilities,
    and criminal justice agencies; a prescriptive package,
    by Lisa Brodyaga. Sponsored by Law Enforcement As-
    sistance Administration, Department of Justice. Wash-
    ington, DC, November 1975. 339p. ED 120612.
    This book is addressed to police administrators, hospi-
tal administrators, prosecutors, and citizens involved in community
action who are prepared to re-examine their agencies' response to
cases of rape. It provides information and analysis to spark such
a review and outlines suggestions for coping with problems that commonly hinder change. The discussion is confined to forcible rape
of adult women, generally defined as the carnal knowledge of a female through the use of force or threat of force by a male other
than her husband. The book is divided into four sections: "The

Police Response," "The Response of Medical Facilities," "The Response of Prosecutors' Offices," and the "Response of Citizens' Action Groups." The material presented in each is based upon the findings of national surveys conducted among each of these four groups, with special emphasis placed on agencies that have begun innovative changes in their approach to cases of rape. Each section presents findings from these nationwide surveys and then suggests guidelines for others seeking ways to improve their procedures in such cases. Insights gained from monitoring rape victim projects or innovations underway in six jurisdictions are presented in Appendix V. A basic finding in these studies was that the function of police departments, hospitals, prosecutors, courts, and citizen groups are highly interdependent.

87. Women in transition; volunteer counselors for women in a county jail; a report. Sacramento, California State Commission on the Status of Women, 1977. 137p. ED 163359.

Women in Transition was conceived as an action project of the California Commission on the Status of Women. The purpose of the project was to test the effectiveness of community volunteers in providing much-needed services to women incarcerated in the county jail. Findings were varied. Community women were interested in the women in jail and did not violate the security of the facility. They were able to relate to inmates despite many differences and were helpful as paraprofessional counselors. Volunteers needed to be motivated by factors beyond usual satisfactions; continuous recruitment and training of new volunteers required a great deal of effort. In addition, the project acted as a catalyst for new programs for ex-offender women in the community as well as being useful as a focus for community education.

88. Birth control as obscenity; Margaret Sanger and "The Woman Rebel," by Lynne Masel Walters. Paper presented at the annual meeting of the Association for Education in Journalism, August 1978. 24p. ED 163518.

In spite of the negative aspects of her determination to be the sole motivator, controller, and martyr for the birth control movement, Margaret Sanger was a positive social force in testing and denouncing the Comstock law. The law, named for Anthony Comstock, a postal inspector who had lobbied Congress to forbid the distribution of obscene materials throughout the United States, equated birth control and sex education with obscenity. After Comstock declared two issues of a socialist newspaper unmailable because Sanger had mentioned the names of venereal diseases in her articles on sex, Sanger resorted to publishing her own newspaper, "The Woman Rebel." The first issue and six of the next eight issues were suppressed for their controversial content and Sanger was indicted on nine counts of law violation, despite the fact that the articles contained only general discussions of contraception. After Sanger fled to Europe, alleging that the courts were treating her unfairly, her estranged husband was arrested for passing on one copy of her birth control pamphlet. Resentful of his publicity, Sanger returned seeking a court trial in order to achieve publicity for her cause. When the government decided not to prosecute her, she achieved publicity by forming an organization to promote contraception.

89. Depression: a social or a mental health problem? Implications for the health of Women, by Myrna M. Weissman. Paper presented at the annual meeting of the American Orthopsychiatric Association, March 1978. 22p. ED 160931.
There is no doubt that women have more depression than men--both treated and untreated--and that depression affects women in their most productive years, impairing personal satisfaction and ability to fulfill social roles. A review of the various therapeutic approaches to depression shows that there is good evidence that the traditional treatments, both pharmacotherapy and psychotherapy, have value, as well as a combination of both approaches. Self-help groups can be used as a supplement to traditional therapies, and a deeper understanding of non-traditional therapies is warranted.

90. Black views of American women; the view from black newspapers, 1865-1900, by Bess Beatty. 1978. 21p. ED 161987.
Although black journalists from 1865 to 1900 were more sensitive to stereotyping and discrimination than their white counterparts, the black papers approached women idealistically, rather than through the realistic situation in which black women existed or through their own awareness of the fact of oppression. The images and proscriptions of women in black papers did not change significantly in this time period, nor did they differ from those found in white papers. Surviving papers make it possible to discern an image of woman as a frail, often frivolous and scatterbrained gossip whose mission was caring for her home and children, serving as her husband's helpmate and maintaining the highest standards of morality. In fact, the experience of slavery had blunted delineations in male and female roles among blacks. Following emancipation, efforts to more sharply define sex roles were counseled and practiced. Black journalists challenged the negative stereotypes of black people fostered by whites, and upgraded the self-image of a usually degraded people. However, in a time period that required most black women to work for survival, newspapers presented irrational expectations, drawn from the white-inspired "cult of true womanhood."

91. Debilitating attributions of the woman alcoholic undergoing treatment, by Irene H. Frieze and Maureen C. McHugh. Paper presented at the annual convention of the American Psychological Association, August 1977. 38p. ED 159520.
Alcoholism is becoming an increasingly significant problem for women. At one time, women rarely drank and the female

alcoholic was an anomaly.   Estimates of the total number of women
alcoholics in the United States today are over 900,000.   Women now
constitute from 20 to 35% of all alcoholics in this country.   This
paper attempts to gain understanding of psychological factors which
may underlie female alcoholism.   The approach used was to apply
a theoretical model derived from social psychology: attribution
theory.   In order to assess causal attributions, expectancies, and
affect, a group of alcoholics were asked to state their causal attributions for a number of success or failure achievement and interpersonal situations.   Their responses were compared with those of
the general population.   The alcoholic sample included 41 male and
28 female recovering alcoholics in a halfway house treatment center.   The nonalcoholic sample included 31 males and 33 females re-
cruited from neighborhoods similar to the former neighborhoods of
the alcoholic subjects.   Alcoholics of both sexes saw success most
resulting from effort.   Female alcoholics saw failure as more due
to their personalities than to lack of effort.   Employment seemed
to be a particularly important situation for understanding alcoholic
attributions.

92.   The Equal Rights Amendment in Washington State; an analysis
            and interpretation of voting patterns, by Viktor Gecas.
            Sponsored by the Department of Rural Sociology, Wash-
            ington State University, 1977.   22p.   ED 160507.
            A study was undertaken in Washington state to investigate
voting behavior on the Equal Rights Amendment (ERA), which was
approved by Washington state voters in 1972.   Specifically, research
objectives were to determine who was for or against the ERA, to
assess the nature of objections to the ERA, and to consider implications of the ERA for family relationships.   A random sample of
over 800 Washington state residents was interviewed by telephone in
December 1972.   Information was obtained on respondents' age, sex,
marital status, occupation, education, family size, political and religious affiliation, and vote (or attitude) regarding the ERA.   Findings indicated that men were more favorable toward the ERA than
women: single and divorced respondents were more favorable than
were married respondents: young were more favorable than old:
white collar workers were more favorable than blue collar workers:
and individuals with more education were more favorable than those
with less education.   Favorable decisions regarding the ERA appeared to be influenced by psychological variables (attitudes, values, self-
concept) and by situational factors such as responsibilities of women
and men in the home and outside employment.   Additional research
is suggested on the unequal division of labor in the home as an obstacle to sex equality and as a major reason for women's opposition
to the ERA.

93.   The Mature woman in higher education; what's a nice old girl
            like you doing in a place like this? by Monnie Ryan.
            1979.   35p.   ED 174295.
            Mature women are returning to colleges and universities

in ever-increasing numbers. These women have special goals and special needs and it is essential that institutions of higher education respond to these needs. The problems faced by the older woman student are numerous and may be characterized as either institutional or personal. Institutional problems include: the availability of accurate program information; financial aid restrictions; lack of counseling and support services and of child care; rigid class scheduling; and failure to receive credit for earlier education and various life experiences. Personal problems involve fear of academic competition; insecurity about learning ability; guilt that results from conflicting home and school demands; and lack of spousal support, either financial or emotional. Institutions of higher education can respond to these problems by offering formal orientation programs and peer support organizations; financial aid for part-time students; and flexible and nontraditional class formats, utilizing evening classes, televised instruction, and satellite and mobile campuses. Personal and career counseling services should be provided by staff members trained to understand the needs of mature women re-entry students.

94. Choices and careers; free to choose; women today and tomorrow, by Cathaleen Finley. Madison, University of Wisconsin Extension Service. 22p. ED 158941.
    Nine out of 10 girls can expect to work for pay; six of them will be part of the labor force for 30 years. Today five out of ten women between the ages of 18 and 64 are working outside the home. A young woman must plan to be a worker as well as wife and mother. One fourth of all American Indian women who work for pay are clerical workers, one-fifth service workers, and another one-fifth do factory type work, all relatively low paying jobs. The world is changing; women expect to live longer and have fewer children; and there are more widowed, divorced, separated, and unmarried women. Greater attention must be given to career planning. This document is the introduction to the "Choices and Careers: Free to Choose" program for young tribal women, which endeavors to help girls think through the choices they have and to plan so that options are open for career choices. It discusses new career opportunities for women, including the non-traditional jobs becoming available, the value of higher education, and early conditioning that creates the passivity, dependence and non-competitive attitudes that hamper girls in realizing their fullest potential.

95. The League of Women Voters of the United States; a case study in organizational communication, by Ileen N. Kaufman-Everett. Paper presented at the Speech Communication Association convention, December 1977. 20p. ED 159099.
    The paper analyzes structure and organizational communication within the League of Women Voters. The document is presented in three major sections. The first section traces the history of the League of Women Voters from its origins in the women's suffrage movement to its current involvement with international re-

lations, human rights, and environmental quality. Section two discusses the League's structure and membership. It is a large multi-
organization which stresses differentiation into units, integration of
activities among units, and adaptation of activities to changing conditions. The League is divided into local, state, and national units,
and comprises approximately 140,000 members. Approximately
4,000 members are men. Members work on local, state, and national issues in cooperation with league units concerned with those
issues. Section three analyzes the League's approach to organizational communication. The League encourages communication among
members as well as integration and cooperation among units. Each
unit has its own officers and Board of Directors responsible for
management of their particular League and who act as representatives of the general membership. Leagues at all levels sponsor
committees, workshops, discussion units, and general membership
meetings. All members are encouraged to participate in as many
activities as possible and to share leadership roles.

96. A Consciousness-raising program for adult women, by Marylou
     B. Kincaid. 1972. 31p. ED 116064.
          This program is a structured, 16-session consciousness-
raising group for adult women which can be used in a university
setting with women in continuing education or in a community setting
with noncollege women. The program is designed to help women
identify the influence of sex-role stereotyping on their lives, learn
ways for effective sex-role conflict resolution, and define interests
and personal goals. It has been given as a one credit course by
the Counseling Service staff at Phoenix Community College in Arizona for groups of 12 to 15 women. Participants have become more
self-achievement-oriented and inner-directed following the course and
report an increased appreciation for other women.

97. Mothers too soon. Washington, DC, Draper World Population
     Fund, 1975. 29p. ED 113270.
          Six articles provide an overview of the problems of early
marriage and/or adolescent pregnancy in both developed and developing nations. The first article reveals that social factors outweigh
the biological in the reproduction process and reports that each year
over 15 million babies are born to girls under 20, who become
mothers too soon to achieve their full potential as educated active
citizens and too soon to provide optimal care and support for their
babies. The second article examines early marriage and pregnancy
in traditional Islamic society. An expert on Chinese population policies, in the third article highlights the priority which the Chinese
have given to raising the marriage age to increase female participation in national development and to reduce population. Sex and reproduction, which are constantly rising, among American teenage
women are examined in the fourth article. The fifth article presents the problems of teenage pregnancies as high risks for infants.
Marriage law reform in Indonesia is examined in the sixth article
with respect to the struggle for equal rights for women. The last

article presents the biological aspects of teenage pregnancy. Also
included in the report are memorial tributes to William Draper by
leaders in the international population field.

98. An Historical review of women in dentistry; an annotated bib-
    liography, by Constance Boquist and Jeannette Haase.
    Rockville, MD, Health Resources Administration, DHEW,
    June 1977. 112p. ED 148223.
    A brief introduction is given to the bibliography, which
contains 263 citations and 162 original abstracts of articles on the
topic of women dentists. The citations cover the period of 1865-
1977, and include some from popular publications. The majority
are from professional and scientific journals and books.

99. Rediscovering women mathematicians, by Karen D. Rappaport.
    1978. 23p. ED 160444.
    The lives and mathematical contributions of seven famous
women mathematicians are presented. They are: Hypatia, Agnesi,
Sophie Germain, Mary Sommerville, Augusta Lovelace, Sofya Kova-
levsky, and Emmy Noether.

100. Women in science and technology; U.S./USSR comparisons, by
     Gerhard Schilling and M. Kathleen Hunt. Santa Monica,
     CA, Rand Corporation, June 1974. 72p. ED 125886.
     This report compares the roles and utilization of women
in science and technology in the Soviet Union and the United States.
Changes in demographic and population data in both countries during
this century are examined and compared. Differences in policies
and organization of scientific enterprises are also examined and used
in comparing the participation of women in scientific and professional
occupations in the two countries. Results of the analysis indicate
that over the last 30 years, Russian women have been educated and
have achieved all but the highest offices equally with men. The
authors observe that use of women's capacities is essential to the
Soviet economy, and that if any change in women's status should be
expected in the USSR, it will be one of declining need for women
in the work force. By contrast, the status of women in the United
States is changing from one in which their talents have been untapped
or underdeveloped. It is conjectured that societal changes in the
United States will cause an increase in the proportion of women in
the professions.

101. Out of the cage; women emerging, by Sophie Ann Aoki. Hono-
     lulu, Hawaii State Commission on the Status of Women,
     1976. 52p. ED 146682.
     A history of the status of women in Hawaii, particularly,
and the United States, in general, is documented in this publication.
Two case studies of women encountering employment discrimination
in Hawaii because of their sex and their actions to obtain equal
employment conditions are summarized. Present employment conditions in Hawaii are followed by a section on women of old Hawaii.

The history of the women's movement in the United States is discussed in terms of individual rights, religion, education, and employment.   The final sections discuss combating sex discrimination
by the political activities of voting, party participation, holding office, and uniting diverse groups in supporting the ratification of the
Equal Rights Amendment.

102.   A Woman's guide to apprenticeship.   Washington, DC, Wo-
        men's Bureau, Department of Labor, 1978.   28p.   ED
        167837.
        This guide informs women about the apprenticeship sys-
tem and how it operates, provides some background on the problems
that women sometimes encounter in seeking apprenticeships, and
outlines the apprenticeship application process.   Statistics are given
concerning the growth in the number of women participating in the
apprenticeship system.   In the section, Women as Skilled Craft
Workers, the current status of these workers as well as their ability, interest, and availability are discussed.   The system itself is
analyzed in terms of the role of federal and state apprenticeship
agencies and committees, training, standards, and types of apprenticeable occupations.   Barriers to women in apprenticeship, such
as sex discrimination, inadequate preparation, and age, are examined in the third section.   A section on how to become an apprentice
includes choosing a trade, sources of occupational and program information, and the application process (containing data on tests, interviews, and probation).   Another section summarizes federal laws
and regulations affecting apprenticeship.   Addresses for the Women's
Bureau Regional Offices and for the Bureau of Apprenticeship and
Training Regional Offices are appended.

103.   Women and the American economy; a bicentennial appraisal;
        proceedings of the Air Force Academy Assembly.
        Colorado Springs, March 1976.   82p.   ED 136090.
        The proceedings delve into facets of the women's move-
ment in America and, particularly the effect of women on the national economy.   Highlighted are the speeches to the Assembly of
Ms. Betty Friedan, Mrs. Catherine East, Dr. Peggy Kruger, Dr.
Jean Lipman-Blumen, and Mrs. Phyllis Schlafly, as well as a final
report adopted by the Assembly.   The personal, social, and economic factors which have altered the awareness of traditional sex roles
and have given impetus to the "sex role revolution" are enumerated
and discussed.   The impact of the changing sex stereotype upon the
family and society is detailed.   Pros and cons of the Equal Rights
Amendment are presented.

104.   The Consequences of early childbearing; research summary,
        by Kristin A. Moore and Sandra L. Hofferth.   Sponsored
        by the National Institute of Child Health and Human De-
        velopment, National Institute of Health, December 1977.
        25p.   ED 149002.
        The effects of early childbearing on a woman's later

social and economic status are examined in this paper. Previous
research has documented an association of early motherhood with
lower educational attainment, marital instability, higher subsequent
fertility, and later economic poverty. However, these associations
have not been tested in multivariate models of attainment that include important controls for social, economic, and motivational factors. Therefore, it is not clear whether the attainment of young
women is inhibited by having a first birth at a young age, or whether
the achievements of early childbearers are limited by personal and
social characteristics other than age at first birth. The analyses
summarized in this paper evaluate the attainment of approximately
5000 contemporary young American females as it is affected by the
age when they bear their first child. In addition, the effect of the
legitimacy status of the birth is evaluated. Quantified results and
analytical discussion focus upon education; family size (fertility);
marital stability; and occupational and income status. Additional
foci include an examination of the relationship between female headed
families, welfare dependency, and poverty. Some means are suggested by which the government, the schools, and other institutions
could ameliorate the problems of high teenage fertility.

105.   Forty-six pioneers; Louisiana women in non-traditional jobs.
        Baton Rouge, Louisiana State Department of Health and
        Human Resources, November 1977. 53p. ED 150432.
        This report concerns forty-six Jobs Unlimited placements
of women in Louisiana into nontraditional jobs (mostly blue-collar or
skilled craft fields) between April 1976 and January 1977. (Jobs
Unlimited was a project which informed the public, especially women,
of opportunities available in nontraditional employment.) The report
researches the demographic background, employment history, and
social characteristics of the women placed, explores client adjustment and progress in the new job, and examines the attitudes of
personnel administrators toward women in nontraditional jobs, and
those of women toward their nontraditional work. Some of the major conclusions presented follow: (1) For most of the forty-six women placed, the greatest strides came in the areas of wages and
chances for advancement, (2) the job retention rate of 85% with an
average eight months of service indicated that, with proper counseling and screening of prospective employees, excessive turnover rates
for women workers can be avoided, (3) the experience of nontraditional employment has been a positive one for the majority of women
involved, (4) as a whole, company administrators failed to notice
any significant effects from the employment of women, and (5) neither
foremen nor administrators perceived any considerable advantages
in the hiring of women, although overall reactions were generally
positive. (Recommendations concerning the hiring of women in nontraditional jobs are included in this report. Twelve biographical
sketches of women who served as subjects are appended to reflect
the diversity of the women adn their experiences in their new employment.)

106. Four traditions; women of New York during the American
Revolution, by Linda Grant DePaaw. Albany, New York
State American Revolution Bicentennial Commission,
1974. 42p. ED 111732.
The role of New York women in the American Revolution
is discussed in a survey of four cultural traditions in 17th and 18th
century New York--Iroquois, African, Dutch, and English. The
purpose is to provide a historical record on the subject of women's
history. Women from the four cultural traditions were bound by
different conventions which influenced their reactions to the Revolutionary crisis and affected the ways in which that crisis would change
their lives. American women were as deeply influenced by the Revolution as were American men, though not always to their benefit.
The successful war for independence marked a significant turning
point in the status of women. Documented stories are recounted of
individual women's activities during the Revolution in each of the
chapters titled: Four Traditions; Choosing Sides; Soldiers, Refugees, and Camp Followers; Treason and Espionage; and Aftermath.
Some of the stories depict heroic acts, but some show wrongdoings
as well. They all indicate the importance and necessity of the roles
women played and the tasks they undertook during the Revolution.

107. Mary Abigail Dodge; journalist and anti-feminist, by Maurine
Beasley. Paper presented at the annual meeting of the
Association for Education in Journalism, August 1979.
28p. ED 172238.
Mary Abigail Dodge, a Washington, D.C., correspondent before and after the United States Civil War, was one of the
most acclaimed women journalists of the nineteenth century. Unknown today, Dodge wrote on politics, religion, and contemporary
issues for newspapers and magazines and commented prolifically
on the role of women in society. After feminist leanings as a young
woman, she became increasingly conservative as she grew older.
Her most celebrated articles appeared in the "New York Tribune"
in 1877 and 1878 and attacked the efforts at civil service reform
attempted under the administration of President Rutherford B. Hayes.
Throughout her 40-year career, Dodge insisted on writing under the
pseudonym, "Gail Hamilton." Dividing her life into two totally different spheres, she remained "Abby" to her family and refused to
acknowledge in public that she was also "Gail," the famous literary
figure. Well-known as a brilliant and witty conversationalist, she
had wide-ranging contacts in literary and political circles. Her
career illustrates that an able woman could carve a place for herself in Victorian journalism, but it also illuminates the self-doubts
and insecurities of a woman trying to function in a man's occupation.

108. Hannah Bruce Watson; patriot printer in the American Revolution, by Susan Henry. Paper presented at the annual
meeting of the Association for Education in Journalism,
August 1978. 26p. ED 163515.
Although Hannah Watson had had little printing training

prior to her husband's unexpected death, she assumed his job as
publisher of the "Connecticut Courant" newspaper, a vehement advocate of the patriot cause, for 16 months during the Revolutionary
War. In spite of problems such as wartime printing shortages, the
burning and reconstruction of the paper mill, inflation, and the responsibility of settling her husband's estate, Watson's paper was
financially successful and maintained a patriotic editorial policy that
reminded readers of the war and the principles behind it in every
issue. The paper supplied battle descriptions from all of the colonies, analyses of significant events, and news of British home events
and criticisms of Parliament, while calling for colonist support and
economic sacrifice. Excluding advertising and short local items,
the paper carried only nine nonpolitical articles during this period.
When Hannah Watson married a successful businessman, she turned
over her position and property to him and retired to private life
and the newspaper assumed a conservative editorial policy.

109. Women in sports and games in the colonial period, by R. A.
        Howell. Paper presented at the annual convention,
        North American Society for Sport History, May 1977.
        27p. ED 150132.
        The physical activities of women in the colonial period
in the United States were limited. Social attitudes differed between
the northern and southern colonies on appropriate activities for women. In the north it was not considered unseemly for women to
participate in ice skating, while in the south women were encouraged
to become good equestriennes. In the colonies as a whole, women's
recreational activities were limited to less strenuous pleasures, such
as dancing, quilting, and decorous swimming (bathing). As spectators, women were permitted to view horse races and boat races.

110. Covering women; women's publications and the mass media,
        by Sheila J. Silver. Paper presented at the annual
        meeting of the Association for Education in Journalism,
        August 1977. 24p. ED 153210.
        Before reporting on a study of the relationship between
the mass media and advocates of women's rights who edit periodicals for women, the first half of this paper discusses the following:
the problematic area of the coverage of women in newspapers, feminist criticism of the restricted content of women's pages, the press's
controversial coverage of the women's movement, journalists as advocates of feminism, and feminist periodicals. The second half of
the paper reports on a questionnaire designed to find out how 210
editors of women's publications felt about communication for women.
Questions asked for specific information about the publication and
limited the range of responses on opinion questions. The survey
results are both demographic and related to the relationship between
the mass media and the respondents. The study revealed no hostility between feminist editors and the press; dissatisfaction that exists on the part of the editors surveyed lies mainly in the frustra-
tions of reaching women when limited by unsophisticated equipment,

low budgets, and small staffs, while the mass media, with wider influence and range, are uncertain and inconsistent in assigning stories about women and giving them prominent play.

4.
ETHNIC GROUPS
AND
MINORITIES:
INDIANS,
BLACKS,
CHICANOS

111. <u>Minority contributions to science, engineering, and medicine,</u>
        by Peggy Funches. San Diego, City Schools, 1978.
        179p. ED 156382.
        Offering an historical perspective on the development
of science, engineering, medicine, and technology and providing current role models for minority students, the bulletin lists the outstanding contributions made by: (1) Blacks - medicine, chemistry,
architecture, engineering, physics, biology, and exploration; (2)
Hispanos - biomedical research, botany, biology, physics, chemistry, space education, physiology, mathematics, pharmacology, me-
teorology, oceanography, sociology, geology, anthropology, psychology, engineering, electronics, and computers; (3) Asian Americans
- astronomy, engineering, technology, mathematics, medicine, health,
physics, dentistry, chemistry, and space education; (4) American
Indians - engineering, botany, physics, architecture, chemistry,
biology, agronomy, forestry, environmental science, weather fore-
casting, science education, audiology, otolaryngology, archeology,
nursing, mathematics, anthropology, psychology, dentistry, medicine, and pharmacology. Also listed are Hispanic Nobel Prize win-
ners, scientists of the 20th century, and professors; Moslem and
Jewish scientists of Medieval Spain (circa 900-1400), statistics on
the representation of Hispanos in science; programs designed to
meet the Hispanos' health service needs; programs for Indian students and agencies to contact for possible financial aid; groups of
special interest to Indian students; and available resources and
creative ways to incorporate knowledge and appreciation of minority
contributions into the regular instructional program.

112. <u>Land and minority enterprise; the crisis and the opportunity,</u>
        by Lester M. Salamon. Durham, NC, Institute of
        Policy Sciences and Public Affairs, Duke University,

June 1976. 94p. ED 139852.

The location, uses and changes of minority land resources are examined. The utility of an "expanded ownership" approach is demonstrated. Practical ways to implement a minority
business development strategy utilizing existing minority-owned land
as a base are considered. One idea in particular is discussed: the
possibility of giving minority landowners access to federally owned
land in ways that would contribute to the viability of existing minority farm enterprises. It has been found that black landowners have
been losing their land at a rapid rate in the South in large part because the size of their individual holdings is not sufficient to generate an adequate income. Federal landownership is quite extensive
in the South, where most black-owned land is concentrated. Commercial activity is already quite extensive on federal landholdings
in the southeast. The use of public lands to accommodate the graz-
ing needs of minority-owned beef cattle enterprises is one of the
most interesting possibilities for systematically utilizing public land
in a land-based minority development strategy. Public lands could
also contribute substantially to other minority enterprise development
operations as well, including a variety of specialty crop production
activities and timber operations.

113.   Toward a new bill of rights. New York, National Urban
         League, 1977. 215p. ED 148956.

The theme of the 1976 Urban League Conference was
"a new bill of rights" for all Americans. Rights of blacks and other
minority groups were particularly emphasized. The subject of the
right to black representation in the American political system was
addressed by Samuel Du Bois Cook. The keynote address by Vernon E. Jordan, Jr., considered such issues as the rights of all
citizens to education, economic security, health, family stability,
political representation, and the right to safe communities. Andrew
Billingsley, James G. Haughton, Andrew F. Brimmer, Edythe J.
Gaines, and Thomas A. Bradley all spoke to at least one of these
issues. Carla Hill's address reviewed the progress of federal urban programs in the year preceding the Conference. Henry Kissin-
ger spoke about foreign affairs, particularly the U.S. relationship
with Africa. W.J. Usery, Jr., and William M. Ellinghaus stressed
black participation in the American private enterprise system.
Yvonne Braithwaite Burke, Arthur A. Fletcher, Hubert H. Humphrey,
and Charles McC. Mathias discussed the role of black voters in the
1976 presidential race. John Hope Franklin mentioned important
events in the history of black Americans. The introductions, texts,
and discussions of all the above mentioned speeches are included in
this document. Also included are texts of press conferences held,
statements of concern released by the Urban League, lists of Conference exhibitors, and a listing of League members and Conference
participants.

114.   Minorities and malnutrition, by Francis A. Kornegay. De-
         troit, Detroit Urban League, December 1975. 60p. ED

129937.
Various aspects of the relationship between minorities
and malnutrition are discussed in this brief paper. Malnutrition,
one of the byproducts of low economic status, is creating a crisis
proportion health problem affecting minority citizens. Malnutrition
seriously affects children, older people in poverty, and chronically
unemployed or underemployed youth. It is also most likely to be
found among the drug and alcohol addicted population. Frequently,
malnutrition leads to tuberculosis and other diseases among older
people and results in infant mortality and diseases of the newborn.
Poverty has been identified as the cause of malnutrition, and a cor-
responding proportion of difficulties children experience in school
and later in their career development may be due to deficit nutrition affecting brain growth during early life. Because Detroit's
over fifty percent black population is the worst affected economically in the entire nation, the city is most likely to be affected by malnutrition on a scale greater than the national average. The Detroit
Urban League intends to direct research effort in evaluating the nutritional problems of minorities in order to find productive outlets
for channeling their resources.

115.   The Melting of the ethnics; education of the immigrants, 1880-
       1914, by Mark Krug. Bloomington, IN, Phi Delta Kappa,
       1976. 128p. ED 128284.
       This book, one in a five-volume series dealing with per-
spectives in American education, discusses the education of ethnic
groups in the United States. The purpose of the series is to create
a better understanding of the education process and the relation of
education to human welfare. Chapter one discusses multicultural
education, examining the concept of the melting pot, the "Americanization" idea, and the theory of cultural pluralism. Chapter two relates the story of three major immigrant groups: Italians, Jews,
and Poles. In chapter three ethnic loyalities and affiliations are investigated. Chapter four examines the educational philosophy of
Jane Addams, founder of Chicago's Hull House. Public schools and
the upward mobility of immigrant children through them is the theme
of chapter five. Specifically examined are bilingual education programs, curriculum materials dealing with ethnic cultures, how public education did or did not meet the needs of ethnic groups, and
the "- mainstream" American culture. The book contains a selected
bibliography.

116.   Look how far you've come. Harrisburg, Pennsylvania State
       Department of Education, 1977. 43p. ED 173182.
       This pamphlet contains 28 articles written by high school
students based on interviews with community members from 17 ethnic groups. The interviews are conducted by the students as part
of a unit on immigration within their social studies course. The
interviews illustrate many aspects of ethnic studies which are based
on the human rather than the academic dimension. Among the ethnic groups represented are Yugoslavs, Czechoslovakians, Poles,

Serbians, French, Sicilians, Austrians, Mexicans, East Germans, Koreans, Scottish, English, Italians, and Albanians. Many of the interviewees were older adults who had immigrated to the United States early in the 20th century. Their stories describe life in their native countries, holiday customs, immigration experiences on Ellis Island, first impressions of life in the United States, their first jobs in the United States, marriages and deaths of family members, and benefits of living in the United States.

117.   WASPs and others; the immigration debate on the prairies, 1896-1920, by Howard Palmer. Paper delivered to the annual Western Canadian Studies Conference, February 1978. 58p. ED 163146.
       The public controversy which developed between 1896 and 1920 in the Canadian prairie provinces over the question of immigration is examined in this paper. It is shown that although many of the social, political, religious and cultural characteristics which have differentiated the prairies have been a result of ethnic diversity, the predominantly white Anglo-Saxon Protestant population which pioneered the prairies was initially resistent to many immigrant groups. The non-restrictive immigration policy, developed by Minister of the Interior Sifton to stimulate agricultural and economic growth of the region, and its social, political, and economic effects are considered in detail. Acceptance or rejection of various groups (Asians, Central and Eastern Europeans, blacks) and their subsequent assimilation processes (particularly with regard to language) are explained. The issues of racism, social reform, feminism, radicalism, prohibition and naturalization are described in light of the changing social situation and the prevailing political and intellectual currents. Attitudes towards assimilation and immigration legislation are detailed for each ethnic group and, finally, effects of the immigration process on various groups up to 1970 are summarized.

118.   History of Westport and Norwalk, by John L. Mahar. Westport, CT, Westport-Weston Arts Council, 1979. 21p. ED 167446.
       The history of immigration to Norwalk and Westport, Connecticut, from the Revolutionary War period to 1979 is presented. The reading is part of a project to investigate the ethnically varied cultural heritage of the Norwalk-Westport area. It is arranged in two major sections. Section I focuses on Westport--described as an attractive suburban town with a history of involvement in the Revolutionary War, rapid economic growth during the 19th century, and a high degree of interaction among immigrants from many European nations. Groups identified as most common in the 1900 census of Westport are Irish, German, Swedish, Danish, Russian, and Hungarian. Information is presented for each of these groups on life-style, work, recreation, schooling, and religious observances. Section II traces development and settlement of Norwalk. Purchased in 1640 from the Indians, Norwalk developed in

the 1800s as a regional industrial center. Among immigrants who
were attracted to Norwalk with the hope of securing jobs were Irish,
Italians, Hungarians, and Slavs. Beginning in 1950, a new wave of
immigrants settled in Norwalk. Most recent immigrants are Puerto
Ricans, Costa Ricans and blacks from North Carolina, South Carolina,
and Virginia. The document concludes with information on the intense rivalry that has characterized Norwalk proper and South Norwalk from 1870 to the present.

119. Cape Verdeans in America; our story, by Raymond A. Almeida.
        Boston, American Committee for Cape Verde, Inc. , 1978.
        62p. ED 161773.
        Immigration and acculturation of Cape Verdeans in the
United States from the mid-19th century to the present are discussed. Emphasis is on the period prior to 1922, at which time the
United States Congress enacted new laws restricting the immigration
of people of color. The Cape Verde islands are located in the At-
lantic off the coast of West Africa. Because of their location, they
served as a safe harbor to generations of slavers, pirates, smug-
glers, and sailors. The document is presented in four chapters.
Chapter I discusses the historic link between the Cape Verde islands
and New England. Chapter II examines the practice of hiring Cape
Verdeans as crew members for New England's whaling ships from
the period before the American Revolution to the latter half of the
19th century. Chapter III discusses the Cape Verdean-American
packet trade during the 1800s and the settlement of Cape Verdean
seamen in New England towns. Chapter IV characterizes experiences
of Cape Verdeans in America during the period 1900-24. Topics
discussed include processes of immigration to the United States, employment, income, and living conditions. Numerous photographs
are incorporated into the text.

120. The Forgotten minority; Asian Americans in New York City.
        New York, New York State Advisory Committee to the
        U.S. Commission on Civil Rights, November 1977. 59p.
        ED 156784.
        Approximately 2.1 percent of New York City's population
is Asian American. This report is concerned with the difficulties
faced by members of the Chinese, Japanese, Filipino and Korean
communities in the areas of immigration, employment, and as a
result of media stereotyping of Asians. An overview of individual
Asian communities in New York is presented, including brief histories and immigration statistics. Government policies, such as exclusion acts, regulation of visas for Asians, and the eligibility of
immigrants for social security and public assistance, are reviewed.
The employment of Asian Americans in New York is examined in
terms of their representation in traditional and nontraditional industries. Statistics of Asian representation in restaurant, laundry and
garment work, as well as in city and State government, the construction industry, and the health field, are presented. Government
sponsored employment services and programs available locally to

Asian immigrants are described. The effects of the stereotypic
images of Asians projected by the media upon Asian American opportunities are described.

121. An Ethnic anthology. Olympia, WA, Olympia School District,
        1975. 47p. ED 152867.
        The main purpose of this anthology is to provide a
sampling of insights related to racially and culturally different experiences, with an emphasis on the Asian American experience.
The anthology focuses on the experiences of minority children as
portrayed by both children and adults. Impressions written by five
Asian American children in Grades 7 through 9, along with fifteen
poems, and three short stories form the major part of the anthology.

122.   Asian Americans; a case of benighted neglect, by Tom Owan.
         Sponsored by the Social Security Administration, DHEW,
         May 1975. 77p. ED 159254.
         The undercount of the Asian American population, the
phenomenal rise of Asian immigrants, the projected doubling of the
Asian American population by 1980, and the concentration of this
population in urban areas are significant reasons for the reordering
of program priorities so that Asian Americans are not excluded from
Federally funded benefits and services. The stereotyping of Asian
Americans as success models for other immigrants has lulled the
American public into considering Asian American concerns secondary to the problems of other minority groups. Despite the fact
that the Asian Americans attained lower median incomes in the major metropolitan areas, lowest average public assistance incomes
and lower average social security incomes, they continue to be ignored in their efforts to raise themselves into the economic mainstream. Asian Americans also have serious health problems. For
example, they suffer a disproportionate percentage of tuberculosis in
San Francisco and the Chinese have especially high hospitalization
rates for mental illness in the State of California. Furthermore,
the Asian American elderly in major metropolitan areas are facing
serious survival problems due to a history of racism, evacuation
into concentration camps, and denial of citizenship and job opportunities. An effort should be made to provide needed bilingual and
bicultural social services to Asian Americans and other minority
groups.

123.   Asian Americans; Chinese Americans, Japanese Americans,
         Korean Americans, by Keiko Panter. Atlanta, GA,
         Public Schools, 1976. 83p. ED 173513.
         This report presents information on the experiences of
three different Asian-American groups (Chinese, Japanese and Koreans) in the United States. Historical and geographic overviews of
each group's country and a brief chronological history of each
group's country of origin are included. Additional information provided deals with the cultural heritage of the three groups. Specific
topics considered include social norms, verbal and nonverbal com-

munication, music, literature, art and performing arts, and calli-
graphy. Differences between the groups in each of these areas are
illustrated.

124. People of Japan; building bridges of understanding. Provo,
UT, Language Research Center, Brigham Young University, 1976. 47p. ED 140625.
This booklet was designed to facilitate interactions and
communication with the people of Japan by providing information
about their customs, attitudes and other cultural characteristics
which influence their actions and values. A brief description of
Japan is given, covering the following: history, government, the
economy, education, transportation, communications, health facilities,
the people, the family, religion, language, diet, the arts, and sports.
The cultural traits and values involved in the Japanese modesty and
reserve, saving face, traditionalism, passiveness, the situational
ethic, and nonindividualism in a vertical society are explained through
brief descriptions of realistic situations involving American visitors
to Japan. A self-test is given after each situation. Information is
also given on: greetings, visiting, eating, gestures, punctuality,
general courtesies, telephone, shopping, the bath, homes, weddings,
funerals, dress, the postal system, eating out, holidays and festivals, and signs. A list of useful Japanese phrases is given. In
an appendix, descriptions are given of Nihon and nationalism, the
emperor, and the samurai, and several stories about Japanese feelings and attitudes are provided. An annotated bibliography is also
provided.

125. Persistence of ethnicity; the Japanese of Colorado, by Russell
Endo. Paper presented at the Symposium on Ethnicity
on the Great Plains, 1978. 27p. ED 164366.
This paper presents an overview of the history of Japanese in Colorado. Japanese immigrants first came to Colorado
between 1900 and 1910 as railroad laborers. Some became coal
miners in southern Colorado; most others became farm laborers.
Although the Japanese population during this period was small, communities developed in several locales. The largest was in Denver,
and included some small businesses, ethnic churches, and a Japanese newspaper. During the period 1910-1940, the Japanese population in Colorado stabilized at about 2,000. Because they were
prohibited from becoming naturalized citizens, the Japanese became
self-sufficient within their own business and community organizations.
However, they encouraged their children to become educated and to
participate in non-Japanese institutions. The Buddhist church and
several Japanese newspapers continued to be active in Denver. The
period 1940-1970 began with an influx of more Japanese from the
West Coast due to white hostility there caused by the outbreak of
the war. Despite resistance of white Coloradans to Japanese re-
settlement in the state, the Denver community grew and many Japanese obtained more professional jobs. Toward the end of the
period a third generation of Japanese Americans appeared in the

population, and most of the ethnic associations in Denver served
the second-generation Japanese instead of their immigrant parents.
By the 1970s many Japanese had entered the middle class and were
fairly well assimilated into the mainstream culture.   Denver no
longer has major residential concentrations of Japanese.

126.   The Asian American employment market; the Japanese experi-
            ence.   1979.   22p.   ED 173497.
        The Japanese Americans are numerically the largest of
all the Asian American ethnic groups.   In contrast to the other
Asian American groups in the United States, the Japanese Americans
are predominantly native born.   Although first and second generation
Japanese Americans had been subject to intense employment discrimination before World War II and over 100,000 were interned in relocation centers during the War, they have since come to be viewed
as the model minority.   The important factors contributing to their
success are their heavy emphasis on education as the key to success, their upward occupational mobility into professional and technical jobs, and their eastward migration after the War in pursuit of
less discriminatory geographic areas and jobs.   The present day
geographic distribution of Japanese Americans is conditioned by socioeconomic factors.   By a process of adaptation and accomodation,
the first generation Japanese American paved the way for subsequent generations.   The success of the second and third generations
now raises the possibility of their total absorption into the 'melting
pot' and their loss of identity as Japanese Americans.

127.   Chinese youth gangs; an investigation of their origins and ac-
            tivities in Vancouver schools, by Delbert Joe and Nor-
            man Robinson.   Paper presented at the American Edu-
            cational Research Association annual meeting, March
            1978.   25p.   ED 152925.
        This study investigated the origins and activities of
Chinese youth gangs in the northeast section of the city of Vancouver,
Canada over a three year period (1975-1978).   More specifically,
the study attempted to identify and document the existence of several
youth gangs that were believed to be operating in the schools and
community; to collect data on their origins and activities; and to
consider ways of overcoming some of the school and societal problems caused by the gangs.   Structured interviews were held with
13 gang members and with individuals in schools and the community
who had some contact with them.   There were four gangs operating
in Chinatown and its environs at that time.   They were composed of
recently arrived Hong Kong teenagers between 13 and 19 years of
age.   The learning problems that this group of Chinese youth experienced gave rise to behavior problems in schools.   There were
many community problems caused by the gangs.   These included
shoplifting, theft from automobiles, pickpocketing, and others.   This
study also makes comparisons between the Chinese youth gangs studied earlier by other researchers.   Recommendations are made for
the improvement of educational provisions for Chinese youth.

128. Gangs in New York's Chinatown, by Betty Lee Sung. New
     York, Department of Asian Studies, City University of
     New York, 1977. 106p. ED 152894
          In order to examine the phenomenon of gangs among
Chinese youths in New York, interviews were conducted with members of the Chinatown community and with persons working in this
community.   In this document the texts of the author's discussions
with eight individuals are presented.   A social worker who works
with delinquent Chinese youth and a former gang member now working in an outreach project characterize gang members and their
motivations, and describe gang activities.   A Young Chinese man,
not a member of a street gang, talks about life in Chinatown.   Two
policemen and a Chinatown civic leader also discuss gang related
problems.   In addition, information obtained in an interview with
two "hard core" gang members, and the author's assessment of
their comments, are presented.   Changes in the character of Chinese
youth gangs over the years are evident through these interviews.
Some immigration figures, as well as arrest statistics, are offered
to help illustrate these changes.   Recommendations for remedying the
youth gang problem are addressed to government, community and
school officials, and to the youths and their parents.

129. Chinese children's songs, compiled by Irene Kwok. San Fran-
     cisco, Unified School District, 1977, 52p.   ED 144387.
          Singing can be an enjoyable and effective way to motivate
children to learn a second language.   This booklet consists of contemporary and folk songs that are related to Chinese festivals, transportation, the family, seasons, Christmas and other topics.   Each
page gives the music to a song with the words in Chinese and in
English.   The songs are illustrated with black-and-white drawings.
A cassette of the songs was developed to accompany this booklet.

130. The Magic of Chinese music, by Betty S. J. Wong. San
     Francisco, Unified School District, 1974. 63p.   ED
     123156.
          Although this booklet is intended for use in the class-
room, the author cautions the reader that it is an adventure into
Chinese music rather than a teaching or history experience.   By
learning how to play the music, students "travel" through China,
giving them a better understanding of this country.   The author
describes the invention of ancient Chinese instruments, the construction of several of the instruments used in ancient times, the
sounds used in Chinese music, and tells also of the multiple uses
to which many of these instruments can be put.   Included are descriptions of the Chinese people who developed and who now listen
to the music, the sounds of nature from which the music is taken,
the score for drum, gong, cymbals, and a Chinese orchestra from
a piece called "Chinese New Year," and a general look at the different kinds of Chinese music that exist today (traditional, contemporary, and experimental).   The four chapters are entitled: "Believe
and You Shall Receive Magic"; "Through a Chinese Looking Glass";

"Play Time-How to Play"; and "Chinese Music Lives." A bibliography and a listing of available records and tapes are included.

131. Glimpses of Hmong history and culture, by K. Yang See
     and G. L. Barney. Arlington, VA, Center for Applied
     Linguistics, 1978. 45p. ED 159901.
          The two essays in this guide are intended to provide
Americans with an introduction to the history and culture of the
Hmong refugees from Laos. In the first essay, "The Hmongs of
Laos: 1896-1978," the following topics are discussed: (1) the
Hmongs' history until 1940; (2) the emergence of Hmong leaders
during and after World War II and the guerilla army after the take-
over by the Pathet Lao; (3) the effects of relocation into new regions and inhospitable climates between 1955 and 1975; (4) the fall
of the Royal Lao government and the period between 1972 and 1975;
and (5) the problems arising from the flight into Thailand since 1975.
In the second essay, a description of Hmong life and culture during
the early '50s is provided to give a picture of the life that the older refugees remember. The following subjects are discussed: (1)
the origins, history and way of life of the people and the mountain-
ous regions in which they live; (2) their patrilinear clan system,
which is the basis for their social organization and is a primary integrating factor in their culture as a whole; (3) their political organization, rooted in respect for the authority of the elders; (4) the
economy and division of labor; (5) folklore and beliefs, particularly
as these influence their daily life and customs; and (6) their life
cycle, that is, family and household beliefs, customs and values.

132. Koreans; building bridges of understanding. Provo, UT,
     Language Research Center, Brigham Young University,
     1976. 32p. ED 140623.
          This booklet was designed to facilitate interactions and
communication with the people of Korea by providing information
about their customs, attitudes and other cultural characteristics
which influence their actions and values. A brief description of
Korea is given, which covers the following: geography, weather,
history, government, international attitudes, the economy, language,
education, transportation and communications, the family, religion,
the arts, and sports. Attitudes toward self-esteem and reputation,
nonindividualism, and a vertical society are explained through brief
descriptions of realistic situations involving American visitors to
Korea. A self-test is given after each situation. Information is
also given on: greetings, visiting, gifts, gestures, general courtesies, eating, useful Korean phrases, signs, the monetary system,
public transporation, housing, diet, family rites, festivals and holidays, work, names, and clothing. A brief bibliography is provided.

133. Slavs in America, by Adele K. Donchenko. 1976. 44p. ED
     137164.
          The history of Slavic immigration in America is traced
and the characteristics that define Slavs as an ethnic group are

identified. Focusing on the difficulties experienced by Slavs in melting into accepted American patterns, the paper records the rise in
Slavic ethnic consciousness. Topics discussed are Slavic language,
geographic concentration of Slavs in Eastern Europe, cultural identity, physical characteristics, and religious differences. The section
on early immigration discusses the reasons which attracted Slavs to
America from earliest colonial days. These reasons include religious convictions, military obligations, adventure, and political
idealism. Case studies of individual Slavic immigrants are presented. The greatest wave of Slavic immigration occurring from
1880-1920 is described, followed by discussion of the constant but
less intense immigration after 1920. Reasons for later immigration include the Bolshevik Revolution, displacement due to political
events in Europe, and religious persecution. The major contributions of Slavs to American science, music, industry, politics, and
education are noted.

134. Lithuanians in America; contributions to America, relation-
       ship to homeland, integration into American life, re-
       tention of ethnicity in America. Chicago, Consortium
       for Inter-Ethnic Curriculum Development, 1976. 114p.
       ED 130982.
          This ethnic heritage unit is about Lithuanians in the
United States. The first section presents basic facts, such as a
map of Lithuania, map of Eastern Europe, facts about Lithuania,
principal dates in Lithuanian history, Lithuanian historical figures,
bibliography about Lithuanians, and a list of Lithuanian organizations in the United States. The second section discusses early
Lithuanian settlement in North America and some traditions about
Christmas, folk celebrations, and Easter. The third section offers
information about Lithuanian immigration to America, Lithuanians in
the labor force, and Lithuanian cultural continuities in the United
States. Cultural patterns in Europe and the USSR are presented in
another section in light of 20th century Lithuanian Americans, Lithuanians in the economics field, and historical consciousness. The
next section presents Lithuanian community organizations and the
Lithuanian independence day celebration as conflicting interests within the United States. The last section discusses the challenge of
an interdependent world by focusing on Lithuanians for a free Lithuania, Simas Kurdirka, Lithuanian language, Saturday schools,
parish schools, and Lithuanian English-language publications. Each
section is divided into two parts--one denotes the theme of contributions of Lithuanians to American life and/or their integration into
American life and the second part refers to the relationship of Lithuanians to Lithuania and/or their retention of ethnicity in the
United States.

135. Ukrainians in America. Chicago, Consortium for Inter-Ethnic
       Curriculum Development, 1976. 130p. ED 130983.
          This ethnic heritage unit is about Ukrainians in the
United States. The first section presents basic facts, such as a

map of Ukraine, map of Eastern Europe, facts about Ukraine, principal dates in Ukrainian history, ten outstanding figures in modern
Ukrainian history, milestones of Ukrainian communities in the United
States, bibliography about Ukrainians, and a resource guide of community organizations in the United States. The second section discusses early Ukrainian settlement in North America, religious feasts,
and celebration of family occasions. The third section presents
Ukrainian immigration, musical instruments, easter eggs, Pysanka,
and Christmas puppet theater "Vertep." Cultural patterns in Europe
and USSR are presented in the next section in light of the Ukrainian-
American artist named Archipenko, two adventurers from Ukraine,
historical consciousness, aspirations to freedom, and the modern
and united Ukraine. The following section presents conflicting interests within the United States such as community organizations
and the Ukrainian independence day celebration. The last section
focuses on challenges of an interdependent world for Ukrainians that
involve concern for human rights, religion, language, cultural activity, visiting Ukraine, and taking vacations. Each section is divided into two parts--one denotes the theme of contributions of
Ukrainians to American life and/or their integration into American
life and the second part refers to the relationship of Ukrainian
Americans to Ukraine and/or their retention of ethnicity in the United
States.

136. The Hungarian-Americans of South Bend, by Darlene Scherer
     and Karen Rasmussen. South Bend, Ethnic Heritage
     Studies Program, University of Indiana, June 1975.
     34p. ED 174555.
     Developed as part of an ethnic heritage studies program,
this historical narrative of Hungarian Americans in South Bend, Indiana, is intended to increase cultural awareness and appreciation.
The document is divided into three sections. Section I offers a
brief history of Hungary and describes the background of the three
emigrant groups; lower working class World War I refugees, upper-
class professional displaced persons from World War II, and young
urban upper-class Freedom Fighters of 1956. Section II discusses
Hungarian American life and social development in South Bend, emphasizing differing values, social attitudes, economic opportunities,
social conditions, and assimilation patterns for the three groups.
The first group of immigrants established a Hungarian community
based on Hungarian folk culture and festivals, churches, social clubs,
political groups, benefit societies, and social centers. Later groups
were more interested in rapid assimilation. Section III identifies
major aspects of South Bend's Hungarian cultural heritage, including the family as a basic social and economic unit, the importance
of land and home, and respect for hard work and self-reliance. A
discussion of Hungarian food concludes the booklet.

137. Greeks in America, by Demetrius Mazacoufa. Atlanta, GA,
     Public Schools, 1976. 76p. ED 173512.
     Information is presented on various topics related to

Greek-Americans, including the different phases of emigration and immigration, language difficulties and other problems encountered in America, and Greek-American organizations and institutions. Particular attention is given to describing the cultural, social, and political characteristics of the Greek community in Atlanta. An appendix provides additional information: (1) Greece is compared in size to the United States: (2) the Greek flag and U.S. flag are compared: (3) statistical data which compare the weather in Greece to that of Georgia are provided: (4) the extent of Greek immigration to the U.S. between 1923 and 1960 and the distribution of the Greek population throughout the U.S. are shown: (5) nonverbal forms of Greek communication are illustrated: (6) recipes for Greek dishes are presented: and (7) notable Greek Americans are listed. A selected bibliography is attached.

138. In quest of a cultural identity; an inquiry for the Polish community, by Stanley S. Seidner. 1976. 45p. ED 167674.
This report concentrates on the problems associated with the negative image of the historical, social, and cultural backgrounds of Polish immigrants to the United States. It provides a perspective on the problems this immigrant group encountered in establishing and maintaining its cultural identity. Specific problems with negative stereotyping, discriminatory attitudes, bias in employment, and poor self-image are discussed. Factors contributing to the negative stereotyping such as "Polish jokes" and other forms of prejudice are also discussed. Suggestions are made for rectifying this "negative ethnocentrism." Reference is made to psychological studies which indicate that bicultural programs foster positive self-image. Specific cultural approaches suggested include a gain in political influence and the exposure of ethnic Polish and other minorities to Polish foods, music, and literature.

139. German-speaking people of Europe. Provo, UT, Language Research Center, Brigham Young University, 1976. 47p. ED 140621.
This book attempts to provide cultural information which will enable an American to communicate effectively with German-speaking people of Europe. The book discusses differences between American and Germanic culture in such areas as food, laws, customs, religion, language, dress, and basic attitudes. Background information is given on Austria, Germany, and Switzerland and on the characteristics of their people. Problems in intercultural communication are presented via situations built around such themes as: the concept of time, attitudes toward knowledge, formality, individual pride and sense of privacy. Facial expressions and gestures are also discussed. Short cultural notes on such topics as shopping and holidays are followed by "survival phrases" and a translation of common signs, clothing sizes, and weights and measures. A brief bibliography completes the volume.

140. Mormons and Mormon history as reflected in U.S. Government

documents, 1830 to 1907, by Carol W. Christensen.
November 1977.   53p.   ED 146930.

This annotated bibliography contains over 250 sources
on Mormons and Mormon history from 1830 to 1907 found in government publications.   The nineteenth century documents reflect the
controversy, issues, and sentiments concerning the Church of Jesus
Christ of Latter-Day Saints, and with the twentieth century, mark
a new era of tolerance and understanding.   The sources include
congressional publications, census reports, legislative publications,
and court cases.   Arranged chronologically, subject divisions include: Mormons' Relations with Neighbors--in Missouri, in Utah,
Non-Mormons, Indians, Federal Officials in Utah; Splinter Groups;
Mt. Meadows Massacre; Territorial Status for Desert; the Mormon
War; Movement for Statehood for Utah; Power and Influence of the
Mormon Church in Utah; Polygamy; Women's Rights in Utah; Mormons and Education; and Mormons in Mexico.   The bibliography
was compiled from the sources available at The University of Texas
at Austin.

141.   The Kibbutz; the Hebrew word for "group, " by Bobbie H. Row-
       land.   1973.   24p.   ED 095990.

This paper provides a descriptive summary of the historical development, the basic features, the organizational structure,
the patterns of childrearing and education, and specific research
findings concerning the Kibbutz Movement in Israel.   Four main
types of collective settlements are described, along with the main
characteristics and tenets representative of all kibbutzim.   The philosophy of 'collective education' is presented, and the educational
structure from birth through high school is outlined in detail.   A
brief review of some of the research dealing with the psychological,
sociological, physiological, philosphical, educational, and occupational
aspects of this lifestyle is reported.

142.   Jewish holidays, by Joan Abrams.   1977.   57p.   ED 150589.

This paper examines the development of Hebrew literature since the recording of Genesis and provides resources for teaching about Jewish holidays and folklore.   Although originally designed
for use in teaching a six-week junior high school unit, the materials
included may be adapted for use with students at the elementary
through senior high school levels.   Following a brief overview of
Hebrew literature, the paper discusses the story of the Creation,
the Jewish Sabbath, the Jewish New Year, the holiday of Tishah
Ba'av, the Exodus from Egypt and the related holiday of Passover,
the "Book of Esther" and the origin of Purim, and the story of
Chanukkah.   Annotated bibliographies of resources related to each
of the topics are included.

143.   Jews in America.   Chicago, Consortium For Inter-Ethnic
       Curriculum Development, 1976.   122p.   ED 130981.

This ethnic heritage unit is about Jews in the United
States.   The first section presents basic facts, such as a map of

Israel, map of Eastern Europe, facts about Israel, a bibliography
about Jews, and a list of Jewish organizations in the United States.
The second section discusses early Jewish settlement in North
America, Jewish contributions to the discovery of America, Jewish
life in the colonies, Jewish holidays, and Jewish traditions of Passover, Bar Mitzvah and Bat Mitzvah, and circumcision. A third
section presents background information concerning immigration, the
revolutionary war, immigration from Central Europe in the early
19th century, Jews on both sides of the civil war, and Jewish contributions to the American labor movement, as well as the Yiddish
theater and newspapers as a bridge between two worlds. Cultural
patterns in Europe and USSR are discussed in another section in
light of some 20th century Jews who contributed to American life,
Jewish historical consciousness, and Theodore Herzl in particular.
Another section presents Jewish community organizations, Yom
Ha'atzmaut, and "The Law of Return" as conflicting interests within
the United States. The last section focuses on current Jewish concerns for human rights, separation of church and state, religion,
higher education in Israel, archaeology in Israel, Jewish education
in the United States, and travel to Israel by American Jews. Each
section is divided into two parts--one denotes the theme of contributions of Jews to American life and/or their integration into American life and the second part refers to the relationship of Jews to
Israel and/or their retention. of ethnicity in the United States.

144.　　Puerto Ricans in the continental United States; an uncertain
　　　　future, by Kal Wagenheim. Washington, DC, Com-
　　　　mission on Civil Rights, October 1976. 168p. ED
　　　　132227.
　　　　　　The purpose of this Commission on Civil Rights report
is to: (1) provide policymakers and the general public with greater
insight into the unique history of mainland Puerto Ricans, and the
continuing grave difficulties that afflict a large sector of the community; (2) provide useful source material for further research;
and (3) recommend government action to address the special needs
of mainland Puerto Ricans. The facts contained in this report con-
firm that Puerto Ricans comprise a distinct ethnic group. This report also documents uses of specific government laws and programs
that are designed to assist Puerto Ricans and other minority groups,
and yet have fallen far short of their mandated goals. The data in
this report stem from several sources: the Commission hearings
on Puerto Ricans conducted in New York City in February 1972; a
series of regional studies and open meetings conducted between 1971
and 1976 by the Commission's State Advisory Committees in New
York, New Jersey, Pennsylvania, Massachusetts, Illinois, and Connecticut; research and personal interviews conducted by Commission
staff; data developed by the U.S. Bureau of the Census, the U.S.
Department of Labor, and the Commonwealth of Puerto Rico; and a
number of other studies by various scholars, organizations, and
government agencies.

145. <u>American Indian reference book</u>. Alexandria, VA, eARTh, 1976. 307p. ED 134391.
Designed to aid librarians, school teachers, and others in need of American Indian references and reference sources, this compilation covers a wide variety of material which has generally been scattered throughout various individual references. Specifically, this reference book includes: (1) Location of Tribes by State; (2) Locations of Tribes by Tribal Name; (3) Reservations, Rancherias, and Villages (by name, population, and acreage); (4) Population by Reservation Tribes; (5) Population by State; (6) Cities with Large Indian Populations: (7) Tribal Classifications (based upon historic data, geographic location, and linguistic stock as identified by the U. S. Census Bureau); (8) Tribal Names--Past and Present; (9) Industrial Parks (by tribal name and geographic location); (10) Schools; (11) Bureau of Indian Affairs Field Offices (the 13 Area Offices and associated field offices); (12) Past Commissioners of Indian Affairs; (13) Powwows, Festivals, Dances, and Other Annual Events (listed by date and place); (14) American Indians of the Past; (15) Wars, Campaigns, Uprisings, Disturbances, and Expeditions; (16) Organizations (by states); (17) Craft Sale Shops (by state); (18) Radio Stations (by state); (19) Periodicals (by time of publication); (20) Books (575 citations); (21) Films; (22) Filmloops; (23) Filmstrips; (24) Phonograph Records; (25) Tape Recordings; (26) Museums with Outstanding Indian Collections.

146. <u>Historical backgrounds for modern Indian law and order,</u> compiled by Robert W. Young. Washington, DC, Department of Indian Affairs, April 1969. 29p. ED 116887.
Focusing on the development of American Indian law and order, this monograph presents basic historical data chronologically ordered under the following headings: (1) Indian America (tribal and linguistic groups, migration, the American cultural zones); (2) Colonial America (early colonization, Indian legal land title vs. title of occupancy, Indian external and internal sovereignty, the French and Indian Wars, development of Indian Affairs after 1763); (3) The War of Independence and the Post Revolution Period (Indian neutrality and Indian Affairs, the erosion of tribal sovereignty with adoption of the U. S. Constitution, creation of the Bureau of Indian Affairs-BIA); (4) The Period of National Expansion (forced removal of tribes to new lands and the "- Trail of Tears," treaties, Indian Wars of the 1860's); (5) The Post Civil War Period (western Indian reservations established, breakdown of tribal economy and the "feeding policy," Federal paternalism, the allotment system and further loss of land, and the Competency Act of 1906); (6) The Indian of the 20th Century (voting rights, the Meriam Report and reform, the Indian Reorganization Act of 1946); (7) The Administration of Justice by Tribal Governments (limited internal and external sovereignty, tribal vs. European-American concepts of justice, tribal vs. State and municipal governments).

147. <u>Indian law enforcement history,</u> by David Etheridge. Wash-

ington, DC, Bureau of Indian Affairs, February 1975.
80p. ED 116888.

Written as a tribute to American Indian law enforcement
officers and the Indian Criminal Justice System, this monograph details the history of the legislative, judicial, financial, and cultural
problems associated with the development of Indian law enforcement.
Citing numerous court cases, pieces of legislation, and individual
and organizational conflicts, this history emphasizes the people, both
Native American and white, who helped to establish tribal, reservation, and Federal systems of justice and law enforcement. Among
the many people mentioned and pictured via photographs are: (1)
San Carlos Police Captain, Eskinilay; (2) Indian Agent John Clum
and the San Carlos Apache Police; (3) Sinte-Galeska; (4) San Six-
killer, High Sheriff of the Cherokee Nation; (5) Red Tomahawk, the
Indian policeman who shot Sitting Bull in 1890; (6) Crow Dog, a
Captain of Indian Police at Rosebud; (7) Gall, a judge on the court
of Indian Offenses at Standing Rock; (8) Quanah Parker, a Comanche
who served as chief judge of the Kiowa Court; (9) Julia Wades in
Water, the first woman to serve as an officer in the Indian Police;
(10) William "Pussyfoot" Johnson, a Special Officer for the Bureau
of Indian Affairs hired to keep alcohol out of the Indian Territory;
(11) the Honorable Virgil L. Kirk, Sr., Chief Justice of the Navajo
Nation.

148. Transformation of tradition; autobiographical works by native
      American women, by Gretchen Bataille. 1978. 31p.
      ED 173002.

The Indian woman has been viewed as a subservient and
oppressed female; often overlooked were the economic, social and
political positions women held within tribal societies. The biographies and autobiographies of Indian women that have been obtained
over the last century can be used to examine this contradiction in
perspectives. These accounts have undergone changes in several
significant ways over the years, including changes in the perception
of audience, purpose of revealing the life story, and the economic
and/or political climate of the period of recording. The earliest
material was told by the women through an interpretor to an anthropologist. The purpose was not to focus on an individual life but
to illuminate a culture and the scientist or editor chose what was
significant. Emphasis in early accounts was placed on the roles of
males and females, the familial relationships, material culture, and
a regret for the changes from the old ways. In recent narratives
Indian women often are writing their own stories and choosing the
material they themselves want to include. Many of these stories reflect the dilemma of the pulls between the traditional ways and the
pushes toward acculturation. The Indian woman is and has been
strong within her culture and the life stories of Indian women support
this perspective. This document discusses specific biographies of
Native American women; it provides bibliographic citations for the
sources quoted and additional listings for other autobiographical works
and resource material.

149. American Indians in transition, by Helen W. Johnson. Wash-
     ington, DC, Economic Research Service, Department of
     Agriculture, 1975. 42p. ED 111589.
         The American Indian population is in a period of transi-
tion. It is young, growing, and becoming more urban. There were
some improvements in income, housing, education, and health in the
1960-70 decade, but Indians remain the most disadvantaged of the
minority ethnic groups in the United States. By most of the above
measures, Indians, especially rural Indians, are not as well off as
the U.S. population as a whole. But the Indian people are moving
toward self-determination, or self-government, in programs to enhance their lives. Both excessive paternalism and termination of
the trust relationships have become discredited as national policy
regarding Indians. As the President's Message of 1970 states,
"Federal termination errs in one direction, Federal paternalism errs
in the other." It is also widely accepted that the integrity of the
Indian culture should be preserved, not only as a contribution to
cultural pluralism which enriches society as a whole, but also as
a reflection of the desires of the Indian people themselves. The
Indian culture is in a transition period, but the roots of Indian customs and values are deep and will not yield quickly or easily to
alien customs and values. The process of moving toward self-
determination is underway, and some measure of change is in the
Indian picture today.

150. Information profiles of Indian reservations in Arizona, Nevada
     and Utah. Phoenix, Bureau of Indian Affairs, 1978.
     202p. ED 158903.
         Based on information provided by Bureau of Indian Af-
fairs (BIA) Agency Offices and by the Indian Health Service, this
publication provides profiles of 45 Indian reservations located in
Arizona, Nevada, and Utah. These profiles include data on reservations located partially or totally in the adjoining states of Oregon,
Idaho, California, and New Mexico which are under the administrative jurisdiction of the BIA Phoenix and Navajo Area Offices. Primarily based on data collected during 1977, the profiles provide information on the people and area, education, employment, housing,
industrialization, resources availability, income, health, resource
development, and additional attainments. Each profile includes addresses and phone numbers of BIA and tribal officials and offices
as of March 1978. Reservations covered include the Camp Verde,
Colorado River, Fort Apache, Fort Yuma, Gila River, Havasupai,
Navajo, Papago, Yavapai-Prescott Community, Battle Mountain,
Duck Valley, Fallon Colony, Goshute, Las Vegas Colony, Pyramid
Lake, Reno Sparks Colony, Uintah and Ouray, and Yomba. Tabular
data are given on the service population of Phoenix Area by state,
lands under BIA jurisdiction as of June 30, 1977, Indian population
and labor force as of April 1977, reservation populations and acreage recapitulation, and estimates of resident Indian population and
labor force status by state and reservation.

151. Indian women and the law in Canada; citizens minus, by Kath-
     leen Jamieson. Ottawa, Advisory Council on the Status

of Women, April 1978. 113p. ED 158913.
To be born poor, Indian, and a female is to be a member of the most disadvantaged minority in Canada today. For 109 years the Indian Act of 1868 has discriminated against Canada's Indian women on grounds of race, sex and marital status. It states that an Indian woman marrying a non-Indian man ceases legally to be Indian. She must leave her parents' home and her reserve. She may not own property on the reserve and she may be prevented from inheriting property from her parents. Her children are not recognized as Indian, and she may be prevented from returning to live with her family on the reserve even if she is in dire need, sick, deserted, widowed, separated, or divorced. Indian men may marry whom they please without penalty; their non-Indian spouses and children receive full Indian rights and status. The effects of this legislation on the Indian woman and her children can be very grave materially, culturally, and psychologically. The Indian Act is presently under revision, but displaced Indian women have no voice in the negotiations. This monograph, using both historical and sociological approaches, documents and analyzes discriminatory legislation and explores the consequences.

152. Indian projects funded by EDA, 1965-1977. Washington, DC, Economic Development Administration, Department of Commerce, December 1977. 134p. ED 165966.
Since 1967 the Economic Development Administration (EDA) has carried out an Indian program that emphasized economic development of Indian reservations and trust lands. In the past 12 years Indian tribes in 32 states have received community and industrial development grants to assist them in developing a viable economic base on their lands. Tribes in Arizona have received the greatest amount of assistance with $113,263,174 awarded in the period from August 26, 1965 to September 30, 1977. New Mexico tribal groups received $37,927,795, and Indians in Washington received $37,467,572. Indians in Massachusetts received the smallest amount of assistance: $146,050. EDA grants were made for such projects as planning and impact studies, water and sewer systems, tourism facilities, industrial parks, and community facilities such as fire stations, community centers, and health centers. Assistance was also given to national Indian groups for conferences, training programs, studies, and other types of activities, including those related to industrial development. In addition to listing the total Indian project funding by state for the 12 year period, this document itemizes the amounts and kinds of assistance given to specific tribes in each state. It also lists the amounts and kinds of aid awarded to the national level projects.

153. American Indian influence on the American Pharmacopeia, by Virgil Vogel. Paper presented at the American Association for the Advancement of Science, February 1976. 14p. ED 138390.
The first U.S. Pharmacopeia, issued in 1820, listed 296 substances of animal, mineral, or vegetable origin in its primary and secondary lists. Of these 130, nearly all of vegetable

origin, represented drugs used by American Indians. The number
grew at each decennial revision during the 19th century, though
some drugs were listed only for a decade. About 220 drugs of Native American use were listed altogether in the U.S. Pharmacopeia
or the National Formulary (which began in 1888) up to the present
time. Although the number of such listings has declined since the
advent of synthetic drugs about 1890, it is significant that 41 new
substances of American Indian usage have become official since 1890.
However, only 30 substances of Amerindian origin survived in the
17th revision of the U.S. Pharmacopeia in 1965. These drugs were
not always used in the same form by Indians and whites. In the
preparation of drugs, whites have used processes, i.e., distillation,
which were not known to the Indians. Moreover, Indian usage of
remedies has not always corresponded with white usage. This paper
presents a brief overview of some of the drugs borrowed by white
medicine from the American Indians. These drugs have been grouped
into: anesthetics, narcotics, and stimulant drugs; astringents; cathar-
tics; childbirth medicines; febrifuges; vermifuges; emetics; poisons;
antibiotics; diabetes remedy; and contraceptives.

154. The Indian elder; a forgotten American, compiled by Juana
        Lyon. Final report on the National Indian Conference
        on Aging, June 1976. 619p. ED 158897.
        A culmination of the efforts of many Indian and con-
cerned non-Indian people, the conference, attended by almost 1,500
American Indians and Alaska Natives representing 171 tribes, aimed
to promote effective and adequate services needed by the Indian elderly. Based on input from the Indian community and service providers,
five concurrent workshops were scheduled to address the topics of
income, environment, legal problems, physical well-being, and legislation. This report presents discussions of the: events which led
to the conference; recommendations and resolutions submitted into
the conference record; conference objectives and agenda; organization of workshops; background of the conference recommendations;
implications and the follow-up. Also included are the highlights of
conference background, planning, implementation, and evaluation;
the questionnaire given to the Indian community and a summary of
the Indian community and a summary of the responses; and the responses by the Administration on Aging at the regional and state
levels. Appendices include discussions of the historical and legal
perspectives of Tribal sovereignty and Tribal government, the National Congress of American Indians' position on aging concerns, the
Indian Health Care Improvement Act, and social services to Indians
through Title XX; comparative population data for Indians aged 65
and over living on identified reservations in selected states; statistical data of such tribes as the Mississippi Band of Choctaws, St.
Regis Mohawk, Jicarilla Apache, and Miccosukee; and testimonies
before various committees and subcommittees on aging.

155. Sir William Johnson and the Indians of New York, by Milton
        W. Hamilton. Albany, New York State American Revo-
        lution Bicentennial Commission, 1975. 55p. ED 114349.
        In order to make the vast literature about the history of

Indian and white relations in New York readily accessible to teachers, students, and general readers, this booklet brings together the main points of the relationship between the Indians and Sir William Johnson. Johnson is a key figure in the Indian story of New York state during the 1770s. The topics covered in this document are Indians of New York, coming of the white men, management of Indian affairs, William Johnson comes to America, the Indian trade, French and Indian War, Battle of Lake George, Sir William Johnson, the close of the war, taking Fort Niagara, Sir William--colonial statesman, culture on the frontier, life at Johnson Hall, failure of Indian management, American independence, Indians and the Revolution, and importance of Sir William Johnson. Both the white man's and the Indian's views on major events are incorporated into the booklet.

156. American Indian recipes, edited by Katherine J. Gurnoe and
     Christian Skjervold. Minneapolis, Public Schools, 1974.
     28p. ED 160269.
        Presenting some 60 to 70 Native American recipes, this document includes a brief introduction and a suggested reading list (15 citations related to American Indian foods). The introduction identifies five regional Native American cuisines as follows: in the Southwest, peppers and beans were made into chili, soups, guacamole, and barbecue sauces by the Pueblo, Papago, and Hopi tribes; in the Northwest, seafood recipes were the contributions made by the Tlingit, Kwakiutl, Salich, and other tribes; in the Great Plains, roasted buffalo was the contribution made by the Sioux and the Cheyenne; in the South, the Cherokee and other tribes contributed stews, soups, and an assortment of cornbreads; in the Northeast, the clam bake and baked beans were contributions made by the Narragansetts, Penobscots, and Powhatans. Exemplary recipes found in this document include fry bread (Navajo, Chippewa, and Dakota style), water cress soup, berry soup, fried wild rice casserole, venison and beef jerky. Zuni mutton stew, buffalo steak with wild rice dressing, smoked venison, muskrat, quail, fruit leather, thistle salad, wild teas, Seminole sour bread, Shawnee blue bread, etc.

157. Indian legends, edited by Katherine Gurnoe and Christian
     Skjervold. Minneapolis, Public Schools, 1976. 37p.
     ED 160268.
        Presenting American Indian legends, this material provides insight into the cultural background of the Dakota, Ojibwa, and Winnebago people. Written in a straightforward manner, each of the eight legends is associated with an Indian group. The legends included here are titled as follows: Minnesota is Minabozho's Land (Objibwa); How We Got the Rainbow (an extension of the Ojibwa Minabozho legend); How the Birds Came to Have Their Many Colors (no tribal designation); The Story of Coyote and Moradjawinga (Earth Wanderer--a Winnebago legend); The Four Winds (Sioux); The Great Circle (Dakota); Legends of the Pipestone Quarry: The Three Maidens and the Dakota Buffalo Maiden Story (both Dakota). Each of the narratives includes complementary illustrations. A five-item bibliography is also included.

158. Alaskan folktales, by Katherine Peter and Mary L. Pope.
        Anchorage, Alaska State Operated Schools, 1976. 72p.
        ED 127824.
        This volume of Alaskan folktales contains eight stories
written in English and Gwich'in. The book is designed with the
English and Gwich'in versions facing each other on opposite pages.
It is illustrated with line drawings.

159. Trail of broken promises; an assessment of HUD's Indian
        housing programs, by Thomas H. Stanton. Washington,
        DC, Center for Study of Responsive Law, 1977. 35p.
        ED 152441.
        Documenting the inefficiency of the Housing and Urban
Development (HUD) programs for American Indians, this report discusses HUD program administration and presents specific recommendations. The report is divided into the following sections and
subsections: (1) 1977 is the ninth consecutive year HUD has promised more Indian housing than it has delivered; (2) Indian housing is
desperately needed: (3) HUD's administration of Indian housing is
disorganized and inefficient (HUD's Indian programs are disorganized, HUD has failed to assure coordination with the Bureau of
Indian Affairs and the Indian Health Service, resulting in unnecessary
delays; and HUD Indian housing lacks quality); (4) Indian housing programs are flawed by HUD's poor relationship with Indian housing
authorities, (background; HUD has a poor relationship with Indian
housing authorities; the HUD Indian housing regulations and handbook
are not based upon reality and, therefore, are impossible for the
Indian housing authorities to implement; and HUD is mismanaging
its program to improve management of local Indian housing authorities); (5) recommendations (HUD should maintain a commitment to
Indian housing authorities) high Indian housing goals; given the special nature of Indian needs, HUD should combine all Indian program
activities into one Indian program office reporting directly to the
Secretary; HUD should take the lead in the Federal Indian housing
effort; and HUD must face squarely the responsibility to help build
institutions as well as houses).

160. Indian justice; a research bibliography, by Vincent J. Webb.
        Monticello, IL, Council of Planning Librarians, 1976.
        69p. ED 139580.
        Compiled for educators, social workers, police officers,
planners, and others interested in the problem of criminal justice
for Native Americans, this bibliography cites 911 materials pertaining to American Indian justice. Covering the period from 1966 to
1975, citations were extracted from the following indices and abstracts: Readers' Guide to Periodical Literature, Social Sciences
and Humanities Index, Index to Legal Periodicals, Crime and Delinquency Literature, Abstracts of Criminology and Penology, Crime
and Delinquency Abstracts, Poverty and Human Resources' Abstracts,
Psychological Abstracts, and Sociological Abstracts. The 10 sections
cover: general works which deal with the socio-historical situation
of Indians in the U.S.; bibliographies and indices which deal specifically with Indian justice and other relevant topics; cultural and social

organization; social psychology of Native Americans; social problems, i. e., alcoholism, criminal behavior and deviance, racial discrimination, poverty, health instability, protest confrontations between Native Americans and the state and Federal government; urban problems; administration of Indian justice; Indian law and civil rights; property and resource rights; and social policy and reform.

161. A Better day for Indians, by Vine Deloria, Jr. New York, Field Foundation, 1977. 38p. ED 138418.

Vesting Congress with implied powers over American Indians produces attitudes and assumptions which are extremely influential. There are seven such controlling assumptions: Congress is presumed to act in good faith toward Indians; the belief that past policies were based upon some intelligent criteria that incorporated an understanding of conditions, the approval of Indians, and a far-sighted intention of Congress; the paternalistic assumption that the solution of Indian problems is a simple matter of adjustment of already existing programs; the perception of Indian lands and communities as laboratories which can be used to test various theories of social engineering, the Federal government can use Indian lands at its discretion; sanction of the privilege of the Federal establishment to avoid difficult decisions; and tribal rights are nuisances that can be abated as need be. In view of the impact of these assumptions, the following specific recommendations are offered to affect fundamental shifts in direction, simplification of complex problems to their elemental factors, and expansion of the manner in which Indians believe they perceive themselves today: uniform recognition of Indian communities; clarification of tribal membership; a standard definition of the status of an Indian tribe; creation of a "Court of Indian Affairs"; arbitration of long-standing Native claims; rejuvenation of the Indian land base; and universal eligibility for government aid based on need.

162. The Native American woman; a perspective, by Bea Medicine. University Park, ERIC Clearinghouse on Rural Education and Small Schools, New Mexico State University, March 1978. 122p. ED 151122.

Presenting varied perspectives describing the Native American woman, this book is divided into six chapters as follows: (1) Native Americans and Anthropology (this chapter illustrates the way in which anthropologists have helped stereotype American Indian women); (2) The Native American Woman in Ethnographic Perspective (emphasizing role variations and tribal differences, this chapter points up the importance of cultural background); (3) The Native American Woman in Historical Perspective (emphasis on the negative stereotyping of American Indians by historians, with the assertion that the historian typically, stereotyped more severely than the anthropologist); (4) The Plain's Native American Woman (emphasis on Cheyenne sexual roles, sexual rites, and sexual taboos); (5) The Native American Woman in Transition (lengthy excerpts from a biographical account by Bonnin and a semi-autobiographical account by Qoyawayma, both women who have experienced change agent roles); (6) A Perspective of the Issues and Challenges

Facing the Contemporary Native American Woman (low income; legal problems; sexism; the Women's Movement; questions re: marriage, identity, and inter-tribal marriage; education; and religion).

163. The North Dakota Indian reservation economy; a descriptive study, by James J. Harris. Grand Forks, Bureau of Business and Economic Research, University of North Dakota, August 1975. 137p. ED 127062.

Economic development remains one of the most important objectives of American Indian reservations. Various programs for developing the reservations' resources have been implemented. Due to the multiplicity of needs, development policy has been multi-faceted: health programs to upgrade physical well-being; educational programs to enhance scholastic achievement; manpower programs to increase skill levels and employability; and job-creation programs and industrial projects to reduce unemployment. Thus, reservation life has improved. However, in order to determine the degree of improvement, the economic position of reservations needs clarification. This study describes the present economic status of North Dakota's Indian population and relates the current situation to major development programs of the last decade and other identifiable factors. Data pertains to: social and economic characteristics--age, sex, family characteristics, labor force participation, employment status, occupational structure, income for persons and families, health and education; health, education, and welfare trends and programs; manpower and community developments--role of the Office of Economic Opportunity, employment and adult training programs, overall assessment of manpower programs; and land and capital resources.

164. Menominee Indian tribe of Wisconsin, by Wayne E. Stephens. Billings, MT, Bureau of Indian Affairs, April 1975. 176p. ED 131992.

Designed to provide data and resource materials needed by the Menominee Restoration Committee and others involved in reservation organizational and development planning, this report covers the present status of the Menominee tribal resources and presents an annotated bibliography. The resource inventory includes maps, tables, and charts and is divided into the following sections: (1) The Setting (historical background, forestry, disenchantment with farming, Menominee land today, transportation, communications, electric power, schools, medical facilities, financial institutions, housing, water and sewer, industrial development, entrepreneurship and managerial development); (2) The People (Menominee County residents, general population characteristics, employment, income, education, vocational training, housing, and health); (3) Physical Environment and Resources (climate, topography and drainage, geology, minerals and nonmetalic deposits, hydrology, soils, agriculture, vegetation and forestry, recreation, and wildlife resources). Arranged under six subject headings, the annotated bibliography includes sections on: culture and history (71 citations); resources (91 citations); feasibility studies (39 citations); legal matters (63 citations); reports (138 citations); and Menominee Enterprises Inc. File Headings.

165. Native Americans in the southwest, by Bryce Washington.
Paper presented at the Society for Intercultural Education, Training, and Research, February 1977. 39p.
ED 147061.

In theory Arizona Indian tribes can be represented by five major cultural groups: Athapascan, Pueblo, Yuman, Plateau Rancheria, and Desert Rancheria tribes. Each of these tribes has its own distinctive way of life or culture. They do not want to lose their cultural identity, nor do they want to become "like Anglos". They "do" want to pass on to posterity their heritage, their lands, their past and the ability to get along in both worlds--the Anglo world and the Indian world. Therefore, an educator must have some understanding of the lifestyle, religion, historical background, and the political, economic and social conditions of those living within the area served by his school. The educator should know that the economic and political emphases in the Southwest center about two major areas--water, land and mineral rights, and the sovereignty of the reservations. He should also know that the social conditions of Native Americans in the Southwest are strongly affected by stereotypes which have persisted since the pioneer days. This paper discusses the history of Arizona Indians, the current litigation between various tribes and various levels of government, political and economic conditions, the "integrity" of tribal officials, the Navajo-Hopi joint-use land dispute, the controversial Central Arizona Project, the water allocations disputes, the problems found in Indian education, the social conditions, and the current Indian educational conditions.

166. Maine Indians; a brief summary. Augusta, ME, State Department of Indian Affairs, December 1975. 21p. ED 119882.

Divided into five major sections, this revised summary of the socioeconomic development of Maine American Indians presents the following: (1) General Information (prehistoric development of these Algonquian-speaking Indians including the most recently accepted tribal and band subdivisions; their cultural and historical development; and their position today including reservation size and locations, tribal government, and the State-tribal relationship); (2) The Development and Influence of the Catholic Indian Missions in Maine, 1611-1820 (comprising the major portion of this document, this section deals with: Early French Missions; Capuchins at Castine; Jesuits on the Saint Lawrence; Missions on the Kennebec; Mission on the Penobscot; Missions on the Saint John River; After the Fall of Quebec in 1763; and Under the United States); (3) Maine's Department of Indian Affairs (initiation, purpose, branch offices, goals, and objectives); (4) Indian Education in Maine (a summary which details the Maine Department of Education's responsibility for reservation based day schools and presents information relative to on- and off-reservation enrollment statistics, regular and special programs, personnel, and construction); (5) Forest Resources of the Indian Township Passamaquoddy Reservation (land use, multiple use policy, timber management, and forest protection).

167. Schools for the Choctaws, by James D. Morrison. Austin,
TX, Discrimination and Assessment Center for Bilingual
Education, February 1978. 378p. ED 164207.

The educational system developed by the Choctaw Nation
during the nineteenth century began with annuity funding from early
treaties which ceded Choctaw land to the U.S. and ended with Choctaw loss of control over their schools in 1899 to the U.S. government. Starting in 1818, missionaries from American Protestant de-
nominations became an important factor in Indian education, establishing early mission schools in Choctaw lands in Mississippi and
Alabama which promoted "agriculture, homemaking, Christianity,
and citizenship". With the Indian Removal Act of 1830, mission
schools were uprooted to follow Choctaws to their new Oklahoma
home. The 1830 Treaty of Dancing Rabbit Creek (continuing previous support for education, instituting the "Forty Youth Fund"
which financed college education for Choctaws) and the Public School
Act of 1842 (funds for seven boarding schools--two for boys, five
for girls) were landmark decisions. Largely administered by missionary groups, schools were under Choctaw support. While boarding academies and seminaries were the backbone of the school system, neighborhood and Sunday schools (including weekend adult education) were also underway. Interrupted by the Civil War, Choctaw education efforts resumed in 1866 with boarding schools, neighborhood schools, and support for higher education. Federal control
of the Choctaw school system resulted from the Curtis Act in 1898.

168. Iroquois culture, history, and prehistory. Proceedings of the
1965 conference on Iroquois Research, edited by Elisa-
beth Tooker. Albany, New York State Education Department, 1967. 116p. ED 164200.

Although the Iroquois are one of the most thoroughly
studied Indian peoples of this continent, many important aspects of
their history and culture remain unexplained. For the past 20 years
the Conference on Iroquois Research has reported on current research and discussed needs and opportunities for future research.
Twenty papers are included in this document. These deal with such
subjects as aspects of recent change on the Allegany Reservations,
early years of the Seneca nation, etymology of the word "Iroquois,"
the Onodaga Bowl Game, and acculturation on the Tyendinaga Reserve
in Canada. Another paper suggests the Huron and Iroquois may not
have had as strong a matrilocal rule of residence in the 17th century as previously believed. Interest by the Tuscaroras to revive
their language is also discussed. An ethnohistorical study of Hochel-
oga made in connection with the restudy of the Dawson site is given,
as well as a discussion of some hitherto unreported pottery types in
Eastern Ontario and Southern Quebec. Five papers report on archaeological work at the Kelso, Howlett Hill, Garoga, Simmons, and
Cornish Sites. Three reports are concerned with other aspects of
analysis and interpretation of archaeological data; these deal with
pottery analysis in terms of "attributes" rather than types, pottery
analysis as a source for inferences on social relationships and organizations among the Straits of Mackinac peoples, and the use of
ethnographic data to interpret archaeological data from the Mohr site.

The final paper deals with the Anthropology Study Curriculum Project. History and purposes of the Conference on Iroquois Research are also given.

169. **Myths and legends of the New York Iroquois,** by Harriet M. Converse. Albany, New York State Education Department, 1974. 211p. ED 164199.
   Adopted for 22 years into the Seneca nation, Harriet Maxwell Converse devoted much of her life to the study and defense of the Indians of New York. The position of friendship and trust she enjoyed enabled her to record extensive information on the customs and institutions of the Iroquois. Material for this volume was taken from her notes found after her death in 1903. The manuscript as found included 22 legends; 14 additional ones were revised from her rough notes. The tales are written in a graceful, poetic style and reflect great understanding and knowledge of the culture. Parts I and II record the myths and legends of the Iroquois. These deal with the story of the creation of the earth, good and evil, sun, stars, and animals. Other stories explain the forces of nature--the spirits behind the winds, thunder, drought, rain, seasons, and death. Some tales relate how certain constellations came to be or explain how the bear lost his tail or the frog his teeth; still others tell of the journey of the soul, the legend of the tall pine, the invisible little people, and the spirits of corn, rock, and lake. Part III includes miscellaneous papers found among her notes. These describe aspects of Iroquois history and culture, including women's rights, wampum belts, the game of lacrosse, the Secret Medicine Society, and Mrs. Converse's initiation into the Seneca Medicine Lodge. The forward to the book includes an account of Harriet Converse's life and her work among the Iroquois.

170. **How stories from Alaska,** by Minnie Gray. Juneau, Alaska State Department of Education, 1978. 41p. ED 173045.
   Four simple "how" stories from Alaskan legend are presented in large type and amply illustrated. In "How the Caribou Lost His Teeth", Siqpik's only son is eaten by the sharp-toothed caribou, so Siqpik feeds the animal sour berries to make his teeth fall out. "How the Loon Got His Spots" relates how the raven paints the loon's back with soot then throws ashes on the loon's head in anger. "The Pike and the Mudsucker" tells why the pike has a boney body and the mudsucker has a boney tail. In "How the Beaver Got His Tail" the beaver and the muskrat exchange their original tails.

171. **More how stories from Alaska,** by Minnie Gray. Juneau, Alaska State Department of Education, 1978. 42p. ED 173046.
   Taken from Alaskan oral tradition, the five "how" stories are written in simple English prose. "The Four Qayaqs" explains why the porcupine has no fat on his stomach and the beaver has none on his back. "Ptarmigan and the Sandhill Crane" tells how the two very different birds come to look alike. In "Why the Dall Sheep Lives in the Mountains", Qayaq's wiggling toes scare a man into the mountains where he becomes a sheep. "Why the Caribou

Has Long Legs" relates how the Qayaq uses a stick to beat the short hind legs of his caribou wife to make her legs grow. "How Three Boys Became Animals" is the story of three brothers left alone who turn into a wolf, a fox, and a raven so they can go outside. The large print book has illustrations on each page.

172. The Tides people; Tlingit Indians of Southeast Alaska; a narrative account of Tlingit culture and values written by a Tlingit, edited by Cyrus E. Peck. Juneau, Borough School District, March 1975. 100p. ED 139550.
    Written by a Tlingit for purposes of affirming Tlingit life style, values, and laws, this narrative account of the Alaskan Tlingit culture and values presents illustrations of the cultural values and value systems manifest in Tlingit language, art forms, music, ceremonies, and rituals.

173. Alaska native population trends and vital statistics, 1950-1985, by George W. Rogers. Fairbanks, Institute of Social, Economic, and Governmental Research, University of Alaska, November 1971. 22p. ED 125846.
    Utilizing U. S. census data and vital statistics (births and deaths adjusted to residence as provided by the Alaska Department of Health and Social Services), this statistical report presents a comparative analysis of Alaska Native population trends. Specifically, the following are presented via tabular and narrative analysis: (1) general population trends in Alaska from 1740-1960 (Native and non-Native); (2) significant Native population movement within regions (Southeast, Southcentral, Southwest, Interior, and Northwest Alaska) for 1950, 1960, and 1970 and by average annual rate of change between 1950-60 and 1960-70; (3) comparison of 1950 census of Native population with 1960 and a vital statistics projection based upon the 1950 and 1960 census; (4) comparison of 1960 census of Native population and other estimates; (5) estimated total Native population and vital statistics (1950-70) for each of Alaska's five regions; and (6) Native population projections by regions for 1970-85. Emphasizing the discrepancy between past official census counts and major demographic changes such as migration, this report indicates: a Native population decline in all but the Southcentral region, though an overall population growth; differing growth rates in the different regions; greater geographic mobility; increased Native urbanization; and a high probability of error and undercounting in the official reports.

174. Yesterday still lives; our native people remember Alaska, edited by Pat DeMarco. 1978. 39p. ED 168754.
    In the summer of 1978, seven teenagers and several staff members from the Fairbanks Native Association-Johnson O'Malley program set out to record some of Alaska's past by interviewing a number of older Alaska Natives and writing their biographical sketches. Some of the students spent a week along the Yukon River taping and photographing people; others travelled to Homer for the same purpose. This book is the result of that project. The sketches about nine native Alaskans present a picture of life as it was in the

early years of this century. Oliver Amouak tells of the sled the caribou hunters used to transport meat; it was made from a curved tree trunk with the jawbones of the bowhead whale serving as sled runners. Kitty Harwood tells how she helped her mother during the fish runs by pulling her boat upstream to the family fish wheels. Lilly Pitka tells of the 1949 flood in Ft. Yukon when she sat on a neighbor's roof and watched her home float away. Some of the tales describe seal hunting, fishing, mining and trapping; others tell of coming of age ceremonies, of superstitions associated with that time, and of celebrations like the blanket toss and potlaches. Some folk medicines are mentioned, including stinkweed as a cure for stomach cancer. Concluding that although the times were hard, they were good, some of the old people regret the loss of the old ways, of respect for older people, and of the quiet times of the days gone by.

175. The Alaska Eskimos; a selected annotated bibliography, by Arthur E. Hippler and John R. Wood. Fairbanks, Institute of Social and Economic Research, University of Alaska, 1977. 335p. ED 165963.
   This annotated bibliography, containing approximately 732 entries, provides a general overview of English literature concerning Alaska Eskimos and cities. Although the earliest date of publication is 1843, the majority of the works have been done since 1900; there are no entries published later than 1975. Section I lists the works alphabetically by author and includes date of publication, title, abstract number, and page in the bibliography. Listed alphabetically by author, Section II provides complete bibliographic information and annotations. Section III classifies Eskimo literature by one general and four specific linguistic categories: (1) General Eskimo; (2) Inupiaq (including Diomede and King Islanders) with subgroups (a) Taremiut (Arctic Coast) and (b) Nunamiut (inland North Slope); (3) Siberian Yupik (including St. Lawrence Islanders); (4) Central Yupik; and (5) Pacific Gulf Yupik. Section IV organizes Eskimo literature according to the time of observation: precontact and early contact to 1900; 1901 to 1940; and 1941 to present. An appendix citing important bibliographic works for Eskimo references, and an addenda consisting of new entries and additions to existing notes completes the document.

176. Navajo wisdom and traditions, by Ethelou Yazzie. Paper presented to the International Conference on the Unity of the Sciences, November 1975. 34p. ED 124366.
   The oral literature of the Navajo people generally falls into two categories: the sacred stories and the folk tales, which often, but not always, point a moral. Sacred stories relate the Navajo's emergence history. These stories tell how the universe holds two kinds of people: the "Earth Surface People" (both living and dead) and the "Holy People" (powerful, mysterious beings that belong to the Sacred World). While the Holy People who travel on lightning, sunbeams, and rainbows are very powerful, they are not all-knowing, all-powerful, and all-good. They make mistakes and have human emotions. They can be invoked, supplicated, propitiated,

and coerced to help the people of the tribe, or to cease doing damage.
The Holy People also serve as ideals of behavior for the Navajo
people to follow or emulate. Although the sacred stories differ from
story teller to story teller and from time to time, the outstanding
lesson remains the same. Basic lessons taught by these stories are:
the universe is a very dangerous place; to survive you must maintain order in those areas of life that you can control; avoid quarrel-
ing, avoid excess, and stay in harmony with your community and
with nature; be wary of non-relatives; when in a new and dangerous
situation, do nothing; and if the situation is really dangerous, escape.

177. Survey of Navajo community studies, 1936-1974, by Eric B.
     Henderson and Jerrold E. Levy. Washington, DC,
     National Science Foundation, March 1975. 157p. ED
     127089.
        Extant Navajo community studies conducted since the
1930's were surveyed. Data for selected social, economic, and
demographic variables as reported in these studies were compared.
Each community study was placed in one of three geographic classifications: western Navajo, eastern Navajo, and off-reservation.
Each on-reservation area was subdivided into rural and wage work
communities for comparison purposes. Comparisons among variables were made on three axes: rural-urban, east-west, and early-
recent. Processes of change from rural traditional life to a modern-
ized wage work economy was elucidated by comparing rural communities with wage work communities studied within the same decade and, whenever possible, within the same region. Since the
eastern portion of the Navajo Reservation was thought to have had
more intense exposure to national influences, east-west comparisons
were made to highlight the directions change was taking in the absence of comparable diachronic data. Throughout the review, comparisons among studies were made difficult by a lack of uniformity
in the use of definitions and techniques of data gathering. Also
differences among areas were exaggerated by the use of small sample populations even when the research design and method were adequate. Regularities of variation over time, from region to region,
and between wage work communities and pastoral communities were
described.

178. The Navajo nation; an American colony, by Carol J. McCabe
     and Hester Lewis. Washington, DC, Commission on
     Civil Rights, September 1975. 155p. ED 111561.
        The major portion of this report is devoted to the Anglo
and American Indian testimony from the 1973 Commission on Civil
Rights Hearings on Navajo economic development, employment, education, and health care. Among the major recommendations cited
are those calling for: (1) legal recognition of the Navajo Tribal
Council to provide for favorable tax classification and Federal Agency
grant and loan qualification; (2) a system by which the Tribal Council could make decisions with greater independence from the Bureau
of Indian Affairs (BIA); (3) legislation to support program development until tribal revenues are adequate to maintain both infrastruc-

ture and development investments; (4) a program to provide superior technical expertise in planning and decision making; (5) a Department of the Interior policy providing for joint enterprises on a 50/50 (tribal and contractor) basis; (6) Federal augmentation of the Navajo Revolving Credit Fund; (7) BIA enforcement of the Navajo preference policy in Federal employment; (8) creation of a tribal agency with jurisdiction over employment discriminiation complaints; (9) full Navajo representation in the educational decision making process; (10) curriculum development to include Navajo cultural awareness; (11) elimination of the Navajo teacher shortage; and (12) appropriation of funds for the Indian Health Service to make Navajo health care comparable to that of the U.S. in general.

179.   Navajo biographies, by Virginia Hoffman and Broderick H.
       Johnson.   Chinle, AZ, Rough Rock Demonstration School,
       1974-1978.   Volume 1, 212p.   Volume 2, 141p.   ED
       164178 and ED 164179.
            The life stories of eight Navajo ("Dine", their term for themselves) leaders are presented in volume one of this collection of biographies.   Interspersed with portraits, drawings, and maps, the narrative chronologically covers the time period from 1766 when the Navajos lived on land under the rule of Spain into the twentieth century and dealings with the government of the U.S. (including the years at Bosque Redondo) and other Indian tribes.   Biographical information was drawn from historical documents and Navajo oral history.   Leaders were selected from a field of hundreds as representative of the quality of Navajo leadership from the late eighteenth century to the present.   The volume contains a message to Navajo students stressing the importance of learning about their past as well as a bibliography and a pronunication guide for Navajo and Spanish words used.   The biographies are of Narbona, Antonio Cebolla Sandoval, Zarcillos Largos, Manuelito, Barboncito, Ganado Mucho, Jesus Arviso, and Henry Chee Dodge.   The second of two volumes contains biographies of seven Navajo men and women chosen to represent Navajo leadership in the twentieth century.   Originally appearing in a 1970 publication of the Rough Rock Demonstration School, the biographies appear here unchanged in order to make them available once again.   In addition to the life stories, which are interspersed with portraits, drawings, and photographs, the volume contains a letter to Navajo students stressing the importance of learning about their heritage, a bibliography, a pronunciation guide for Navajo and Spanish words used, and a description of the approach to education at Rough Rock Demonstration School--one which emphasizes Navajo language and culture.   The biographies in this volume are of Sam Ahkeah, Albert George Chic Sandoval, Paul Jones, Chaba Davis Watson, Annie Dodge Wauneka, Dr. Taylor McKensie, and Raymond Nakai.

180.   Navajo and Zuni; a bibliography of selected materials.   Gall-
       up, NM, Gallup-McKinley County Schools, 1975.   166p.
       ED 165921.
            No attempts at selectivity, critical appraisal or value judgment are made in the revised, partially annotated bibliography,

which focuses on materials printed by and about Navajo and Zuni
Indian Tribes and is intended to acquaint elementary and secondary
educators with the wide variety of materials available for classroom
use to enhance the self-concept of the Indian student. About 1500
entries are organized into 6 sections. Entries for books published
between 1928 and 1974 are contained in two book sections, one for
Navajo themes and one for Zuni. Entries are alphabetized by author
and divided into Fiction, Non-fiction and General. Publication date,
publisher's name, latest price (if available), and type of binding are
given for each book. Arbitrary judgments as to reading and interest
levels are sometimes included. Annotated listings of films, filmstrips, discs, tapes, cassettes, multimedia kits, pictures, maps,
transparencies, museums and agencies are alphabetized by title and
organized by type in the Audiovisual Aids Section. Prices, times,
availability, interest level and other pertinent data are included.
The price and publisher's name of those Indian periodicals of interest
to educators in Zuni-Navajo areas are included in the annotated
Periodicals Section, organized alphabetically by title. A Book Publisher's Index and Media Publisher's Index are included.

181. Keesda; a coming out feast, by Filomena P. Pono. Dulce,
       NM, Independent School District, 1976. 51p. ED
       129497.
       The Jicarilla Apache people celebrate a young girl's
coming of age by having a feast called "Keesda". Derived from
the Spanish word "fiesta", "Keesda" is a Jicarilla Apache word
meaning "feast". This feast is held for four days, usually during
the summer months. However, it may be held at any time during
the year whenever a young girl comes of age. When this happens,
a quiet ceremony is held and the celebration and feast are held the
following summer. The ceremony for the feast follows strict Jicarilla customs since the people believe that the girl's future happiness and well-being depend on following the details exactly. Keesda is a busy but happy occasion for the family who is celebrating
it. Relatives and friends join in the celebration, festivities, and
preparations for the feast. A young brave is chosen by the girl's
father to dance with his daughter in the teepee. The girl's family,
with the help of the brave's family, prepare all the necessary details of the feast. This illustrated booklet describes the activities
held during the 4-day feast and gives a young brave's account of his
role during the ceremony.

182. From Carver to Hill and on, by Samuel P. Massie. New
       York, Research Corporation, 1978. 15p. Ed 162015.
       The story of blacks in chemistry is one of determina-
tion, expectation, participation and contribution. Between 1910 and
1945, despite George Washington Carver's significant agricultural
contributions and St. Elmo Brady's scholarship, white graduate
schools and industry had little interest in accepting blacks. There
was slow progress, despite these attitudes, by black scholars in
black schools and a foundation was laid for future research and publications. Beginning with World War II, changing social conditions
provided more chances for scientific growth in universities, industry,

textbook writing, government agencies, and professional organizations. The effects of desegregation began to be felt in universities and black scholars were hired away from exclusively black colleges. By the mid-1960s, black scholars were less hampered by prejudice and several black chemists became leaders in industry, administration and university programs. Presently, black schools face financial and identity crises because they have lost many of their black teachers. In order for blacks to continue to progress in chemistry, black scholars must serve at black schools, participate in professional organizations, and must write and publish. High level education must be provided for black students.

183. Black contributors to science and energy technology. Washington, DC, Department of Energy, 1979. 28p. ED 170154.
Presents biographical and pictorial information about 12 black scientists and inventors who were selected to serve as models for children who have little opportunity to learn of black contributions to science and technology, and as motivation for students who are uncertain about continuing their studies or about selecting professions. Much of their work has been in the use of energy, as in space technology, transportation, construction and many other military and industrial applications.

184. Proceedings of the First National Sickle Cell Educational Symposium. Arlington, VA, Public Health Service, DHEW, 1978. 183p. ED 155297.
This conference was organized around presentations about the cases of an adult and a pediatric sickle cell anemia patient. Following the presentations of the patients' case histories, and clinical and laboratory findings, the cases were discussed by specialists from various areas of expertise. Among the perspectives offered were those of internal medicine, hematology, ophthalmology, endocrinology, genetics, pediatrics, cardiology, nursing and social work. A series of symposia were conducted on the topics of clinical management, genetic counseling, educational techniques and current research relating to sickle cell disease. Also addressed were the need for and approach to parent education; some educational techniques; international perspectives on sickle cell disease; and the importance of education and sickle cell services as a part of comprehensive health. In addition to the full texts of the conference discussions and presentations, a list of participants is included in this report.

185. Community mental health, behavior therapy, and the Afro-American community, by Gerald G. Jackson. Paper presented at the annual conference of the Association for Advancement of Behavior Therapy, December 1977. 64p. ED 159501.
A preliminary step toward the establishment of a mental health system in the United States that is congruent with the socio-cultural circumstances of Afro-Americans calls for an analysis of the relevance of behavior therapy to the Afro-American com-

munity.   Considerable attention and analysis is given to the socio-
cultural antecedents that interact to produce a set of reactions by
the Afro-American community to behavior therapy and the possible
relationship between specific socio-cultural factors and the effective
practice of behavior therapy.   The two systems are not antithetical
but are congruent in a number of areas.   Multimodal behavior therapy can be viewed as an approach that is in keeping with the holistic
and spiritual dimension of Afro-American culture.   Its effective use
in the Afro-American community is the consequence of a recognition by behavior therapy of the influence of the American ethos on
its conceptualization and practice.   Acceptance of behavior therapy
by the Afro-American community is contingent upon the behavior
therapists and not their theoretical proclamations.

186.   Desegregation and Black achievement, by Robert L. Crain
            and Rita E. Mahard.   Durham, NC, Institute of Policy
            Sciences and Public Affairs, Duke University, October
            1977.   57p.   ED 160682.
            A majority of seventy-three studies dealing with the ef-
fect of desegregation on black achievement conclude that desegregation has a beneficial effect on black achievement scores.   These
findings are in agreement with various national surveys that have
found black achievement higher in predominantly white schools.   However, a number of desegregation studies have not found higher black
test scores after desegregation.   This may be accounted for by the
following: (1) weaker studies are less likely to find positive desegregation effects: and (2) certain kinds of desegregation plans are
less likely to have positive effects than are others.   A comparison
of the 73 studies does lead to the important conclusion that desegregation is more likely to have a positive impact on black test scores
if it begins in the earliest grades, and effects are especially likely
to be positive for first graders.   Another finding suggested by the
studies reviewed is that voluntary desegregation plans are less likely
to yield results than are mandatory plans.

187.   Black colleges as a national resource, by James E. Black-
            well.   Atlanta, Southern Education Foundation, 1976.
            38p.   ED 124094.
            A conference of primarily black college presidents and
of heads of foundations and agencies, which are devoted to the
strengthening of black colleges and higher education for blacks, focused on the role of black colleges beyond 1975, discussing critical
issues confronted by black colleges, including legal, economic, education, leadership, and political.   In this summary report of the
conference content, private and public black colleges are examined
separately followed by a statement of consensus that developed around
the following priorities for black colleges as a national resource:
(1) training of black and non-black students; (2) strengthening the
black community; (3) sharing resources and common goals with Third
World Nations; (4) development of major centers of research and
development affecting the quality of life; (5) fostering pluralism; (6)
meeting the challenge of new, untapped manpower needs in academic
and professional spheres and in public/social policy; (7) education

of poor and disadvantaged; (8) producing models of black leadership; (9) functioning as purveyors of black cultural heritage; and (10) training to meet critical manpower needs, e.g., in international diplomacy and law, health professions, and community conversation. Some recommendations are included for implementing the above priorities. The report includes summary discussion on What is a black college? Why were they founded? What did they do? and characteristics and clientele.

188. Rural blacks; a vanishing population, by Lewis W. Jones and
         Everett S. Lee. Paper presented at the W.E.B. Du-
         Bois Institute for the Study of the American Black,
         October 1974. 17p. ED 126219.
         The rural Negro population has been of public concern
since the slave status was defined and an ideological defense of that
status began to take shape. When slavery ended, a definition of the
Negro status in custom and in law was undertaken wherever Negro
people were concentrated. Controls were devised to "keep the Negro
in his place." That place for decades was to be in the rural South
and largely in the agricultural enterprises until the impact of World
War I was felt in the United States. In order to place a discussion
of the rural Negro at a conference identified with W.E.B. DuBois
several references are mentioned and discussed. By 1970, 80 percent of the black population is in urban places and nearly 74 percent are in metropolitan areas. No more than half (53 percent) of
the black population is southern, and in no state is the black population much more than a third. The black farmers who remain are
highly concentrated, specialize in cash crops, and operate small
units with little monetary return. Current trends do not encourage
hopes for a resurgence of blacks in agriculture in the South. Despite what appears to be a high rate of reproduction the black farm
population is diminishing. There is a high rate of out-migration
from rural populations, and the number of children is diminishing
relative to the total population. A high proportion of the black children in rural farm areas are those of people who are dead, who
are living elsewhere, or who are members of subfamilies whose
heads are not household heads.

189. The Black family in American economy; Black capitalism, by
         Peter A. Ezeocha. Paper presented at the Pan Ameri-
         can Studies Conference, March 1975. 28p. ED 126216.
         Black capitalism that is well planned and run is a source
of innumerable benefits to the American society in general and to
blacks in particular. It generates opportunities for blacks to perform in occupations which for many years were closed to them.
For hundreds of years blacks have been despised and often looked
down upon on account of the fact that in the main they possess no
property; most of them are poor amidst plenty. It is argued here
that through black capitalism, all these anomalous treatments could
be combated and alleviated. Since the rebirth of black business
enterprises, black racial has reappeared because now some better
opportunities exist for blacks. Blacks of the modern era are seen
in high government offices, mercantile industries, institutions of

higher learning, and private endeavors. The pace of black capitalism has been slow in realizing its goal of a total economic upgrad-
ing of the black community which requires the ownership and control
of new capital and business opportunity by people within the black
ghetto, but it has made some significant achievements. It is concluded that black capitalism is gradually generating new vitality in
the black-ghetto inner cities.

190.   The Black migrant; changing origins, changing characteristics,
        by A. R. Miller. Paper presented at the W. E. B. DuBois
        Institute for the Study of the American Black, October
        1974. 39p. ED 126226.
        The character of black migration, as well as the signifi-
cance that migration will play in the future of the black population
is examined in this paper. Section I of the paper presents an introduction. Section II addresses recent migration to metropolitan
areas, focusing on the origins of recent migrants, characteristics
of recent migrants (age, education, activity, status, and occupation),
and a summary. This section of the paper notes that black migrants
to metropolitan areas now come predominantly from other metropolitan areas and that the major stream of black migration is now from
one metropolitan area to another. It is also noted that the description of the average black migrant to the city as an ill-trained person of rural background and low socioeconomic status to whom the
social problems of the large metropolitan areas can be largely attributed will not hold. He or she is in fact well educated by current
standards and, judging from the occupational position of those employed, relatively successful at utilizing this education. Section III
discusses interstate migration and multiple movers. It seems clear
from the evidence of the 1970 census, that the black population of
the United States is now in a third stage--when the rural to urban
shift has proceeded to the point where in fact it is a relatively
small part of total migration and when perhaps the differences in
educational opportunities between city and country have diminished.

191.   The State of Black America 1977. New York, National Ur-
        ban League, January 1977. 86p. ED 135914.
        This document contains the National Urban League's
second annual "State of Black America", report which describes the
condition of black citizens during the year 1976. The report examines developments in eleven major areas of life: the economy,
employment, education, housing, health, social welfare, youth,
crime, legislation, political involvement, and foreign policy. It
also includes, for the first time, the results of a survey of Urban
League affiliates from 107 cities across the country. The survey
shows deepened depression and hardship among blacks. Employment and housing are the most crisis-ridden areas. The most important event for blacks in 1976 was the presidential election. They
showed confidence in political leadership as a result of Jimmy Carter's victory.

192.   Keynote address by Vernon E. Jordan, Jr. Speech presented
        at the annual conference of the National Urban League,

July 1977. 21p. ED 148928.
This speech outlines the plight of black people under the
present federal government administration. It is stated that the administration is not living up to the First Commandment of politics;
that is, to help those who helped it. The administration has failed
black people since it has not adequately addressed itself to a new
domestic policy. The urban areas are dying because local politics
are aimed at killing inner city neighborhoods. It is suggested that
a national urban policy be developed. This should have three major
components: (1) federally supported and directed increases in basic
social services, (2) massive creation of housing opportunities for
low and moderate income families and (3) an urban economic development program that includes guaranteed jobs for all who can work
and an income assistance system. Finally the administration should
signal the nation's poor that their interests will be met by meaningful reform of the welfare system. The National Urban League sup-
ports a long-range plan to use a refundable credit income tax as the
means of assuring a minimum income level beneath which no family
could fall. This plan includes four steps: (1) a massive job creation program, (2) food stamp expansion, (3) major improvements
in social insurance programs, including a national health insurance
plan, and (4) a refundable tax credit. This speech concludes by
calling on blacks and upon their leadership to create a new structure
that will enable blacks to act in unison and to maximize efforts that
will help all blacks in need.

193. The Black rural landowner; endangered species; social, po-
        litical, and economic implications, edited by Leo McGee
        and Robert Boone. Nashville, Tennessee State University,
        1976. 177p. ED 138671.
This publication discusses the issue of black owned rural
land decline. Since the turn of the century, it is estimated that
blacks have lost in excess of 9,000,000 acres of rural land. The
impact of this loss is tremendous for blacks, both on the economic
and psychological levels. Developing strategies to arrest the rapid
decline of black owned rural real estate is a high priority on the
agenda of concern of the black community. It is noted that landownership is important because it provides an economic base for
socio-psychological release and/or identification. In a capitalistic
society, landownership is linked with permanence and political power.
Black land capable of being usefully developed or converted into
capital, constitutes an immensely valuable political resource. If
used correctly, a black land base could be critical to the political
base in the black community. The absence of such a base can have
a crippling effect on the mobilization potential of the black community
in the political process. Among the various social, political, and
economic implications of black rural land loss which are discussed
in this publication are: (1) the Emergency Land Fund, (2) attitudes
of blacks toward rural land, (3) institutional procedures for resolving
tax delinquency in the south, and (4) a case study of black rural
land loss in Tennessee.

194. Ebony patriots; participation of Blacks in the battles of the

American Revolution in the New York City area, 1776-
1779. New York City Bicentennial Corporation, 1976.
25p. ED 157805.

Exploits of 20 black men, slave and free, who fought in
battles of the American Revolution in New York state are recounted.
At the beginning of the Revolutionary War, colonies did not allow
slaves or free blacks to join the Continental Army. Only after the
British Army offered freedom to slaves who joined the royal ranks
did the Continental Army accept black men as soldiers. Among the
20 whose stories are told in this pamphlet were Samuel Sutphin from
N. J. , Timothy Prince from Vermont, and Julius Cezar from New
York. Accounts are given of the black soldiers' participation in
three battles; the battle for Long Island and New York City in 1776,
the fight for White Plains in 1776, and the assault on Stony Point in
1779. During these campaigns, black soldiers served as militiamen,
guides, teamsters, and spies. After the Revolution was over, many
black soldiers experienced difficulties in obtaining the freedom they
had been promised for military service. Others were not granted
their pensions until 30 years or more had passed. A concluding
chapter briefly describes black participation in American military
activities from the French and Indian War through the Vietnam War.

195. When the marching stopped; an analysis of Black issues in the
'70's. New York, National Urban League, Inc. , April
1973. 177p. ED 148953.

This volume presents the contents of a conference held
with scholars concerning their perceptions of some of the critical
issues affecting black Americans. The formal presentations and the
discussion that followed are reproduced in this book. The sessions
explored several major forces impinging on the lives of the black
and the poor and developed broad approaches to deal positively with
those forces. What developed from the sessions was not a list of
proposed solutions but a comprehensive examination of where the
black person stands in the present social and economic milieu and
a look at his prospects for the future. There were sessions, addressing the following issues: (1) economic policy and income security, (2) personal security, law enforcement and the administration of justice, (3) the political process and (4) educational policy.
Among the specific issues which were discussed are the following:
(1) the economic outlook and employment prospects for blacks, (2)
crime in the black community, (3) drug problems in the black community, (4) the political process and black liberation, (5) full employment, (6) critical issues in the education of minorities, (7) public school reform, and (8) integration.

196. Bibliography of writings on La Mujer, compiled by Cristina
Portillo. Berkeley, Chicano Studies Library, University
of California, 1976. 56p. ED 164216.

The 283 materials cited in this bibliography are chiefly
on Chicanas in the United States. However, books or articles that
discuss Mexicans or women in general and can be related to the
experiences of Chicanas are also cited. Areas covered include the
arts, education, sociology, economics, history, health, and litera-

ture. The materials are principally from the late sixties to 1976, although earlier publications are cited. Part I contains articles, student papers, dissertations, books, and documents pertaining to la mujer. Part II contains serials that are specifically about Chicanas, Mexicanas and women in general, or contain a variety of articles relevant to Chicanas. Both sections are arranged in alphabetical order by authors. A subject index is included. The items in this bibliography are available in the Chicano Studies Library's collection: full bibliographic information is given to help the user locate the material.

197. Profile of the Mexican American woman, by Martha Cotera. University Park, ERIC Clearinghouse on Rural Education and Small Schools, New Mexico State University, March 1976. 280p. ED 119888.

The second largest group of minority women in the U.S., Mexican American women share multitudinous histories, vast differences in lifestyles, experiences and realities. A Chicana may have recently arrived from Mexico, or her ancestors may have been in the Southwest since 1520 (or before) or in the Midwest since the 1880's. She may be rural, urban, poor, middle class or Ph.D., a high school dropout, a teacher, or a migrant. She does share some basic, and heterogeneous, roots in the development of Indian and Spanish culture and history. She also shares the history of involvement and participation which has been a way of life for the Chicano community in the U.S. since 1848. Documenting the development of Mexican American women in Mexico and the U.S., this monograph discusses: the Chicana's historical legacy during Mexico's Pre-Columbian and Colonial Periods, its War for Independence, the 1910 Revolution, and during the United States Colonial Period and history between 1840 and 1960; Chicanas in the U.S. today--their education, employment status, income, health, housing, roles, and attitudes; the Chicana and her family; today's Chicana and her achievements in education, literature and journalism, political activities, and labor; Chicanas in the feminist movement; and the Chicana and the future. Appended are a 119-item bibliography, addresses for 35 Chicana organizations, and various resolutions passed between 1970 and 1975 in 10 Chicana conferences.

198. The Mexican American woman and mental health, by Guadalupe Gibson. Paper presented at the Arizona conference for Spanish-speaking women, June 1975. 28p. ED 143469.

For a long time Chicanas have been self-denying, self-sacrificing. Well, it is time that Mexican American women began thinking of themselves. It follows that if women love and cherish others, they must begin by loving and cherishing themselves. From the mental health perspective it is essential that they do so, not only for their sake, but for that of those around them; for how can they truly value others if they do not value themselves. Since the Chicana has always been the mainstay of the family, the mental health of her family is dependent on her positive self-image and self-identity. In freeing herself to be herself, she is freeing others to be themselves too. This paper discusses the indicators of the

Chicana's mental health--self-identity, self-image, understanding and acceptance of herself, her perceptions of the world around her and her relationships with others, her ability to handle crises and cope with stress, and her flexibility to shift roles without discomfort; the Mexican American woman within the bicultural milieu; attitudes held by mental health professionals; the concept of women from the Mexicano point of view; sexism in the language and literature; the Chicana's attitudes toward and role in the women's movement; the stereotypic views of the Mexican American woman; and the importance of the Chicana having a positive self-image and self-identity of herself.

199. The Chicana image, by Judy Salinas. Paper presented at the Popular Culture Association meeting, March 1975. 16p. ED 106032.
    Literature has perpetuated through the centuries the cultural and traditional roles and stereotypes of woman, particularly the Hispanic woman. Two main categories or images of woman, with variations and generalizations, have been: (1) the "good woman", symbolized by a woman who can think or do no evil, is pure, understanding, kind, weak, passive, needs to be protected, but yet has an inner strength and a capacity for enduring and suffering; and (2) the "bad woman", symbolized by one who is a temptress and seductress, representing evil through love and the perversion and excess of its passions. The "bad woman" is morally judged and condemned by all and must suffer a severe punishment for her evil actions, usually death by murder or suicide. A third gray-area category is one which blends these two principal images: yet, one image consistently dominates the other. These principal images of woman have persisted in Spanish, Spanish American, and Anglo American literature from their respective beginnings to contemporary examples. These categories are examined in various selections and passages of several Chicano works. Among these are Roland Hinojosa's "Estampas del valle y otras obras"; Jorge Isaacs' "Maria"; Jose Montoya's "La jefita"; Estela Portillo's "The Swallows"; and Rodolfo Anaya's "Bless Me, Ultima."

200. La mujer Chicana; an annotated bibliography, by Evey Chapa. Austin, TX, Chicana Research and Learning Center, 1976. 94p. ED 152439.
    Intended to provide interested persons, researchers, and educators with information about "la mujer Chicana", this annotated bibliography cites 320 materials published between 1916 and 1975, with the majority being between 1960 and 1975. The 12 sections cover the following subject areas: Chicana publications; Chicana feminism and "el movimiento"; education; health--birth control, folk medicine, mental health, and health in general; history; labor/ employment; culture: the family; machismo; politics; social issues-- child care, prison, rape, religion, sex-role stereotyping, welfare, and youth related; and "Third World Women". Entries in the section on Chicana publications fall under two categories: publications initiated and produced by mujeres, and special editions of existing Chicano periodicals or journals. Among the topics covered are the problems

Chicanas face in education; historical events which occurred before 1960, primarily concerning Mexicanas and Latinas; Chicana involvement in literature and the arts; political activities of Chicanas; problems in attaining equality in employment; and Chicana involvement in boycotts and strikes. Many of the sources are cross-referenced under a second subject area. Entries are consecutively numbered and the cross-referenced annotation refers the reader to another number in the bibliography. In order to facilitate the acquisition of the materials not easily located in most libraries, a list of addresses for their source is appended.

201.   Through Anglo eyes; Chicanos as portrayed in the news media, by Felix Gutierrez. Paper presented at the annual meeting of the Association for Education in Journalism, August 1978. 20p. ED 159693.
        Coverage of Chicanos by the news media, almost nonexistent until the mid-1960s, still has not achieved full balance or objectivity. It is important for media personnel to develop greater competence in handling Chicano coverage since the Latino group, of which Chicanos are the largest segment, are the nation's fastest growing population group and--contrary to their portrayal by the media as a regional group--are dispersed throughout the United States. Research studies on media coverage of Chicanos have shown that coverage, generally low, has been concentrated in periods when Chicanos are either the subject of public issues or perceived as posing a threat to the established order; that stereotypical symbols, often with negative connotations, have been used to designate Chicano groups; that reporters covering Chicanos tend to rely on non-Chicano sources; and that coverage of Chicanos has tended to emphasize negative aspects of the community. A study of 1977-1978 California newspaper coverage of undocumented Chicano workers, or "illegal aliens," shows that reporters relied heavily on Anglo law enforcement and public officials as sources, rather than on representatives of immigrant organizations, legal agencies, Latino groups, and the academic community, and consequently portrayed the undocumented workers as law enforcement or public problems.

202.   A Voting rights handbook for Chicanos. San Francisco, Mexican American Legal Defense and Educational Fund, Inc., 1977. 162p. ED 148528.
        In the summer of 1975, the protective provisions of the 1965 Voting Rights Act were extended to parts of the Southwest. This marks a significant point in the history to secure for Chicanos a meaningful participation in the political process. The basic purpose of the Act assures that minorities can participate in the election process without any unreasonable barriers which might discourage voting. Although the Act will not eliminate all forms of voter discrimination, it will serve to discourage states, counties, school districts, and cities from making discriminatory election law changes. In addition, the Act provides other protections to insure fair registration drives and elections. Important parts of the Act which apply to states, counties, school districts, cities, and other special districts in certain areas of the Southwest are: covered

jurisdictions must show that any changes in election laws do not
have a discriminatory purpose or effect.   Federal examiners can
be assigned to an area to encourage minority voter registration;
Federal observers may also be sent to an area to observe election
day activities and document any instances of voter discrimination;
bilingual elections must be conducted in those areas covered by the
Act.   This handbook, written in English and Spanish, describes the
Act's protective features and lists the circumstances by which Chicanos can have direct input into the enforcement of these provisions.

203.   The Chicanos of El Paso; a case of changing colonization, by
        Oscar J. Martinez.   May 1977.   69p.   ED 153780.
        Using historical statistics and key indicators, data were
synthesized to identify longitudinal trends and patterns in the social,
economic, and political status of El Paso's Chicanos.   Data related
to group achievement were analyzed.   A framework adapted to local
conditions based on the internal colonialism model was used for the
periodization of El Paso Chicano history.   Data indicated a historical
division along economic, political, and social lines.   This separation
was partially explained by the perpetual presence of poor immigrants
and protracted job competition from cheap labor in Juarez.   Such
factors affected local wage, working, and living conditions and caused
some outmigration.   Yet structural discriminatory barriers such as
job exclusion and wage differentials, segregation, lack of educational
opportunities, and political domination have greatly reinforced such
disadvantages and created others, thus contributing to a marked
absence of progress among local Chicanos until recently.   Several
stages were identified in the Chicano community's evolution.   There
was an initial period of "traditional internal colonialism" (1848-1900),
followed by "modified internal colonialism" (1900-1945), and the years
1945-1965 characterized by the emergence of "conditions for incipient decolonization."   With the onset of the Chicano Movement in
1965, El Paso's Chicanos entered into "incipient decolonization",
and this phase continues to the present.

204.   School desegregation and the Chicano community, by Sheldon
        Rosen.   Washington, DC, National Institute of Education,
        DHEW, 1976.   104p.   ED 131974.
        A profile of Chicanos on the basis of key indicators of
socioeconomic and political status reveals remarkable gaps between
them and the Anglo segment.   Chicano incomes are much lower,
their educational attainments are inferior, their occupational range
is narrow and unfavorable, and their returns on educational attainments are lower.   Finally, their access to policy making is negligi-
ble.   These patterns of political, economic, and social exclusion
are the result of the historical application of the mechanisms of internal colonialism.   The intentional isolation of Chicanos in the public schools of both the rural and urban Southwest has been a pervasive feature of the region's educational systems for many decades.
This educational segregation, whether de jure or de facto, is sustained by official policies and institutional arrangements.   This
paper outlines the public practices that limit desegregation efforts
in communities with large Chicano populations and suggests which

community types are most susceptible to attempts at integration. The paper also explores the historical and current consequences for Chicanos of their subordinate ethnic status, and their evolutionary role as a forcibly included population; examines present patterns of social, economic, and political marginality characteristic of Mexican American society; analyzes the mechanisms of internal colonialism; examines the population's adaptive responses to its status as an internal colony; and discusses future problems and implications for public policy.

5.
HANDICAPPED AND DISADVANTAGED

205.   A Handbook on the legal rights of handicapped people. Wash-
        ington, DC, President's Committee on Employment of
        the Handicapped, 1976. 96p. ED 125181.
        Summarized and organized for easy reference are feder-
al and state (Virginia, Maryland, and the District of Columbia) laws
and results of court cases regarding the rights of the handicapped
in the areas of architectural barriers, benefits, civil rights, education, employment, hospital and medical matters, housing, insurance, transportation, vocational rehabilitation, and lawyers and organizations. Provisions are organized within each category by lo-
cality. Sources of further information or procedures for filing a
complaint are provided whenever appropriate. Also included are
lists of lawyers referral services, legal aid societies, and other
resources.

206.   Independent living for the physically disabled. Denver, Atlan-
        tis Community, Inc., 1976. 450p. ED 136470.
        Findings are presented from a 1-year planning study of
independent living for severely physically disabled persons. Funded
by a federal grant through the city and county of Denver, the study
focuses on the following 10 necessary services (with subtopics in
parentheses): income assistance (subsidies and typical expenditures),
attendant care (recommendations for long-term solutions and a sample budget for a cluster client), medical services (health insurance
and health planning), counseling (the effects of the 1973 Vocational
Rehabilitation Act), transportation (the Urban Mass Transit Administration), education (mainstreaming), employment (architectural and
psychological barriers), recreation (active vs. passive involvement),
housing (financing and detailed design standards), and legislation
(antidiscrimination laws). Each chapter lists specific recommendations. The report also contains results of two surveys concerning
the disabled population of Denver. Among four appendixes is the
format of the needs assessment survey.

207.   The Long beginning; an overview of the first 150 years of
            Federal legislation and funding for the handicapped, by
            Charlotte Hawkins-Shepard. 1978. 39p. ED 161211.
            Presented is an overview of the first 150 years of

90

federal legislation and funding for the handicapped.   Seventeen terms
are defined and the position of the Bureau of Education for the Handicapped within the federal structure is examined.   The congressional
process of authorizing federal funds for special education is explained and 50 specific federal laws are described.   Special education funding for fiscal years 1978 and 1979 is also discussed and
future trends pertaining to financing of special education are considered.

208.   The Arts and handicapped people; defining the national direc-
       tion. Washington, DC, Bureau of Education for Handi-
       capped, DHEW, April 1977. 78p. ED 158445.
          Proceedings from an April, 1977 conference focus on
the current status and future directions of arts programming for the
handicapped.   M. Appell provides an overview of the field; while W.
Kalenius, Jr. reviews data from 138 current research studies which
indicate that handicapped children were able to learn the art forms,
enjoyed the activities, increased feelings of self worth and learned
academic skills as a result of arts activities.   S. Madeja discusses
the role of aesthetic preception, the critical process, and knowledge
about the arts in arts instruction for the handicapped.   L. Molloy
discusses architectural and program accessibility factors for public
arts facilities.   Methods of facilitating career development and leisure time enjoyment of the arts are discussed by J. Goldstein.
Papers by J. Newberg and J. Kukuk deal with the artist's role in
working with handicapped people and the major components of comprehensive arts education programs for the handicapped.   G. Barlow
cites the negative attitudes of society toward the handicapped in general, and suggests the need to identify attitudes specific to the handicapped in the arts.   Further research needs are projected by J.
Morrison.   A conference summary outlines conclusions (regarding
the Federal role, research, and arts in education, public facilities
and attitudes), implications, and projections.

209.   Home in a wheelchair: house design ideas for easier wheel-
       chair living, by Joseph Chasin. Bethesda, MD, Para-
       lyzed Veterans of America, 1977. 33p. ED 150795.
          Intended to aid in the building or purchase of a home
suitable for use by a handicapped individual in a wheelchair, the
booklet provides detailed design guidelines.   Included is information
on the decision process, finances, ramps, a car shelter, doors, communication devices, electrical needs, windows, elevators and chair
lifts, the kitchen, an exercise area, the laundry, storage, floors and
floor coverings, the bathroom, the bedroom, mobility in the home,
three demonstration houses, alteration of a builder's plan, the wheelchair, and safety.   Also included are a listing of 12 relevant books,
and sources of special equipment.

210.   The Uncounted poor; an ethnological excursion to an institution,
       by William Roth. Madison, Institute for Research on
       Poverty, University of Wisconsin, 1977. 33p.
       ED 146290.
          The upcoming Bureau of the Census document titled, "The

Survey of Institutionalized Persons" will provide complete information
and data on long-term institutional care. Because this document
provides data basically devoid of context, this discussion paper presents an ethnology of a total institution. In it, the author conveys
his impressions and observations formed during a guided tour of
this institution which is simply labeled, "Palm Breeze". Although
the grounds of the institution are aesthetically beautiful with green
lush gardens, there are no people on the grounds. The people are
inside the buildings exhibiting varying degrees of inactivity. There
is a special language at Palm Breeze, shared by the inmates, but
incomprehensible to nurses and guards. Power relationships are
very clear at this institution. Actions are determined according to
what is allowed, and one of the things seemingly not allowed is
English. Ways of discouraging its use include drugs and a day
structured to yank people away from any situation in which English
could be employed, to name but two. The children's wards and the
women's wards are visited, and each is replete with its individual
horrors. The children are over drugged, under stimulated and forgotten. In the women's wards, women can be found drinking from
unflushed toilets. The reason for this is that the water fountains
are broken and some women crawl rather than walk. Palm Breeze
is an inhuman and brutal institution. Its socialization is fast and
efficient. It is a model for changing attitudes, behavior, and personality.

211. The Last suffrage frontier; enfranchising mental hospital resi-
     dents. Harrisburg, Pennsylvania State Advisory Com-
     mittee to the U.S. Commission on Civil Rights, June
     1978. 40p. ED 163117.
          This report addresses the denial of suffrage to mentally
disabled persons institutionalized in Pennsylvania. The case study
of Pennhurst Center patients who tried to vote in the 1976 election
is described. Pertinent Pennsylvania statutes and current voting
practices are analyzed. A national overview of the problem along
with community and institutional attitudes toward voting by the mentally handicapped are discussed. State directives in support of voting rights of institutionalized Pennsylvanians and guidance to election
officials and institutional administrators are outlined. Recommendations are made to institutions concerning how to assist in all aspects
of the voting process, how to decrease community hostility toward
mentally disabled voters, and how to help insure legal voting rights
of institutionalized persons.

212. Health of the disadvantaged; chart book. Bethesda, MD,
     Health Resources Administration, DHEW, September
     1977. 101p. ED 147440.
          This chart book on the health of the disadvantaged con-
tains major published and previously unpublished data. The major
areas that are covered are: health status, utilization of services,
manpower, and financial expenditures. Also included are supplementary tables which present more precise data, and additional information. The charts show that: (1) for most critical measures
of disease, the poor compared to the non-poor and racial and ethnic

minorities compared to whites had higher incidences, (2) the higher
incidences of disease for racial and ethnic minorities were partially
accounted for by socioeconomic factors, (3) the amount of contact
with medical services increased significantly for the poor and racial
minorities between 1964 and 1973, (4) racial minorities and the poor
use medical services to a lesser degree relative to their need in
comparison to whites and the non-poor, respectively, (5) racial
minorities constitute five and one-half per cent of the health professionals and fourteen percent of all health occupations, (6) out-of-
pocket expenses were twice as great for both whites and the non-
poor as compared to racial minorities and the poor, respectively,
(7) disparities existed between whites and racial minorities as to
the benefits received from medicare and medicaid; for instance,
75% greater payments were expended per white as compared to racial minority medicaid recipients, and (8) the poor and minorities
were at a twofold disparity healthwise: they were in poorer health
and they had less spent on them for health services. Poor minorities were at the greatest disparities on both accounts.

213. An Analysis of optacon usage, by Loren T. Schoof II. Palo
    Alto, CA, Telesensory Systems, Inc., 1975. 30p. ED
    108449.
        Use of the Optacon, a reading aid for the blind, was
explored in regard to user occupations, factors affecting reading
speed, and how the machine is used on the job. Data were obtained
from a survey of 250 Optacon users: from statistical analyses of
information gathered about 41 Optacon trainers; and from a telephone
survey of 17 blind people in different occupational groups who use
the Optacon as a job tool. Results included findings that students,
housewives, computer professionals, social workers, and business
personnel are major Optacon users: that young people read more
quickly at the end of Optacon can be a useful tool in any occupation where
retrieval of printed information is useful; [sic] that persons in entry-
level positions are strongly motivated to use the Optacon on the job;
and that the Optacon enables users to plan and to organize their
work more efficiently.

214. Television for deaf people; selected projects, by Thomas
    Freebairn. New York, Deafness Research and Training
    Center, New York University, 1974. 104p. ED 091909.
        Television projects for the deaf are described with spe-
cial focus on activities by the Deafness Research and Training Center to develop a cable television cooperative to produce and distrib-
ute programs for the deaf. The chapter on cable television considers principles of cable television, the model for a cable television
cooperative, steps in establishing the cooperative, television training and production workshops for deaf people, program production by
agencies other than cable television operators, and distribution models for the cooperative. Among conclusions noted is that cable operators are willing to telecast but reluctant to produce programs
for the deaf. Discussed are aspects of original television programing
derived from a national survey of programing needs of deaf people
and activities of the Deafness Research and Training Center. Con-

clusions and recommendations center on increasing the production, dissemination, and evaluation of television programs appropriate for deaf viewers. Alternative visual supplements including sign language inserts and captions are compared. It is concluded that use of the insert is easier and cheaper for the broadcaster, while captions can be understood by more people. Research is urged in all areas of television for deaf people. Local broadcasters are encouraged to produce original materials for the deaf, modify regular programs, and rent specially modified programs. Local deaf communities are encouraged to ask broadcasters for special programing. Publicity brochures, illustrations, and survey results are appended.

215. Alexander Graham Bell; teacher of the deaf, by Robert V. Bruce. Northampton, MA, Clarke School for the Deaf, March 1974. 14p. ED 094520.
     The lecture on Alexander Graham Bell by Dr. Robert V. Bruce, the author of a biography of Bell, focuses on Bell's association with the Clarke School for the Deaf in Massachusetts. Noted are Bell's employment by the school at 25 years of age and the preceding period during which Bell taught elocution at a boys' school in Scotland and used his father's system of Visible Speech at a London school for the deaf. Also described are his early commitment to lipreading and the oral approach to deaf education, his development of the telephone as a byproduct of his inventions to aid deaf students, his lifelong involvement in problems of the deaf, his marriage to a deaf woman, his financial support of schools for the deaf, his support of partial integration of deaf students with hearing students, his controversies with Edward Gallaudet, his investigations into the heritability of deafness, his role in directing Helen Keller's father to the Perkins Institution, his correspondence with Helen Keller, his interest in heavier-than-air flight, his service on the Board of Governors of the Clarke School, and his death in 1922.

216. Mediagraphy on deafness and the deaf, compiled by Thomas R. Harrington. Washington, DC, Gallaudet College, 1979. 269p. ED 169721.
     The annotated mediagraphy listing of nonprint media contains information on 951 titles available from 277 sources for the instruction, information, or entertainment of the hearing impaired. The mediagraphy is divided into four main parts: the main entry section, containing the title, medium, physical description, release date, cost availability, subject group, and a brief annotation; a title cross reference section, a sources section (including names, addresses and voice and TTY telephone numbers of sources where items in the main entry section may be obtained); and source cross reference section. Among subject groups included are audiology and speech, deaf/blind, religion, and hearing impairment. A brief bibliography of additional helpful sources is included.

217. 100 essential signs. Austin, Texas School for the Deaf, January 1978. 29p. ED 168288.
     The booklet contains illustrations of 100 basic signs for use by school employees in working with the deaf. The signs were

chosen for inclusion in the booklet by a committee which reviewed hundreds of signs and evaluated their importance in communicating with the deaf. The illustrations, taken in large part from the "Preferred Signs for Instructional Purposes" text, appear with the English and Spanish word equivalents. The signs are broken down into three categories - safety signs such as stop, go, wait, cold, and hospital; informative signs such as where, boy, mother, teacher, after, and month; and courtesy signs such as good morning, hi, sorry, and excuse me. A brief explanation of the markings appearing in the booklet and the manual alphabet are also included.

218. Silent minority, by Beth Kramer. Washington, DC, President's Committee on Mental Retardation, 1974. 44p. ED 091915.
Discussed in the booklet are approaches for citizens to use in helping the silent minority--mentally retarded (MR) children and adults--attain their rights to life, liberty, and the pursuit of happiness. The MR person is described to be one of 6 millon retarded Americans, to benefit from education although his ability to learn is limited, to have special needs such as speech therapy, and to be unable to protect his own interests. Discussed under the MR person's right to life are the right to be born healthy, advocacy programs, the dilemma of guardianship seen in parents' concerns for the future of their MR children, health insurance legislation, habilitation, improved institutionalization, and ways citizens can protect the life of MR persons. Discussed under the right to liberty are the trend toward normalization; considerations on institutionalization such as correct diagnosis, court procedures, prison problems, legislative reform, zoning barriers; and what the citizen can do to assure liberty for the MR population. Discussed under the right to the pursuit of happiness are the right to an appropriate education, the right to a place in the labor force, fundamental personal rights such as marriage, the right to be treated as an individual equal to other citizens, and what the citizen can do to protect the pursuit of happiness of the MR person. Sources of information on legal rights of the mentally retarded and background literature are included.

219. State aid for special education; who benefits? by William H. Wilken. Washington, DC, National Conference of State Legislatures, October 1976. 254p. ED 136457.
Intended for administrators, educators, and parents, the document presents information on the management and utilization of state special education aid. An introductory section reviews the history of state aid for special education and notes questions which are addressed in the document, such as the following: "How much state funding is available for special education in each of the states?", "What factors are considered in distribution formulas?", and "Do rich local education agencies obtain more special education aid than poor ones?" Chapter I covers dollar amounts available and what they buy, including past and present procedures and policies. (Data presented in tabular form following the text is listed by state.) The controversy about policies determining distribution of funds is reported in Chapter II. Chapter III provides details of patterns of

distribution and allocation of state aid in two states--Georgia and
Massachusetts, with tables of data following the text. Among issues
noted to be of importance are aid distribution, basis for aid entitle-
ments, and procedural requirements.

220. A Reader's guide for parents of children with mental, physi-
      cal or emotional disabilities, by Coralie B. Moore and
      Kathryn G. Morton. Silver Spring, MD, Montgomery
      County Association for Retarded Citizens, 1976. 148p.
      ED 143179.
      Presented for parents of handicapped children is a list-
ing of approximately 600 references. The books in the first section
deal with the following five topics relevant to all handicaps: basic
information; home teaching and playing techniques; experiences of
other parents; and current issues such as advocacy, employment,
prevention, and sex education. The second section contains references for books on 11 specific handicaps. Books for children about
children with handicaps are cited in the third section, and a final
section lists relevant organizations, directories and journals. Book
citations within each topic area are arranged alphabetically by author
and include title, date, pagination information and a brief annotation.

221. The Parents' manual; a manual of supplementary activities
      for homebound children with severely handicapping con-
      ditions, by Joan Shrensky. New York, Graduate School
      of the City University of New York, 1975. 136p. ED
      140562.
      Designed for parents of homebound severely handicapped
children, the manual presents games and activities for teaching preliminary skills (including body awareness), self help skills (such as
washing hands, eating with a spoon, and brushing teeth), visual
skills, language skills, and mathematics skills. An introduction to
each series of activities provides information on purpose, materials,
and approach.

222. A Theatre workshop for children with learning disabilities, by
      Lotte Kaliski. Paper presented at the World Congress
      on Future Special Education, July 1978. 22p. ED
      158541.
      The paper describes a theater workshop for children
with learning disabilities, and discusses its benefits, including improved oral and written language, self esteem, and self control.
Comments of actors involved in the workshop are included.

223. ToyBrary; a toy lending library for parents and children.
      Lincoln, Nebraska State Department of Education, 1978.
      243p. ED 161228.
      Intended for parents, the catalog lists toys which are
helpful in the education of young handicapped children. Four sections focus on toys for developing muscle control, toys that encourage exploring, toys that challenge the mind, and toys that appeal
to the senses. Each entry includes information on how to use the

toy to develop specific skills, as well as a description of how to make a similar toy from household items. A final section provides information on resources (including information sources, journals, and a bibliography) for parents.

224. Arts for the handicapped child; why? Washington, DC, National Committee Arts for the Handicapped, 1978. 59p. ED 161214.
    Presented is a collection of case studies by therapists, educators, artists, parents, and recreation leaders, dealing with the arts as learning experiences for handicapped children. Each of the ten articles records the positive effects of arts experiences (dance, art, music, drama) on the growth and development of a particular handicapped child or group of children.

225. How to help your child; a guide for parents of multiply handicapped children, by Phyllis B. Doyle. Blue Bell, PA, Montgomery County Intermediate Unit 23, 1976. 70p. ED 161193.
    Developed by Project TRAC-Training-/Resources Acquisition and Control, the three part guide is for parents of multiply handicapped children. Part 1 examines a public school training program for multiply handicapped children. Part 2 gives suggestions for activities that can make home life easier and at the same time provide learning experiences for the child. These activities include communications, lifting and carrying, positioning, motor skills, feeding, dressing, toilet training, and hygiene. In Part 3 are many suggestions about where to do and what to go when parents need special help, including the names and addresses of special services in the Pennsylvania area, such as camping, parent groups, care and training for retarded adults, counseling and help with family problems, and home health care. Also in Part 3 is information on special equipment, such as supports for sitting and lying, chairs, walking aids, and clothing. Special information on how to go about finding a baby sitter, obtaining a special car license plate for "handicapped only" and "no parking" privileges, income tax deductions, and planning for the future is also included.

226. Mainstreaming; idea and actuality, by Anne P. Smith. Albany, New York State Education Department, 1973. 24p. ED 111157.
    The importance of mainstreaming (helping handicapped children achieve maximum participation in regular school programs) is emphasized, and underlying concepts are explained. Methods for implementing mainstreaming in protected settings (such as hospitals) and in regular classrooms (through the use of helping teachers, resource rooms, a modified resource program, or open classrooms) are described. Noted are the following common elements of successful mainstreaming programs: preparation, pacing (selective integration), specificity (redefining the special educator's role), and flexible placement. Also included is an annotated bibliography of 14 references on mainstreaming in action.

227. Recreation and handicapped people; a national forum on meeting the recreation and park needs of handicapped people. 1975. 65p. ED 113902.
   Summarized are recommendations made by handicapped people and recreation and park professionals at a 1974 forum on meeting the recreation and park needs of the handicapped. A statement of the issue and delegates' reactions are provided on 12 topics: segregation vs. integration; the role of the voluntary health agency and its effect on the responsibility of the community recreator; the importance of having especially trained personnel (therapeutic recreation professionals); the problem of architectural barriers; legislation; financing; the attitudes of nonhandicapped participants; insurance costs; recreation as a rehabilitation tool; the value of consumer input into recreation planning and design; employment of the handicapped in recreation and park occupations; and transportation. Where applicable, specific suggestions are given for national, state, local, or college level actions. Sample conclusions are that separate but equal facilities are never an acceptable objective, and that 5 percent of all funds in public recreation projects should be used to insure and maintain their usability by handicapped people. Appended are four speeches and papers presented during the national forum which focus on topics such as financing recreation services for the ill and handicapped, and efforts of the National Park Service to meet the needs of handicapped persons.

228. Preventing mental retardation--more can be done; report to the Congress by the Comptroller General of the U.S. Washington, DC, October 1977. 113p. ED 146752.
   Presented is a report on the current status of implementation of the Presidential goal (made in 1971) to reduce by half the incidence of mental retardation by the end of this century. Major conclusions are as follows: no major agency of the Department of Health, Education, and Welfare (HEW) has been made responsible for seeing that the goal is put into practice, coordinating efforts, clarifying agency roles and resource commitments, and measuring progress in meeting the goal; prevention of mental retardation has not been designated an objective by HEW's agencies responsible for prevention; and systems have not been established or methods developed to assess progress in achieving the goal. Chapters focus on the following topics: mental retardation and its causes, improvements needed in HEW administration of the prevention effort, expanding newborn screening for metabolic disorders, improving prenatal care to reduce prematurity and low birth weight, identifying persons in need of genetic testing and counseling, improving immunization levels for rubella and measles, increased screening to detect lead poisoning, expanding testing and immunization to prevent Rh disease, and improving early childhood experiences. Conclusions, recommendations, and HEW comments follow the discussion in each chapter. Appended are such items as a list of the principal HEW officials responsible for activities discussed in the report.

229. Rehabilitation services program. Chicago, Goodwill Rehabilitation Center, no date. 27p. ED 124779.

The document describes the services offered by the Chicago Goodwill Rehabilitation Center. A brief, general description of the goals and activities is provided for each of the following services: personal and vocational evaluation of clients, community and job placement, vocational orientation and exploration, counseling and psychotherapy, social services, work adjustment and work readiness training, remedial and vocational education, manual communication, job-seeking skills, and residential and referral services. Specific areas are listed and brief course content summaries are provided for job skills training in the vocational education program.

230. Your Down's syndrome child; you can help him develop from infancy to adulthood, by David Pitt. 1974. 35p. ED 091891.

Intended for parents of children with Down's Syndrome, the booklet describes causes and probable developmental patterns of the Downs child. It is stressed that parents need professional counseling to aid in adjustment to and rearing of a Downs infant. Discussed are incidence (1 in 700 births), and the accident of cell development which leads to the condition. Typical behavior and developmental characteristics as well as child rearing suggestions are given for the following age levels: infancy, 2-4 years, 4-8 years, 8-12 years, and over 12 years. In opposing the tendency to institutionalize Down's children early in life, the author notes a survey which showed that three fourths of the families who keep the child at home make a good adjustment. Guidelines for selecting an institution and reasons for later placement (such as behavior problems) are provided as is the suggestion that residential hostels are more suitable than large institutions for adult retardates. Also provided is a listing of 18 suggestions for further reading.

6.
CIVIL RIGHTS,
SCHOOL INTEGRATION,
CONSUMER PROTECTION

231.   The Supreme Court on privacy and the press, by William E.
           Lee.   Paper presented at the annual meeting of the
           Association for Education in Journalism, August 1977.
           50p.   ED 147863.
           This paper examines several United States Supreme
Court decisions to evaluate the Court's stance on an individual's
right to privacy when that right conflicts with the press right to
freedom of expression.   Particular attention is paid to the Court's
"Rosenbloom" and "Gertz" decisions.   The paper concludes that the
Supreme Court is trying to accommodate both individual and press
rights as equivalent yet distinct liberties, and that the Court interprets the law of privacy and the law of defamation as being distinct
from one another.

232.   Index; FOI reports, by Jeanni Atkins.   Columbia, MO, Free-
           dom of Information Center, August 1975.   13p.   ED
           139029.
           This cumulative index provides a listing, by topic, of
the following Freedom of Information Center reports: reports 1
through 340, summary papers S1 through S38, and opinion papers
001 through 0017.   Subject titles include, among many others,
"Academic Freedom," "Book Censorship," "Consumer Protection,"
"Gag Orders," "-Press Councils," "TV News," and "Underground
Press."

233.   The Civil rights of students, by Larry W. Hillman.   Knox-
           ville, Educational Opportunities Planning Center, Uni-
           versity of Tennessee, 1972.   57p.   ED 110552.
           This document on the Civil Rights of Students, pre-
pared by the Educational Opportunities Planning Center, provides
a synthesis of presentations made by the author and of the three
discussion and answer sessions that followed at the three meetings
of the School Law Conferences.   Opening remarks emphasize the
need for educators to respond to demonstrations of student dissent
which stress the rights of individuals both inside and outside of
school.   Groups that advocate for students rights, among them the

American Civil Liberties Union, are cited in relation to their position on key issues in this area. Noting that most violations of student rights have concerned due process, minimum standards that satisfy requirements in this area are listed. The development of handbooks describing what students can do and what administrators should do, the formation of parent ombudsmen as go-between administration and students, and a student board of inquiry are some of the innovations undertaken by the Center for the Study of Student Citizenship, Rights, and Responsibilities, in Dayton, Ohio, which is under a federal OEO Grant to develop a model for students rights advocacy. These, along with a presentation of some cases handled by this center during its first year of operation, are discussed. Questions addressed covered specific areas such as an athletic coach's control over student hair length, in-school suspension, confidentiality of school records, right to counsel, and broader topics. Among the broader topics were rights vs. privileges, student responsibility for his education, and what constitutes an education.

234. Access to medical records, by Nancy Cooper. Columbia, MO, Freedom of Information Center, August 1978. 10p. ED 161094.
    Although confidentiality with regard to medical records is supposedly protected by the American Medical Association's principles of Ethics and the physician-patient privilege, there are a number of laws that require a physician to release patient information to public authorities without the patient's consent. These exceptions include birth and death certificates, reports of wounds caused by firearms or weapons, suspected child abuse, infectious diseases, and medical information that affects performance or status in the military. In addition, medical record releases are required for insurance companies and employment. Health care reviewers, state and federal computerized "human services" data banks, and groups of professionals organized to monitor government-funded health care pose further risks to confidentiality in that they often disseminate health information to credit bureaus, employers, and educational institutions. Ironically, individuals often have difficulty in obtaining their own personal health records. In states with access statutes, individuals must sue to obtain medical records, and in states without access statutes, hospitals can legally deny an individual access.

235. In Search of justice. Chicago, American Bar Association. 43p. ED 155070.
    This monograph briefly examines justice in the United States as it has evolved historically in four areas: (1) the right to vote: (2) the right to freedom of expression and freedom of the press; (3) the rights of persons accused of crimes; and (4) the right to equal protection under the law. Each area is analyzed. Historical background information and constitutional case studies and their effect are contained in each chapter. The intention of the booklet is not to provide a comprehensive history; rather the booklet offers insights regarding several fundamental principles of a democratic society.

236. Governmental surveillance of three progressive educators, by
Murry R. Nelson and H. Wells Singleton. Paper presented at the annual meeting of the American Educational
Research Association, March 1978. 25p. ED 156560.
Governmental interference with academic freedom is
illustrated by F.B.I. surveillance of and unauthorized distribution
of information about progressive educators John Dewey, George
Counts, and Harold Rugg. These three educators attracted the attention of governmental agencies and special interest groups during
the 1930s and 1940s because they advocated educational reform and
participated in liberal movements such as the ACLU and the NAACP.
All three were suspected of communist leanings because they de-
parted from traditional educational approaches and urged students
and community members to become actively involved in social reconstruction. In their educational writings and in their courses at
Columbia University and the University of Chicago, these educators
introduced students to controversial issues such as the depression,
labor-management relations, the distribution of wealth, and lifestyles
in socialist countries. By 1941, the F.B.I. had gathered nearly
400 pages of information on the three progressive educators in the
form of reports by private and governmental agencies, letters, articles, and clippings. The F.B.I. method of accumulating data was
to collect any type of readily available information about the men,
put the information in a file, and add to the file in a random manner from time to time. This investigative process, apparently without clear objective, made use of much false, partially true, and un-
substantiated information. The conclusion is that the F.B.I. in-
vestigations into the activities and writings of Dewey, Rugg, and
Counts were capricious, unmethodical, unconfidential, and deleterious
to freedom of speech.

237. Desegregation; what's best for all of our children, by Ann
Siqueland. Seattle, WA, Church Council, 1978. 121p.
ED 152884.
Members of the Church Council of Greater Seattle decided that the school desegregation plan adopted by that city in 1977
is workable and will help to end racial inequalities in education.
This curriculum guide on desegregation issues is intended for use
in a 2-9 week series of adult education classes in area churches.
It is divided into nine resource sections. Topics addressed include:
desegregation history, desegregation law, segregation remedies,
community opinion, and pluralism. Remaining sections consist of
a slide show, a theological discussion on school desegregation, an
overview of desegregation activities being planned for Seattle and
material concerning community action. Preceding each of these
sections is a lesson plan for a class session. This plan focuses
on the resource material which follows.

238. Integrating schools in the nation's largest cities; what has been
accomplished and what is yet to be done, by Reynolds
Farley and Clarence Wurdock. Ann Arbor, Center for
Population Studies, University of Michigan, January 1977.
39p. ED 146278.

This paper evaluates the effectiveness of governmental actions from 1967 to 1974 to integrate public schools in the nation's cities. Data used were obtained from the Office of Civil Rights and were drawn from school districts in the 100 largest metropolitan areas. The results of this evaluation indicate there are substantial indications of progress in both the North and the South. Federal courts overturned most of the delaying tactics which southern cities were using to avoid integration. In most southern cities, black and white children now attend the same schools and the level of segregation is low. Beginning in the early 1970's, increasing pressure was applied to northern cities. The courts ruled that school board policies were partly responsible for the high levels of segregation still obtaining in many of the northern metropolitan areas. This paper concludes that although progress has been made in reducing segregation, there is still much to be accomplished. A few southern and many northern cities have schools which are as segregated today as they were a decade ago. The litigation process and HEW compliance proceedings are time consuming, and a reluctant school board can still delay integration. A more serious impediment, however, to the integration of big city schools is the city-suburban disparity in racial composition.

239. Impact of desegregation; a historical and legal analysis, by J. John Harris, III. Paper presented at the annual meeting of the American Educational Research Association, March 1978. 40p. ED 154088.

Court cases dating from the 1850s and pertaining to racial integration are reviewed in this paper. The impact that judicial decisions and laws have had on civil rights and on racial integration of the schools is discussed. Cases considered include suits from various states concerning voting rights, segregation of public transportation, segregated schools, and segregated housing. Black access to higher education in the first half of this century is also considered. Specific legal mandates for school desegregation are reviewed from the time of the "Brown" decision in 1954. Reaction to court orders to integrate schools in both Northern and Southern states is described. The contemporary situation is assessed, and some predictions about the future of school desegregation are offered.

240. Busing; implications for social change in urban and rural areas, by Ronald D. Henderson. Paper presented at the annual meeting of the American Educational Research Association, April 1976. 32p. ED 124616.

Busing is examined as a tool of social change in the alteration of school structure from racial segregation to racial integration. A commentary is provided on the nexus between social change in education and other aspects of society and the utilization of busing as a tool of social change. Information is also presented on schools in urban and rural areas status in regard to desegregation and integration. An important perspective of this delineation is whether busing will facilitate social change. To highlight conceptualization of social change as it related to desegregation, integration and busing time frame charts are presented. The rationale postulated is that commitment is needed from other sectors of society in order to facilitate change. Open housing and adoption of schools to desegregate student bodies is suggested as possible strategies along with busing to facilitate social change in education and ultimately the total society. Without meaningful dedication to the goal of integration from other sectors of society, busing alone may be a waste of effort, time and money. Most importantly, the physical and psychological well-being of students may be jeopardized.

241. School desegregation; the courts and suburban migration, by Frederick B. Routh and Everett A. Waldo. Washington, DC, Commission on Civil Rights, December 1975. 213p. ED 142669.

The United States Commission on Civil Rights sponsored a consultation in 1975 to review the relationship between desegregation, court orders, and suburbanization, as well as to assess what further role the Commission might play in discharging its responsibility to advance the constitutional rights of all children to a desegregated education. This book contains four papers which were presented and discussed at the consultation. The first paper addresses the suburbanization of America. It traces the movement of population from cities to suburbs and places this movement in an historical perspective. The second paper focuses on the court, congress and school desegregation. It examines the role of the Federal courts as instruments of social change and the constitutional issues involved in any congressional attempt to limit their power to order remedies, including busing. The third paper written by James Coleman, focuses on school desegregation and the loss of whites from large central city school districts. This paper examines trends in school desegregation between 1968 and 1973. Public school desegregation and white flight is also the topic of the last paper. Its analysis of school desegregation and white flight goes into great detail about the differences of various versions of James Coleman's analysis of desegregation and white flight, Coleman's methodology, and assumptions.

242. Community case studies on school desegregation, by Thomas F. Pettigrew and Rae C. Kipp. Sponsored by the National Institute of Education. 1977. 114p. ED 149001.

Though it has been a much publicized national process for a full generation, racial desegregation of the public schools has not received sustained and rigorous evaluation. This report is an attempt to assess the quality and characteristics of community oriented case studies on school desegregation. The search strategy for accessibility and criteria set for appropriateness of case studies are described. Critical reviews are presented of eleven studies. Based on the bibliographical search and case study reviews, it is concluded that although a number of community studies on public school desegregation exist, they consist predominantly of descriptive reports of widely varying quality. The few research oriented studies found are strongest in the comparative criteria concerned with an adequate political perspective, a focus upon integration, and attention to the multilevel nature of the desegregation process. They are weakest in such criteria as an adequate quasi-experimental design and attention to differential effects across different aggregate units. Focusing on these conclusions, suggestions are offered for future and higher quality community school desegregation studies. An extensive bibliography, a list of case studies in progress, and a list of forty communities which have experienced school desegregation are appended to this report.

243.   A Handbook for integrated schooling, by Garlie A. Forehand and Marjorie Ragosta. Princeton, NJ, Educational Testing Service, July 1976. 118p. ED 131154.

Based on data collected by way of tests, questionnaires, and interviews in nearly 200 schools, representing a wide range of geography, population, economic conditions, and social history, this handbook is concerned with how schools can be integrated more effectively. Chapter 1 focuses on the school and the objectives of integrated education. Chapter 2 addresses the principles of effective integrated schooling, and focuses on the characteristics of effective integrated schools, and on principles such as modeling, reinforcement, and facilitation. Chapter 3 focuses on integrated education in the elementary schools encompassing such topics as curriculum, achievement and grouping, multiethnic teaching, home and school relations, rules and disciplines, staffing, and the principal's leadership. The final chapter focuses on integrated education in the high schools, covering aspects such as the school as a social organization, student focused human relations activities, the faculty and staff in human relations activities, and various factors in teaching in integrated high schools such as curriculum teaching methods, internal integration, and formal and informal integration.

244.   Fulfilling the letter and spirit of the law; desegregation of the nation's public schools; a report, edited by Frank Knorr. Washington, DC, Commission on Civil Rights, August 1976. 328p. ED 128518.

This report contains the Civil Rights Commission's evaluation of school desegregation in a variety of school districts throughout the United States and is based on data obtained from commission hearings, State Advisory Committee to the Commission meetings, mail surveys to 1,291 school districts, and 900 indepth interviews in 29 school districts. Recent commission initiatives which resulted in data gathering included hearings and meetings in Boston, Denver, Tampa, Louisville, Berkeley, Minneapolis, Stamford, and Corpus Christi. The main body of the report focuses on and discusses such topics in relation to school desegregation as: the role of leadership, preparation of the community, restructuring of school districts, desegragation and educational quality, minority staff concerns, classroom integration, extracurricular activities, student attitudes, and discipline in desegregated schools. At the end of the evaluation, the report asserts that the one conclusion that stands out above all others is that desegregation does work. The commission recommends that the following be kept in mind if the "substantial progress being made in school desegregation is to be built upon'': (1) leaders must accept that desegregation is a constitutional imperative; (2) the Federal government must strengthen and expand programs designed to facilitate desegregation; (3) there must be vigorous enforcement of laws contributing to the development of desegregated communities; and (4) a major investment of time and resources must be made in order to deal with misconceptions relating to desegregation.

245. A Citizen's guide to school desegregation law, by Mary Von Euler and David L. Parham. Washington, DC, Educational Equity Group, National Institute of Education, DHEW, July 1978. 57p. ED 160689.

These summaries of recent major court decisions related to school desegregation were prepared in an effort to be of assistance to nonlawyers. As an introduction, the workings of the United States judicial system are outlined, and an overview of school desegregation law since 1954 is provided. Recent decisions by the U. S. Supreme Court that set standards for desegregation cases in all Federal courts are explained. Noteworthy Federal cases in which the U. S. Supreme Court did not make significant rulings during the 1976-77 term are summarized. Some important cases that have arisen recently in the California State court system are discussed. Also provided are guidelines for locating texts of court decisions on desegregation.

246. Community attitudes toward a desegregated school system; a study of Charlotte, North Carolina, by Howard Maniloff. Paper presented at the American Educational Research Association annual meeting, March 1978. 21p. ED 154080.

Charlotte-Mecklenburg, North Carolina, is a metropolitan school district which, in 1969, was ordered by a Federal judge to desegregate its more than 100 schools. Desegregation began in 1970 and continues today. Having found evidence that attitudes among whites toward both busing and desegregation had changed during these years, the author set out to examine when and why these changes took place. Fifty-six persons were interviewed. The interviewees believed: (1) that community attitudes had changed; (2) that having lost their case in the Supreme Court convinced many whites that there was no longer any point in fighting desegregation; (3) that an effort three years into desegregation to involve the community in designing a pupil assignment plan strengthened the acceptability of busing and desegregation; (4) that the busing of children from upper middle income and upper income white families made busing more acceptable to other whites; and (5) that many whites changed their attitudes when they perceived that their children were not being hurt educationally or physically by going to school with blacks.

247. Desegregation; futuristic considerations, by David G. Carter. Paper presented at the annual meeting of the American Educational Research Association, March 1978. 18p. ED 152952.

One premise of the Brown v. Board of Education Supreme Court decision was that racial injustice could be eliminated through court ordered desegregation. Twenty-three years after Brown, segregation continues to be one of the most complex issues confronting the country. The failure to distinguish between means (busing school children) and ends (school desegregation) has caused Americans to ignore the goal to which they are legally committed: the education of all their children. Although progress has been made since 1954, a number of more recent court cases illustrate the problems and complexities of school integration. Some decisions, such as Green v. County School Board (1968) and Swann v. Charlotte-Mecklenburg Board of Education (1970), rather than facilitating de-segregation, actually increased litigation by raising more questions than they solved. The confusion and ambiguities arising from past court decisions indicate that segregation will continue to be one of the nation's more pressing problems in the years to come.

248. Central city white flight; racial and nonracial causes, by William H. Frey. Madison, Institute for Research on Poverty, University of Wisconsin, 1977. 53p. ED 146248.

The cumulative adverse impact of residential white flight from large central cities on the residual population has led policy makers to be wary of instituting programs which will further exacerbate the process. Recent policy debates have evolved over the question of whether white city-to-suburb movement is affected more significantly by racially-motivated causes on the one hand, or by the general economic and ecological conditions in the city on the other. The present study assesses a number of previously suggested racial and nonracial factors for 1965 as "pushes" and "pulls" to 70 white city-to-suburb movement streams in 39 standard metropolitan areas. Utilizing a two-stage model of mobility, this analysis suggests that most factors, both racial and nonracial, affect white flight less through the decision to move, than through the choice of destination. Fiscal and ecological features of the metropolitan area are demonstrated to be just as important as racial factors in the explanation. Finally, a path model is constructed which shows that the greater level of flight exhibited in Southern cities is only marginally explained by racial causes.

249. A Guide to consumer action, by Helen E. Nelson. Milwaukee, Center for Consumer Affairs, University of Wisconsin, 1977. 64p. ED 155360.

Designed for individuals and groups seeking to organize consumer activities, this guide focuses on how to build consumer competence, how to organize others, where to get training, and how to influence policy makers. Chapter I discusses how to educate oneself for consumerism by using product-rating periodicals, libraries, public consumer agencies, television, and radio. Twelve steps are listed for filing a complaint, and various types of solving more serious consumer problems are described (government agencies, business or trade associations, and consumer groups). A brief glossary of dispute settlement language is also presented. Chapter II presents studies of the successful organization of seven

consumer groups and discusses incorporation, funding sources
(grants), and affiliation with other groups. Further sources of information (publications and groups) are suggested. The advice of
eight consumer leaders on group organization and operation conclude
the chapter. Chapter III describes two additional activities for consumer groups: consumer advocacy training programs through universities, consumer groups, cooperatives, and industry; and participation as consumer representatives in government and industry policy
making forums. Notes and availability information on various supplementary publications are interspersed throughout.

250. Consumer education reference manual. Knoxville, State
      Agency for Title I, University of Tennessee, July 1976.
      276p. ED 130056.
         This manual contains information for consumer educa-
tion, which is defined as the process of imparting to an individual
the skills, concepts, knowledges, and insights required to help each
person evolve his or her own values, evaluate alternative choices
in the marketplace, manage personal resources effectively, and obtain the best buys for his or her expenditures. Guidelines for consumers are presented in 20 chapters: (1) Appliances, (2) Automobiles (including automobile insurance), (3) Clothing, (4) Credit, (5)
Education, (6) Funerals, (7) Home Furnishings, (8) Housing, (9) Insurance, (10) Legal, (11) Medical, (12) Medicaid, (13), Medicare,
(14), Money Management, (15) Schemes, (16) Selecting and Buying
Food, (17) Shopping, (18) Social Security, (19) Wages (including unemployment compensation), (20) Welfare (including the food stamp
program). Appendixes list state and local resource information,
federal sources of consumer information and complaints, other agencies for information and complaints, and local consumer agencies
for information, complaints, and legal services. Addresses in each
appendix are listed under topical headings (e.g. family counseling,
handicapped, nursing homes), and a topical index is provided for the
manual as a whole.

251. Consumer handbook to credit protection laws. Washington,
      DC, Board of Governors of the Federal Reserve System,
      1978. 26p. ED 171628.
         The five sections of this consumer handbook are The
Cost of Credit, Applying for Credit, Credit Histories and Records,
Correcting Credit Mistakes, and Complaining about Credit. Each
section discusses relevant legislation: Truth in Lending, the Equal
Credit Opportunity Act, and the Fair Credit Reporting Act. Topics
discussed in section 1 include methods for comparing finance costs,
and explanations of open end credit, open end leases, balloon payments, advertising costs, and costs of settlement on a house. Section II discusses discrimination pertaining to sex, age, and marital
status. Borrower characteristics and circumstances under which an
agency may not legally deny credit are listed. Section III covers
establi shing credit histories for married, divorced, or widowed
women, and methods for maintaining credit histories. Section four
explains action to take concerning defective goods and services,
prompt credits and refunds, second mortgage cancellation, lost or

stolen credit cards, unsolicited credit cards, and discounts for cash payments. Section five discusses procedures for complaining to federal agencies. A glossary and addresses of federal enforcement agencies and federal reserve banks are included.

252. A Consumer's guide to the Federal Trade Commission, by Elizabeth Williams. Washington, DC, Consumer Federation of America, 1977. 48p. ED 149139.

This publication presents consumer information designed to encourage and facilitate active citizen involvement in Federal Trade Commission (FTC) proceedings. Nine chapters are included, covering (1) the FTC and its impact on consumers (discusses the authority of FTC, the Bureau of Competition, the Bureau of Consumer Protection, and lists FTC regional offices); (2) categories of FTC proceedings; (3) opportunities for public participation in FTC proceedings; (4) currently active proceedings in the Bureau of Consumer Protection; (5) how groups have participated in FTC rulemaking; (6) compensation for costs of participating in FTC rulemaking; (7) major consumer protection statutes administered by the FTC; (8) information and materials available from the FTC; and (9) other methods of obtaining FTC records and information. A fifteen-page appendix includes an FTC organization chart, active FTC proceedings, how to apply for reimbursement of FTC rulemaking participation, and a list of groups which have received compensation awards for participating in FTC rulemaking proceedings.

7.
EDUCATION

253. General education and the plight of modern man, by Earl J.
    McGrath. Indianapolis, Lilly Endowment, Inc., 1976.
    192p. ED 139340.
    There is in the higher education profession a strong and
growing segment who believe that although our colleges may be successful in producing well-informed and skilled specialists they do not
turn out citizens broadly informed about the complex world in which
they live. Consequently, as a people we are unable to cope with
our personal and civic problems. These intellectual leaders hold the
firm conviction that success in the effort to equip students mentally
and morally to lead more effective lives will be contingent upon basic reforms in the structure and the substance of our system of higher education. Once the members of the society of learning focus
their attention on the present disordered state of affairs in our culture and the unique resources institutions of higher education have
for restoring "a vision of the world in which reverence and order
will prevent the riot into which modern society appears to be moving," they will undertake the essential reforms in policy and practice.

254. How to plan a college program for older people, by John
    Scanlon. New York, Academy for Educational Develop-
    ment, Inc., 1978. 119p. ED 158668.
    Recommendations are offered in this manual for planning,
organizing, and financing academic programs for older people, based
on the experience of institutions already conducting programs for
older students, on current thinking in gerontology, and on knowledge
and experience of staff and consultants of the Academy for Educational Development. Three major questions are addressed: (1) Why
should a college or university be interested in establishing special
programs for older people? (2) What kinds of courses are older
people interested in taking, and what kinds of supplemental services
do they need? (3) What are the steps that must be taken in planning, operating, and financing such a program? Six program models
are described: The Institute for Retired Professionals at the New
School for Social Research; Fordham University's College at Sixty;
The College of Older Americans at Mercyhurst; Project Elderly at

Miami-Dade Community College; Opportunities for Older Adults at
Hawkeye Institute of Technology; and Elderhostel at several New
England institutions. Suggestions for financing the programs are
discussed, and working tools are described, such as marketing instruments, financial reports, and newsletters. Appended are lists
of colleges offering programs, courses being offered, and state agencies on aging.

255. Academic credit for prior off-campus learning, by David A.
        Trivett. Washington, DC, American Association for
        Higher Education, 1975. 80p. ED 105796.
        The educational and social rationale for granting aca-
demic credit for off-campus learning grows out of the notion that
educational systems now have the capability to change from selective
to adaptive systems. If this change is to occur in ways to permit
access, not just in terms of admission but in terms of credentials,
then concomitant changes in institutional practices must take place.
The granting of academic credit for learning acquired off-campus
is viewed by some as a socially just method to bestow credentials
earned regardless of source and is a logical extension of the access
goal. The focus of this paper is the granting of credit for prior
off-campus learning, a form of credit for prior off-campus learning,
a form of credit awarded for experiential learning that is in contrast to such sponsored programs as cooperative learning and field
experience. Several procedures are in use to grant credit for prior
off-campus learning. A traditional method to grant credit for off-
campus learning is an examination for college-level credit. The
College Level Examination Program (CLEP) is the best known method.
Academic credit is also being granted for off-campus learning from
life and work experience. Special degree programs, such as the
external degree, make great use of the various forms of academic
credit for off-campus learning. The emphasis of this report is on
learner-centered methods of evaluation that permit institutions to
become responsive to the growing market of new students who seek
credentials from higher education institutions.

256. The One-teacher school; its midcentury status, by Walter
        Gaumnitz and David T. Blose. Washington, DC, Office
        of Education, DHEW, 1950. 35p. ED 140992.
        Presenting detailed statistics illustrating trends and the
numerical status of one-teacher schools, this U.S. Office of Education bulletin spans a 30-year period describing, by states, the overall decreases in the number of 1-teacher schools, their proportional
relationship to all public schools and teachers, and the number of
students attending them. Specifically, this report includes the following tabular data: public school consolidation trends revealed by
statistics of 1-teacher schools and pupil transportation for the U.S.
as a whole, 1918-48; number of 1-teacher schools by years specified
and by states, 1918-48; percentage of 1-teacher schools in 1917-18
remaining, by years specified and by states; percentage ratios of
1-teacher schools to all public schools by years indicated and by
states, 1918-48; percentage ratios of teachers in 1-teacher schools
to teachers in all public schools by years indicated and by states,

1918-48; number and percentage of all public school pupils attending 1-teacher, 2-teacher, and 3-teacher schools in certain states, 1947-48. The data presented here indicate that: of the remaining 75,000 1-teacher schools, most are small in building, enrollment, and community served; while generally the 1-teacher school is vanishing, in nearly all the northcentral prairie region it accounts for nearly 75% of that region's public schools, 25% of its teachers, and 20% of its students.

257. Boarding schools. Boston, MA, Boarding Schools, 1976.
        56p. ED 133841.
        This booklet has been prepared to provide students, parents, and counselors with information about America's boarding schools and to help them with the application process. It includes brief descriptions of 139 boarding schools--junior schools, boys' schools, girls' schools, military academies, and coeducational schools. It is offered solely as an introduction.

258. The Truman Administration and federal aid to education, by
        Maurice McCann. Paper presented at the annual meet-
        ing of the American Educational Research Association,
        April 1977. 42p. ED 136380.
        During the Truman administration, the concept of federal aid to education became clearly defined and gained considerable political support. President Truman supported general aid for education as a policy consistent with the administration's overall objectives in domestic programs, but he avoided leadership because of the controversies surrounding it. Those controversies centered around issues such as federal aid to nonpublic schools and the form that such aid should take (Funds for school construction? Equalization funds for impacted areas? Across-the-board grants?). Leadership for the federal aid movement therefore shifted to Congress, and specifically to Senator Robert A. Taft of Ohio. Although the movement for general aid to education failed to obtain legislative sanction, it did leave behind a widespread conviction that a need existed for substantial federal aid to education in some form and stimulated new approaches to this objective.

259. A History of vocational education, by Allan M. Hoffman and
        Diane B. Hoffman. 1976. 43p. ED 132283.
        The historical evolution of vocational education is discussed in an attempt to show that obvious comparisons can be drawn between the industrial education movement and debate of American educational history and the concepts of career education today. The document covers the period from the mid-1800's to the present. Major factors influencing the development of vocational education are highlighted: the establishment of trade schools in the 1800's, Industrial Revolution, the industrial education movement, the American Civil War, federal legislation (e.g. Morrill Land Grant Act), foreign educational influence, the manual education movement, the formation of industrial arts associations, and various industrial shifts and societal changes. A bibliography is appended.

260. A Search for a philosophy of vocational education, by Charles
J. Law, Jr. Paper presented at the annual meeting of
State Directors of Vocational Education, May 1975.   71p.
ED 126368.
In the light of the manifest need for a clear, concise,
definable philosophical base the author presents an historical review of vocational education in the United States, and questions the
validity of its early beliefs and tenets in terms of the needs of today's society.   Five chapters discuss the following topics: (1) the
pressure for reevaluation of the philosophy of vocational education
programs and of program accountability in relation to Federal funding: (2) the historical search for a philosophical base, touching on:
the Land-Grant College movement of Jonathan Baldwin Turner, the
manual training philosophy of Calvin M. Woodward, the trade school
movement, the 1963 Vocational Education Act, and the philosophies
and opinions of John Dewey, Charles W. Eliot, Charles A. Prosser,
Melvin L. Barlow, and other educators; (3) tentative philosophy based
on five factors of vocational education considered in terms of a longitudinal historical perspective of vocational education as a function of
formal education; (4) the salability of theoretical versus concrete
skills; and (5) Leon M. Lessinger's theories regarding curriculum
development.   A summary presents five conclusions.   Lessinger's
paper, "Educational Stability in An Unstable Technical Society," is
appended.

261. Vocational education in the 1980's, by Lawrence F. Davenport.
Papers presented at the annual meeting of the American
Association of Community and Junior Colleges, March
1976.   41p.   ED 124249.
This document compiles three papers dealing with the
past, present, and future states of vocational education.   Lawrence
F. Davenport concentrates on the impact of vocational education on
urban minorities and the disadvantaged.   After identifying potential
problems which must be encountered if vocational education programs
are to be reformed (the need for specially trained, sensitive instructors; the blue collar stigma of vocational education; the reluctance
of employers and trade unions to accept trained minorities),   Davenport emphasizes the need for special educational theories to handle
special educational problems.   Reginald Petty discusses some of
the major areas of debate taking place in Congress, and within the
education and manpower communities, regarding manpower training
needs in general, and vocational education in particular.   Petty provides a brief history of vocational education, gives statistics describing the present state of the art, and identifies problem areas which
will dictate the shape of the field in the future.   Roy G. Phillips
describes a career education model for Seattle Central Community
College for the period of the 1980's and beyond.   The model accounts
for the diverse educational needs of the multiethnic population that
the College is designed to serve.

262. The Education of adults; a world perspective, by John Lowe.
Toronto, Ontario Institute for Studies in Education, 1975.

221p. ED 117463.

A summary of the third International Conference on
Adult Education (Tokyo) by UNESCO, the book examines adult education trends of the last decade, functions of adult education as related to lifelong education, and formulation of adult education policies
in the context of national education plans. During the 12-year period between conferences, organized adult education has made notable
advances throughout the world. However, weaknesses remain in
governmental reluctance to treat adult education as an integral part
of educational systems, the low level of financial support, and the
lack of participation in adult education programs by those most needing education. Chapter I reflects "Changing Ideas and Functions"
while Chapters 2 and 3, "Attitudes, Needs, Motivation, and Learning Ability" and "Unmet Needs and Target Groups", examine the
nature of the demand for adult education. Chapter 4 presents "Changing Structures" on the international scene, and Chapter 5 examines
"Programs and Content." The following five chapters deal with
"Methods and Materials"; "The Administrative, Organizing, and
Teaching Force"; "Administrative Policies"; "The Problem of Financing"; and "Research and Development". Two concluding chapters,
"The International Dimension" and "Towards a Learning Society",
discuss the developed nations/developing nations relationship and
future implications.

263.   The Carnegie Corporation of New York and American Educa-
       tional policy 1945-1970, by David E. Weischadle. Paper
       presented at the annual meeting of the History of Educa-
       tion Society, October 1977. 58p. ED 161329.
       Foundation involvement in policy development for public
education raises basic questions concerning the control of a prime
societal function. During the Cold War era (1945-1970) the Carnegie
Corporation of New York funded projects according to its philosophical
interests, using its financial and organizational prominence and cooperative strategies to capture a national policy-making role. The
power or influence levied by the Corporation rested with its financial
wealth, and the ability of its founder to place it in a trust fund with
special privileges, such as tax exemption. The managerial class
that has developed around these special trust funds holds no special
talent, ability, education, or competence that is not found elsewhere.
They do, however, have a unique quality of influence deriving from
access to the Carnegie wealth. The Corporation was in no sense
a benevolent, impartial, independent broker of innovation and experimentation. Indeed, Carnegie had a cause and sought to establish
that cause as national policy for the schools. Without public debate
or national referendum the Corporation and its president over a 25-
year period sought to achieve dominance in policy-making. The issue now faces American education: Should any group of individuals
with special privileges and resources be able to influence education
as Carnegie did in the postwar era?

264.   A Digest of Supreme Court decisions affecting education, by
       Perry A. Zirkel. Bloomington, IN, Phi Delta Kappa,
       1978. 148p. ED 165275.

This digest is a reference tool documenting 144 of the most important Supreme Court cases affecting education from 1859 to 1977, with emphasis on the decisions made during the past 25 years. Each case is written up in a three-part format that provides the facts and background of the case. The cases are organized into five sections: school district finance and organization; church-state relationships; student rights and responsibilities; employee rights and responsibilities; and race, language, and sex discrimination. Most cases listed affect students and staff in kindergarten through grade 12, but a few cases in higher education and juvenile law are listed. A glossary of legal terms is included.

265. Three early champions of education; Benjamin Franklin, Benjamin Rush, and Noah Webster, by Abraham Blinderman. Bloomington, IN, Phi Delta Kappa, 1976. 36p. ED 120098.

Franklin as a stateman, Rush as a physician, and Webster as a linguist and political commentator believed in a "general diffusion of knowledge" and wrote liberally on education. They sincerely believed in education as a civilizing agent, so all three helped found schools and colleges. Franklin's interests were educational philosophy; starting an academy school (vocational-technological); language; and female, black, and adult education. Rush was concerned with educational and political aims, elementary instruction, discipline, education of females and blacks, medical education, and higher education. Webster influenced educational aims, religious and moral education, female education, teaching, and the Americanization of English. Much of what they fought for is in effect today.

266. Boardsmanship; a guide for the school board member, by Vivian N. Doering. Sacramento, California School Boards Association, 1975. 133p. ED 113810.

To become a capable and successful board member, an individual must be willing to devote many hours to serving as a school trustee-attending board meetings, school functions, conferences, and workshops, and thoroughly studying issues and problems demanding decisions. This manual gives a comprehensive account of these areas of board responsibility and the specific "how to's" of procedure. This issue, which incorporates the significant points of the previous editions, has been aimed at updating information of importance to board members as well as at clarifying the role of today's board member. It is hoped that this manual will give the new board member a mini-course in California public school boardmanship and will refresh and update the knowledge of board members who have already served for a period of time.

267. The National Institute of Education; a brief historical overview, by S. M. Pemberton. Washington, DC, National Institute of Education, DHEW, 1973. 37p. ED 119362.

The change in the role and responsibility of the federal government in education and educational research is traced from the creation of the Office of Education (OE) in 1867 to the National Institute of Education (NIE) in 1972. Developments discussed include the task forces of the 1960's and their recommendations, the national program of educational laboratories, regional research and development centers, and various branches of OE and their functions. The conception of NIE is followed through its evolution, objectives, budget, organizational structure, legislative enactment, and first year of operation. NIE activities summarized are (1) the development of new initiatives, including a field-initiated studies program; (2) the development of organizational structures and the hiring of qualified staff; (3) research and exploratory studies, including the continuation of 16 Educational Resources Information Centers (ERIC); and (4) international efforts.

268. The Role of parents as teachers. Philadelphia, Recruitment Leadership and Training Institute, June 1975. 100p. ED 121482.

This illustrated booklet, designed for parents of preschool children, suggests informal learning activities which have the potential to enhance the social, emotional, cognitive, motor, and language development of preschool children. Three categories of games and activities are presented: (1) language games, (2) mathematical concept games, and (3) creative activities. In each category, from 7 to 12 play experiences are suggested and explained in detail. A chart presenting information on preschool social, emotional, cognitive, and motor development is provided, along with hints for parents on interacting with children. A final section discusses preschool preparation for elementary school.

8.
BUSINESS,
FINANCE,
MATHEMATICS

269. Historical beginnings; the Federal Reserve, by Roger T. Johnson. Boston, Federal Reserve Bank, 1978. 65p. ED
174544.
The booklet presents an historical narrative of banks
and banking events leading to the establishment of the Federal Reserve System in 1914. The document is divided into three chapters.
Chapter I discusses attempts to establish a bank before the 20th
century, describing the creation of two central banks whose chapters
were allowed to lapse, the First Bank of the United States in 1791,
and the Second Bank of the United States in 1816. It hypothesizes
that the National Banking Act of 1863 was inadequate because it failed
to provide a central banking structure and, further, that the financial
panics and economic depression which followed this act were triggered
by inelastic currency and immobile reserves. Chapter II details
financial reform in the 20th century, concentrating on the activities
of the 1908 National Monetary Commission, and the pros and cons
of the Aldrich plan of 1911. It also traces how the Pujo hearings
investigating the "money trust," and the election of Woodrow Wilson
led to the Glass-Willis proposal in 1912. Also described are the
introduction of the Federal Reserve bill into Congress in 1913, and
the ensuing political struggle, compromises, and final adoption.
Chapter III outlines the establishment of the system, including selection criteria for each of the 12 regional centers, organization of
national banks into formal membership, election of local directors,
and Wilson's appointment of and Congressional ratification of the
Federal Reserve Board. Concluding comments recount how, on
November 16, 1914, the Federal Reserve banks opened, without
permanent headquarters and with very little business.

270. Understanding the agribusiness concept, by Jasper S. Lee.
Blacksburg, Virginia Polytechnic Institute, 1976. 28p.
ED 130111.
Designed to aid in learning the main ideas of the agribusiness concept, this document answers the following questions,
treating each answer in a separate explanatory section: (1) What is
the meaning of the terms "agriculture" and "agribusiness"? (2) What

is the relationship of agriculture and agribusiness? (3) What is involved in tracing an agricultural product from origin to consumption?
(4) What were the major contributors to the development of agribusiness? (5) How did the development of agribusiness occur? and
(6) What are the essential components of agribusiness activity? Diagrams are included to supplement the text. A bibliography is appended.

271. Zero-base budgeting, by L. James Harvey. Washington, DC,
      McMannis Associates, Inc., 1978. 58p. ED 164019.
        The concept of Zero-Base Budgeting (ZBB) is discussed
in terms of its application, advantages, disadvantages, and implementation in an effective planning, management, and evaluation (PME)
system. A ZBB system requires administrators to: review all
programs and expenditures annually, set clear cut goals, and analyze all possible alternatives for developing programs. Advantages
of ZBB include: programs and expenditures are reviewed annually;
a cost-conscious staff is developed; new approaches are easier to
add; professional development is increased; and a more confident
justification of the budget is created. Disadvantages include: increased paperwork; increased staff time; difficulty in developing and
ranking decision units and packages; and little motivation for staff.
Implementation of a successful ZBB process entails developing a
plan, defining the system, designing proper forms, educating the
staff, using expert help, using the first time through as a trial,
providing resources for cost estimates, and allowing proper time
for implementation. Decision units and decision packages, which
involve programs, activities, or cost centers, are considered as
the basic elements of a ZBB system, and reasons why ZBB's fail
are noted. Appendices contain a list of decision units, sample
forms, and a bibliography.

272. How to raise money for kids (public and private), by Anne B.
      Dodge. Washington, DC, Coalition for Children and
      Youth, February 1978. 77p. ED 160204.
        This guide for social service organizations provides
basic information concerning proposal writing and grant application
procedures which could be useful to anyone beginning fund raising
efforts. It is organized in three sections. Section 1 covers preparation for proposal writing and components and format of a proposal.
Section 2 outlines a plan of action for locating and contacting foundations. A bibliography of publications related to foundation grants
and a list of Foundation Center information locations are provided.
Section 3 presents background information and identification of important terms and procedures, an analysis of the "Catalog of Federal Domestic Assistance Programs," and a discussion of strategy
for obtaining federal funds. A bibliography on federal grants is
included. The following items are appended: (1) a general bibliography, (2) a glossary of terms, (3) a catalogue of federal domestic assistance programs, (4) federal department regional office locations, and (5) office of human development services organizational
charts.

273. The Case for the charitable deduction; extending eligibility to
every taxpayer. Washington, DC, American Council on
Education, August 1978. 16p. ED 158654.
Extending the charitable deduction to all taxpayers, not
just those who itemize, would help protect the deduction from the
unintended, indirect, and adverse effects of other changes in tax
laws, such as increases in the standard deduction. Recent trends
to simplify the tax law and to induce more taxpayers to utilize the
standard deduction have significantly narrowed the incentive effect
of the charitable deduction and has seriously reduced the flow of
funds to charities. Extending the charitable deduction to all taxpayers would increase the total amount of real revenues available
to support community activities and help alleviate public problems.
Over 85 percent of the revenues "given up" would show up as a
reduction in taxes for current nonitemizers, those 77 percent of all
taxpayers who use the standard deduction and have predominantly
low and middle incomes. The theoretical tax policy arguments for
extending the charitable deduction are presented, and it is contended
that the deduction would not unduly complicate tax compliance. The
nature of the American system has from its inception encouraged
voluntary associations and institutions as one way to serve the public good, and support for charitable organizations has been a cornerstone of this pluralistic society. Background material concerning
the proposed legislation to extend the charitable deduction is appended.

274. Measuring price changes; a study of the price indexes. 4th
edition, by William H. Wallace and William E. Cullison.
Richmond, VA, Federal Reserve Bank, April 1979. 52p.
ED 171632.
This three-part monograph examines the major price
indexes used to measure the intensity of inflation. The first part
discusses the recent behavior of prices as measured by the Consumer Price Index (commodities, goods, and services), the Producer
Price Index (wholesale prices of crude materials, intermediate materials, supplies, components, and finished goods), and the Implicit
Price Deflator for the Gross National Product (GNP). The severity
of the current inflation problem and the importance of good measures
of price changes are emphasized. The second part explains the concept of a price index, reviews the criteria that a good index must
satisfy, and discusses conceptual and statistical problems of design
and construction. The final part describes characteristics and explains recent revisions of each of the indexes. The Consumer Price
Index, revised in 1978, is noted as having the most effect on daily
business decisions throughout the country. Prices are observed in
85 areas and separate indexes are computed in 28 cities. The old-
est continually published measurement, the Producer Price Index,
covers about 2800 commodities. Finally, both previously discussed
indexes are explained in terms of their influence on the Implicit Deflator Index for the GNP in which consumer expenditure of the GNP
is adjusted for price change.

275. Dictionary of marketing terms, by Richard M. Everhardt.

Columbus, Ohio Distributive Education Materials Laboratory, Ohio State University. 104p. ED 112226.

A listing of words and definitions compiled from more than 10 college and high school textbooks are presented in this dictionary of marketing terms. Over 1,200 entries of terms used in retailing, wholesaling, economics, and investments are included. This dictionary was designed to aid both instructors and students to better understand the terminology that appears in texts which are used in distributive education courses.

276. Evaluating the buy or rent housing decision, by Joseph M. Davis. College Station, Texas Real Estate Research Center, Texas A & M University, November 1976. 15p. ED 141615.

This booklet offers guidelines by which a person can make an informed decision about whether buying or renting a house is the best individual alternative. Advantages and disadvantages of both buying and renting are listed. Cost considerations are discussed and compared along with such considerations as selection of the time to buy and estimation of investment value.

277. Management by objectives, by L. James Harvey. Washington, DC, McManis Associates, Inc., 1976. 72p. ED 134271.

This document explains and clarifies the management by objectives (MBO) concept in order to give institutions in the Advanced Institutional Development Program (AIDP) help in understanding and using the concept. MBO is defined as an administrative system whereby an administrator and his subordinates identify areas of responsibility in which a person will work, set standards for performance in quantifiable terms and measure the results against these standards within a specific time frame, all within the context of the mission, goals, and objectives of the organization. Subsequent sections of this publication discuss the advantages and disadvantages of MBO; implementation of MBO in the college/university setting; alternative MBO models; reasons why MBO may fail in the educational setting; procedures for establishing institutional mission, goals, and objectives; and procedures for establishing individual objectives within the institution. Definitions, flow charts, and examples are included throughout. It is noted that MBO may take many shapes and forms that may be modified to meet the specific needs of individual institutions if the president and staff are willing to make the adjustments necessary for a management system to succeed. An extensive MBO bibliography is included.

278. Evolution of management thought in the ancient times, by C. L. Sharma. 1977. 37p. ED 145502.

This paper argues that although systematic management thought is a distinctly modern development, the writings of ancient scholars and records of ancient rulers infer that they understood the rudiments of management principles and concepts. To support this thesis, the author reviews the evidence of management practices and concepts in various ancient civilizations, including the Sumerian, Egyptian, Babylonian, Hebrew, ancient Chinese, ancient Indian, Greek, and Roman.

279. Evolution of management thought in the medieval times, by
      C. L. Sharma. 1977. 25p. ED 145539.
      The medieval times witnessed progress toward the growth
of larger and more complex organizations and the application of increasingly sophisticated management techniques. Feudalism contributed the concept of decentralization. The concepts evolved by
the Catholic Church can scarcely be improved on and are very much
pertinent to the management of modern organizations. The concepts
developed by the military and industry of the period are widely used
today, although in a more refined and elaborate form. The concept
of corporation as a separate entity has been a remarkable and extremely useful contribution of the late Roman law. Although no deliberate attempts toward theory-building are discernible during the
medieval times, the writings of the period do offer an insight into
the practice of management. Of special significance are the works
of Machiavelli. Toward the end of the period, the emergence of
Cameralism signifies an awakening to the need of training in management.

280. Common types of financial problems; brief descriptions and
      suggested solutions, by David C. Myhre. Blacksburg,
      Virginia Polytechnic Institute, 1977. 51p. ED 153149.
      This guide is one of a series of four such guides that
are directed toward those people who provide financial counseling to
consumers who have problems with overindebtedness. Recognizing
that many who serve as financial counselors have little training in
the field (for example, clergymen or social workers), the guides
are not offered as complete courses in financial counseling, but as
practical prototype manuals focusing on the most important areas
for counseling: basic techniques, rehabilitative financial planning,
and an overview of common problems with credit and debt. By
using examples of client-counselor exchanges, as well as detailed
exercises for the counselor, the guides help the counselor increase
his/her effectiveness with the client. This particular guide examines
various types of problems that people have with credit and debt, discusses underlying causes of the problems, and offers some general
suggestions for solving them.

281. Evaluating community development corporations; a summary
      report, by Harvey A. Garn. Washington, DC, Urban
      Institute, March 1976. 154p. ED 127388.
      The evaluation of three Ford Foundation supported Com-
munity Development Corporation (CDC) programs with performance
relative to output targets (milestones) that are both identifiable and
quantifiable are presented in this paper. The milestone targets,
developed in 1973 for the following year, are targets over which
the CDC would legitimately be expected to have some control. In
addition to reporting the findings on CDC performance relative to
these targets, qualitative factors which bear importantly on the
meaningful analysis and evaluation of CDCs are discussed. The
three programs evaluated are listed as follows: the Bedford Stuy-
vesant Restoration Corporation, the Woodlawn Organization, and the
Zion Non-Profit Charitable Trust. Three case studies are also

presented in order to examine the performance of the CDCs in developing major housing complexes and shopping centers. The discussion also takes into account circumstances that bear on the success or failure of these projects. An additional purpose of the case studies is to illustrate some of the opportunities and constraints facing CDCs in pursuing their various program options. The final section of the paper comments on some key aspects of the context and problems faced by CDCs, based on the observations while carrying through the project.

282. The Transformation of the urban economic base, by Thomas Stanback, Jr., and Matthew Drennan. Washington, DC, National Commission for Manpower Policy, February 1978. 86p. ED 153084.

The objective stated for this monograph is to provide some insights regarding the nature of urban economic systems and their growth processes which will be useful in formulating developmental policy. A foreword (by Eli Ginzberg) provides background on the history of and present challenge to reshape manpower policies and programs for cities afflicted by unemployment. The first of three chapters deals with the contribution of urban economic theory: the concept of an export base, the nautre of selected growth processes, the forces of decentralization, the concept of a hierarchical system of cities, and the connections between demography and urban economics. Chapter 2 interprets recent national, social, and economic trends in terms of their implications for metropolitan economic development policy. Six themes are stressed: the limited change in export specialization, the growth of local sector employment, uneven rate of growth in productivity among sectors, the emergence of transfers of a major source of metropolitan income, the economic interdependence of central city and suburb, and the widely divergent impact of national demographic trends. The final chapter examines adjustment and stablization mechanisms as well as sources of renewal in the city (cost-price adjustments; agglomeration linkages; and relative immobility of human, cultural, and fixed capital resources), and implications are suggested for five developmental strategies: getting the export base in focus, looking for linkages, avoiding demographic and economic surprises, getting a line on manpower requirements, and maximizing other income flows.

283. Metrics, the measure of your future; a parent's guide to homework. Raleigh, North Carolina State Department of Public Instruction, February 1976. 23p. ED 160386.

The purpose of this booklet is to make it easier for the parent to help his/her child learn the metric system. Contents include: (1) answers to most asked questions of parents: (2) introduction to metric units; (3) converting from one unit to another within the metric system; (4) a reference table; and (5) a chart entitled "All You Will Need to Know About Metric (For Your Everyday Life)."

284. A User's guide for the fabulous abacus, by Alan R. Hausrath. Olympia, WA, Superintendent of Public Instruction, 1978. 20p. ED 156460.

A guide for using an abacus is accompanied by a heavy-duty paper abacus. The guide includes instruction in how to represent numbers on an abacus as well as in place value, addition, carrying, subtraction, and borrowing. Diagrams are used throughout the guide and a brief English-Spanish vocabulary list specific to the use of the abacus is included.

285. Electronic hand calculators; the implications for pre-college education, by Marilyn Suydam. Washington, DC, National Science Foundation, February 1976. 377p. ED 127205.

This volume reports research conducted to provide the National Science Foundation (NSF) with information concerning the existing range of beliefs and opinions about the impact of the hand-held calculator on pre-college educational practice. A literature search and several surveys of groups of individuals involved in calculator manufacture and sales or in education were conducted. In addition, four position papers by prominent educators were obtained. The body of the report presents summaries of information collected relevant to availability of calculators, arguments for and against their use in schools, ways in which they are now used in schools, and research findings. Five recommendations related to study of and preparation for implementation of calculator use are made. Appendices to the report present an annotated list of references, the detailed findings of the surveys, and the position papers: Immerzeel, Ockenga, and Tarr discuss plausible instances with which to use calculators; Pollak proposes criteria for redesigning the curriculum; Weaver makes suggestions for needed research; and Usiskin and Bell provide some perspectives on curriculum revision.

286. Your electrical hand calculator; how to get the most out of it, by Richard Carney. New Brunswick, NJ, Curriculum Lab. of Rutgers University, September 1978. 232p. ED 159480.

Designed for use by students at beginning high school through adult levels, this manual contains seventeen lessons on uses of the electronic hand calculator. Within each of the eight sections lessons presented include objectives, procedural information, examples, and problems to be solved. Following an introductory lesson to the calculator, section 2 provides lessons on three fundamental operations: addition and subtraction, multiplication and division, and powers and roots. Section 3 lessons are on decimals and percents: rounding off numbers, fractions to decimals, and percentage. Two lessons on special features are given in section 4: multiplication and division by a constant, and memory. Section 5 covers order of operations: basic operations and parentheses. In section 6, special keys are presented: key, negative numbers and sign-change key, reciprocal key, and exchange keys. Section 7 has two lessons on the presentation of numbers: significant figures and scientific notation. Review problems are provided in section 8. Selected answers to problems presented in the various sections are appended, and an index is provided.

9.
SCIENCE,
ENERGY,
ENVIRONMENT

287. Technology and ecology; technology's crossroads, by Eugene
      C. Bammel. Morgantown, College of Human Resources
      and Education, University of West Virginia, September
      1976. 22p. ED 132116.
      This seminar paper investigates the relationship between
technology and environment to determine the impact of technology on
the individual's personal and physical environment. It deals with the
consequences for individuals living in an environment shaped by modern technology. The main focus is that technology has acted as a
leveling force--a destroyer of unique differences of regional diversi-
ties and national identities, and of environments that complement
an individual's life-style. Modern technology has created environments with characteristics of mass production, mass distribution,
and mass consumption. Illustrations of environments that have been
altered by technology are cited. Using urbanity as its vehicle, technology has created an environment containing technological problems
which man can barely control. It is man's responsibility to solve
these problems in order to regain control over his environment.
The use of technology has become a moral issue, involving values
and choices of technological advance versus survival in changed environments. Although man has used technology to better his life,
he has not controlled technology. Thus, man has become the victim
of technology and his resultant environment. He must correct the
problems it has created before his environment is destroyed.

288. Radiocarbon dating; an annotated bibliography, by Suellen
      Fortine. April 1977. 64p. ED 146931.
      This selective annotated bibliography covers various
sources of information on the radiocarbon dating method, including
journal articles, conference proceedings, and reports, reflecting the
most important and useful sources of the last 25 years. The bibliography is divided into five parts--general background on radiocarbon,
radiocarbon dating, laboratory methods, limitations and sources of
errors, and calibration of the radiocarbon chronology. Extensive
introductory materials include characteristics of the literature, discussion of radiocarbon dating, the author's observations based on a

124

personal tour of the Radiocarbon Laboratory at the University of Texas, and a listing of radiocarbon laboratories around the world. The bibliography was compiled from the sources available at the University of Texas as of April 1977.

289. A Primer on artificial intelligence, by Ralph A. Leal. 1975. 33p. ED 114116.
A survey of literature on recent advances in the field of artificial intelligence provides a comprehensive introduction to this field for the nontechnical reader. Important areas covered are: (1) definitions, (2) the brain and thinking, (3) heuristic search, and (4) programing languages used in the research of artificial intelligence. Some examples of artificial intelligence are described. Suggestions for additional reading and a 28-item bibliography are appended.

290. Why man explores. Symposium held at California Institute of Technology, July 1976, sponsored by NASA. 46p. ED 129618.
This document presents a transcript of a National Aeronautics and Space Administration panel discussion held on July 2, 1976, in conjunction with the Viking Mission to Mars. The panel consisted of Norman Cousins, Ray Bradbury, Jacques Cousteau, James Michener, and Philip Morrison, and the principal topic was a philosophical discussion of the question, "Why does man explore?" Also discussed are the implications of finding life on Mars and man's future.

291. The Pioneer Venus missions, Mountain View, CA, Ames Research Center, NASA, 1978. 44p. ED 162852.
This document provides detailed information on the atmosphere and weather of Venus. This pamphlet describes the technological hardware including the probes that enter the Venusian atmosphere, the orbiter and the launch vehicle. Information is provided in lay terms on the mission profile, including details of events from launch to mission end. The pamphlet describes research to be conducted during the mission and relates the importance of the findings to human concerns.

292. Unidentified flying objects; a selected bibliography, compiled by Kay Rodgers. Washington, DC, Library of Congress, 1976. 21p. ED 138464.
This bibliography, intended for the general reader, provides selective coverage of the unidentified flying object (UFO) literature that has appeared since 1969. The coverage is limited to English language works, but does include translations and materials published abroad. Other bibliographies are listed, as are books, congressional and other government reports, articles from journals and magazines, and proceedings of conferences and symposia. Included also is a mailing address for ordering a packet of information on UFOs which includes an annotated list of reprints and books available from the Center for UFO Studies and other sources.

293. Saving money through energy conservation, by Michael H.

Presley. Stillwater, School of Industrial Education,
Oklahoma State University, 1976. 81p. ED 164285.

This publication is an introduction to personal energy
conservation. The first chapter presents a rationale for conserving
energy and points out that private citizens control about one third
of this country's energy consumption. Chapters two and three show
how to save money by saving energy. Chapter two discusses energy
conservation methods in the home such as caulking, insulation, temperature settings, and so forth. Chapter three discusses energy
conservation measures outside the home such as automobile maintenance practices, landscaping for shade and windscreens, and driv-
ing habits. Chapter four discusses future uses of renewable energy
sources such as solar, wind, geothermal, etc. and the various proposed technologies associated with these future sources. All the
energy conservation methods suggested were included because they
were judged cost effective; i.e., enough money would be saved over
a reasonable period of time from using them to return the money
invested initially.

294. Energy management in municipal buildings. Boston, Massa-
        chusetts State Department of Community Affairs Con-
        servation Project, 1977. 158p. ED 164296.

This manual is written for the manager or supervisor
responsible for instituting an energy management program for municipal government in dealing with the need to reduce energy consumption. The guide reviews methods for central coordination of activity
to ensure that resources are wisely applied, that results are com-
municated, and that follow-up on findings takes place. It defines
the techniques of preparation of the energy budget, of organizing and
evaluating a building audit, and the management principles involved
in selecting among alternative conservation measures to determine
the combination most likely to be effective for a particular building.
It discusses the human factors involved in changing wasteful practices of building users. A technical appendix provides detailed technical information and formulated work sheets for carrying out techniques presented in the text.

295. The Energy and environment glossary, by John Jones and
        Edward Dalton. Portland, OR, Energy and Man's
        Environment Inc., 1977. 50p. ED 159042.

This is a glossary of words that commonly appear in
energy education and environmental education materials. With over
750 words ranging from "abatement" to "zooplankton" this publication includes some uncommon terms such as "anadromous," "film
badge," "putrescible," and "tritium." Space is provided after each
alphabetical section for the addition of words not included in the
publication. This publication seems to have been written for use
by upper elementary and junior high school students. The definitions
are non-technical and, where appropriate, include comments on how
the term relates to environmental issues. This glossary should also
be useful to teachers.

296. U.S. energy prospects; an engineering viewpoint. Washington,

DC, National Academy of Engineering, 1974.   149p.
ED 125849.

With the Arab oil embargo of 1973, the United States
became aware of its dependence on foreign fuel to maintain its productive capacity, employment base, political autonomy, strategic
security, and living standard. An engineering Task Force on Energy
was appointed to provide an informed assessment of the realistic
strategies that could be initiated if the United States chose to become as independent as possible of foreign sources by 1985, based
on technology now known or applicable by that date. This publication presents the analysis, findings, and conclusions of that task
force. The task force concludes that the achievement of energy self-
sufficiency in one decade would require enormous efforts including
voluntary reduction of energy consumption and development of available fuel resources. Central to this report are the roles of government, industry, and the public in advancing a comprehensive energy
program in the next decade. Specific considerations discussed in the
report include supply and demand, conservation potentials, oil and
gas, shale oil, coal supply, and electricity prospects, program constraints and responsibilities beyond 1985.

297.   Nuclear power and the environment, by Joseph M. Dukert.
        Washington, DC, Energy Research and Development
        Administration, 1976. 95p. ED 130847.
        Described are the major environmental effects resulting
from the production of electricity by nuclear power plants. Discussed
are effects of waste heat, radioactivity, radioactive waste elimination,
costs, and future prospects. Included are diagrams illustrating cool-
ing tower operation, effects of thermal discharge into water systems,
radioactive waste disposal facilities, and a reading list.

298.   Solar energy, by William W. Eaton. Washington, DC, Energy
        Research and Development Administration, 1976. 56p.
        ED 130848.
        Presented is the utilization of solar radiation as an
energy resource principally for the production of electricity. Included are discussions of solar thermal conversion, photovoltic conversion, wind energy, and energy from ocean temperature differences.
Future solar energy plans, the role of solar energy in plant and fos-
sil fuel production, and public participation in solar energy development are also presented. Diagrams illustrating solar collectors,
availability of solar and wind energy, operation of ocean thermal
power plants, and an appendix listing the basic units of energy are
provided for reference.

299.   Energy Storage, by William W. Eaton. Washington, DC,
        Energy Research and Development Administration, 1975.
        40p. ED 130844.
        Described are technological considerations affecting
storage of energy, particularly electrical energy. The background
and present status of energy storage by batteries, water storage,
compressed air storage, flywheels, magnetic storage, hydrogen
storage, and thermal storage are discussed followed by a review of

development trends.   Included are diagrams illustrating the basic mechanisms of each storage system and energy flow diagrams for 1970 and 1985.

300.   Energy technology, by William W. Eaton.   Washington, DC,
             Energy Research and Development Administration, 1975.
             65p.   ED 130845.
             Reviewed are technological problems faced in energy production including locating, recovering, developing, storing, and distributing energy in clean, convenient, economical, and environmentally satisfactory manners.   The energy resources of coal, oil, natural gas, hydroelectric power, nuclear energy, solar energy, geothermal energy, winds, tides, fuel cells, magnetohydrodynamics, hydrogen, and various storage devices are discussed.   Energy transmission and diagrams illustrating energy demands, electrical generation capacity, and energy converter efficiencies are included.

301.   Geothermal energy, by William W. Eaton.   Washington, DC,
             Energy Research and Development Administration, 1975.
             48p.   ED 130846.
             Described are the origin and nature of geothermal energy source, technological considerations affecting its development as an energy source, its environmental effects, economic considerations, and future prospects of development in this field.   Basic system diagrams of the operation of a geothermal power plant are included.

10.
SOCIAL
AND
PSYCHOLOGICAL

302. Growth control; some questions for urban decisionmakers,
     by Robert A. Levine. Santa Monica, CA, Rand Corpora-
     tion, July 1974. 36p. ED 105024.
        This report is intended to provide urban decisionmakers--
mayors, city managers, planning directors, key staff and line officials, city councilmen--and citizen groups with a guide to some of
the issues that surround the effort to bring urban growth under control. The report attempts to be neutral in regard to whether urban
growth should be controlled, suggesting instead that communities
should ask themselves why they want to control growth (if they do)
as a first question in examining how to control. Two analysis-based
views on urban change must not, however, be concealed. First, it
is very easy to confuse causes and effects in urban growth. Second,
it may be easy to control growth within a limited political jurisdiction, but if the locally determined objective is to control growth
over a broad area, it is very easy for rigorous control of the parts
to allow continued chaos of the whole. Following an introduction,
the second section of this report takes up various possible objectives
of urban growth control and their implications; Section Three discusses the possibilities of different kinds of control; Section Four
goes into some detail on issues raised by "side effects" of attempting to control urban growth. Then Section Five addresses the question of how urban growth might be controlled.

303. The Suburbanization of America, by Robert C. Weaver. Pa-
     per presented at a consultation with the Commission on
     Civil Rights, December 1975. 36p. ED 123303.
        This paper is organized into four parts. Part One, The
Historical Pattern and Its Study, notes that the impulse to suburban-
ize is probably as old as the city itself. However, because of magnitude alone, contemporary suburban settlement would have to be
assessed as a phenomenon that is uniquely different from its pre-
decessors. Part Two, The Changed Role of the Suburbs Since World
War II, observes that, unlike the central city, the basic function
and form of which have changed only in degree, the suburban settlements that have emerged since World War II have little in common

with the ecological type called suburb previous to that time. Part III, Motivations of Housing Consumers in Opting for the Suburbs, asserts that knowing why the millions of American households that opted to live in the suburbs since World War II made that choice can tell us much about the future of our cities. Part IV, The Impact of Race Upon Suburbanization, proposes that because in recent decades that exodus from the central city to the suburbs peaked at the same time that a large number of newcomers to the large metropolitan areas were readily identifiable minorities, there has been much distortion of what has been involved. Some have confused coincidence with causation.

304. Improving urban America; a challenge to federalism, by Richard H. Leach. Washington, DC, Advisory Commission on Intergovernmental Relations, September 1976. 288p. ED 131149.
This report, an update of an earlier report from the Advisory Commission on Intergovernmental Relations, presents a review of urban America and its governmental capabilities. Chapters focus on: (1) urban America today (major aspects of the urban problem, changes in urban problems, changes in the perception of urban problem solving, and programs for meeting urban needs); (2) overcoming the urban fiscal problem (the plight of central cities, Federal action, State action, and the development of an effective and equitable state and local revenue system); (3) improving services in urban America; (4) restructuring local governments (the Federal role, and others); (5) solving the problem of metropolitan areas (urban development, urbanization, building requirements, urban development planning and land use regulation, and urban development policy framework); and (6) intergovernmental problems and strategies for the future. The report concludes that urban society is worth saving. The connection between the high standard of living in America and the urban setting of most American activity today is not coincidental. What is called for is a series of actions which will produce, at the end, a revitalized American urban scene. The Federal system already has begun to change, yet the need for urban statemanship at all levels remains great.

305. Cheating; an annotated bibliography, by Barbara M. Wildemuth. Princeton, NJ, ERIC Clearinghouse on Tests, Measurement, and Evaluation, October 1976. 39p. ED 132182.
This 89-item, annotated bibliography was compiled to provide access to research and discussions of cheating and, specifically, cheating on tests. It is not limited to any educational level, nor is it confined to any specific curriculum area. Two data bases were searched by computer, and a library search was conducted. A computer search of the Educational Resources Information Center (ERIC) data base yielded documents announced in Resources in Education and journal articles indexed in Current Index to Journals in Education which covers over 700 education-related journals. Also searched by computer was Psychological Abstracts, an index providing summaries of literature in psychology and related disciplines. Over 800 journals, technical reports, monographs, and other scien-

tific documents are regularly covered. All data fields in both data bases were searched for any form of the term, cheat. The ERIC data base was searched in October 1976. ERIC began collecting information for RIE in 1966 and for CIJE in 1969. At the time of the search, the data base was complete through September 1976. Psychological Abstracts was searched in October 1976, and the data base dates from 1967. A subject index is provided.

306. Wavelengths, by Lochie B. Christopher. Boston, Massachusetts State Department of Education, January 1977. 77p. ED 158154.

This self-study guide is intended for young people between the ages of 16 and 22. It is divided into nine sections, each dealing with a potential problem area topic such as friends, love, sex, and marriage. A short introduction heads each section and is followed by a variety of activities. The activities include suggestions for verbal, written, artistic, musical and feeling-oriented experiences. The last section draws the whole book together by helping the user of the guide to apply the learnings in the first eight sections to himself as a part of a community. This guide can be used alone, with friends, or with a trained group leader. Its purpose is to help the individual better understand himself and his relations with others.

307. Depression; what it is and how to deal with it; a manual, by Kevin J. Hartigan and Gerald N. Weiskott. 1976. 37p. ED 153160.

This manual is designed to help counseling personnel understand and deal with depression. It begins by defining depression (the "common cold of psychopathology") and listing a number of typical symptthoms, giving mild, moderate and severe manifestations. It then offers seven different treatment approaches or theories. Directly or indirectly, these theories most frequently account for negative expectancy, dejected mood, behavioral deficits, retarded physical activity, loss of libido and appetite and motivational deficits. A majority of the theories acknowledge faulty cognitions, passivity and avoidance as manifestations of depression. The manual concludes by outlining a workshop designed to help college students manage depression and stress. The workshop (two sessions of three hours each) is not intended to replace individual therapy but can be used as a productive adjunct to it.

308. Coping with pain; studies in stress inoculation, by John J. Horan. Paper presented at the annual meeting of the American Educational Research Association, March 1978. 33p. ED 158151.

The stress-inoculation paradigm for helping clients deal with pain consists of education about the psychological dimensions of pain, training in a number of coping skills relevant to each dimension, and practice in applying these skills to the noxious stimulus. Presented are two studies, the first of which represents a component analysis of stress inoculation, and the second, an enhancement of the generalization potential of the paradigm and an exploration of the effect of procedural variations in the exposure component. Additional studies, currently in progress, are also described.

309. Life situations and lifestyles of persons who attempt suicide, by Isaac Sakinofsky. Paper presented at the annual meeting of the American Association of Suicidology, April 1978. 16p. ED 159568.

A Sample of 228 suicide attempts admitted in the emergency rooms of four general hospitals in an industrial city was studied as part of an ongoing follow-up investigation of the interaction of life situations and stresses and coping skills. Approximately 60% of the sample came from chaotic homes torn apart by family conflict. An assortative mating factor which may operate differently between the sexes is suggested, and the probability that female suicide attempters are self-selected and use this form of behavior as a legitimized way of bringing their marital disharmony to a head is indicated. The proportion of the total sample who were unemployed was striking. There was a clear association between coming from a disordered family background and subsequently living on welfare in adult life, whereas those who came from a stable background were more often found to be supporting themselves. Some evidence exists, suggesting that a childhood background characterized by family strife and dissension is damaging to the development of personality (as exemplified in suicide attempters) and severely impairs the ability to form harmonious sexual partnerships as well as impairing the development of constructive attitudes and skills towards work and self-support.

310. Therapists; who are they and what do they do? by George W. Rogers, Jr., and Thomas W. McCann. 1975. 31p. ED 163324.

This article is primarily written for beginning therapists, paraprofessionals, and interested students. The following questions are discussed: (1) Who are therapists?; (2) What do therapists do?; (3) Why do people become therapists?; and (4) What are the characteristics of "good" therapists? The continuum of therapists is examined, ranging from the professional to the amateur. Positive and negative reasons for becoming a therapist are explored, as well as the potentially helpful and/or harmful results of therapy. The list of the characteristics of the "good" therapist is drawn from a variety of schools of thought in accord with the paper's generally eclectic theoretical orientation.

311. The American Psychiatric Association decision on homosexuality, by Malcolm Spector. 1978. 30p. ED 156796.

This paper describes the events leading to and the process by which the American Psychiatric Association decided that homosexuality is not itself a psychiatric disorder. This change was an amendment to the official Diagnostic and Statistical Manual of Mental Disorders. The data come from the analysis of documents and unstructured interviews. The role of gay liberation groups and of liberal factions within the American Psychiatric Association are discussed. Possible consequences of the decision are considered.

312. Outward Bound; a reference volume, compiled by Arnold Shore. Greenwich, CT, Outward Bound, Inc., February 1977. 594p. ED 165926.

The main purpose of this reference volume on Outward Bound (OB) is to provide access to the research literature by giving the reader a sense of the state of literature, providing analysis on salient research and programmatic issues, granting easy access to individual pieces of research, and opening up related research literatures. Section I is an overview of the research literature on OB presented in tabular form and listing title, author(s), topic, type of study, type of course, assessment, and whether or not the study's findings are reported in Section II. Explanations are provided on how to use the table and its relationship to other sections in the volume. Section II is a report on what has been learned about academic and research issues from the literature; it constitutes a review of empirical studies, covering research design, theory, special OB topics, and other observations. Section III consists of two types of summaries: (1) summaries by the author of this volume which include critical commentary; and (2) summaries in the words of the authors of the research. Section IV is an extensive bibliography of related research literatures organized under three major headings: (1) Education; (2) Psychology; and (3) Corrections. A minor heading "Other" is also included. The bibliography includes well over 1000 citations dating from the early 1900's to the present. Section III includes over 100 summaries by Shore and by the research authors covering OB from its inception to the present.

313. Food stamps; a bibliography, by Colin Cameron. Madison, Institute for Research on Poverty, University of Wisconsin, June 1977. 57p. ED 147413.

A voluminous body of literature exists on the topic of food stamps including the administration of the federal and state programs and the question of abuses and fraud. This bibliography describes a portion of that material in print. An introduction provides general information and a chronology of the food stamp program and comments on the place of nutrition in social welfare. Topics in this classified, annotated bibliography include: history of the food stamp program from the late 1930's to 1961; background information on potential recipients; nutrition and food information; continuing Nixon's reforms up to the present; the delivery of the service; advocacy for the poor in need of food stamps; debate on the issue of abuse; citations of related interest; and sourcebooks and ongoing sources of information. An author index is also provided.

314. The Effects of welfare reform alternatives on the family, by Katherine Bradbury. Madison, Institute for Research on Poverty, University of Wisconsin, June 1977. 95p. ED 146315.

This paper analyzes the effects of welfare reform alternatives on the family. Because the family is the basic unit of social organization in society, the effect of public policies on marital sta-

bility is of great concern. The effects of welfare reform on the
family are of particular public policy interest because it is generally
assumed (1) that the number of female headed families is increasing
in relation to the number of families as a whole; (2) that children,
as well as the other members of society, will be better off if their
parents remain married; and (3) that the existing welfare system
contains incentives for families to split up and for female headed
families with children to be created. It is noted that the first assumption is correct. The number of female headed families is increasing in relation to the number of families as a whole. Regarding the second assumption, it is noted that there is no reliable evidence regarding the effects of marital stability on children. Regarding the third assumption, there are numerous incentives in existing income maintenance programs for families to split up. Most
welfare reform proposals would also create incentives for family
splitting. For example, the Income Supplement Program in some
cases leads to reductions in income of up to $1,200 if two adults
marry. In the absence of reliable conclusions about the effects of
marital disruption on children and on society, it is difficult to know
whether public policy should actively discourage family breakup or
whether it should be neutral.

315. It starts with people; experiences in drug abuse prevention,
        by Henry S. Resnik. Washington, DC, Porter, Novelli
        and Associates, Inc., 1978. 84p. ED 167851.
        The question of drug abuse prevention is examined in
this booklet. Addressing itself to a variety of disciplines and professions, the book reveals the effectiveness of prevention programs
implemented in classroom, school and community settings. It draws
on the experiences of several dozen drug abuse prevention programs
that were either visited or assessed as part of an intensive research
and review process. Strategies and educational techniques for prevention programs are emphasized, and organizational models for
schools, communities and minority groups are presented. The emphasis is on how individual people can reach across age and social
barriers to work with youth and help them live without drugs.

316. Alternatives; one approach to drug education, by V. Alton
        Dohner. 1973. 67p. ED 146527.
        This publication attempts to produce greater understand-
ing of the complex problems of drug abuse and drug dependence.
The major emphasis for prevention is through helping children develop to a healthy maturity. Section One discusses various approaches
to drug education (scare and fear, matter-of-fact, styles of use and
motives, society and continuum use, and alternatives to drug abuse).
Section Two discusses motives for using mood-altering drugs (curi-
osity, imitation, peer pressure, well-being, instant achievement,
relaxation, recreation, psychological support, rebellion, insight,
etc.) Section Three discusses alternatives to drug abuse (meaningful relaxation, work and vocational skills, personal awareness,
social-political involvement, etc.) The final section briefly discusses a program of family living courses as they should be presented to various grade levels in school. Appendices include a list of
various drugs and stimulants, and a short glossary of relevant terms.

317. <u>Fathering: a bibliography</u>, by Alice Sterling Honig. Urbana,
IL, ERIC Clearinghouse on Early Childhood Education,
August 1977. 78p. ED 142293.
   This bibliography on fathering contains over 1000 entries
dating from 1941 to 1977. References are organized into 10 sections,
each reflecting a major area of interest to theorists, researchers,
and clinicians. The ten areas include: (1) role of the father, (2)
father and socialization, (3) fathers' contributions to sex role development, (4) fathers and their children's cognitive competence,
(5) fathers and infants, (6) fathering and problem behavior in children, (7) children's views on fathering, (8) nontraditional fathering,
(9) correlates of urbanization and occupations of fathers, and (10)
father absence, loss, or neglect in relation to child behaviors.
Some of the entries are annotated.

318. <u>On becoming a "Modern Parent" in the 1920's</u>, by Libby
Byers. 1977. 32p. ED 148468.
   Child rearing and parenting practices during the 1920s,
the impact of science and scientific discoveries during this period,
medical advances and the concurrent decline in the death-rate of
infants and young children are discussed in this paper. Also discussed is the impact of the theories of psychologists G. Stanley
Hall, Lewis Terman, and John B. Watson, all proponents of a scientific approach to child rearing. Hall, an evolutionist and a pro-
ponent of child study, was responsible for bringing Freud and Jung
to the United States. Terman's contributions were the most influential in the measurement movement and in the area of intelligence
testing. According to the paper, John B. Watson exerted the greatest influence on parents during the 1920s. His behaviorist orientation was reflected in his emphasis on strict schedules, habit training, and a mechanistic approach to child rearing. Other writers
reflected this same orientation. Not until the late 1920s and early
1930s did Freud's theories of unconscious motivation and impulse
expression affect child rearing practices. It is suggested that parents were influenced not only by these conflicting theories, but also
by memories of their own Victorian upbringing.

319. <u>Data on Vietnam era veterans</u>. Washington, DC, Veterans
Administration, September 1978. 66p. ED 167014.
   Statistical data are presented on Vietnam era veterans
for the following topics: employment status, medical status, compensation and pension, education, housing assistance, expenditures,
and demographic information. The estimated number and age of
veterans in civil life, categorized by sex and state, and the educational attainment of veterans at the time of separation, by age groups,
are presented. Information on length of service and estimated gross
separations and number of casualties are included. Employment information includes work experience of civilian male veterans, aged
20-34; seasonally adjusted unemployment rates; and income data.
Medical information includes annual census of patients in VA hospitals on September 28, 1977; outpatient medical care; and dental outpatient activity. Compensation and pension data include active compensation, dependency, and indemnity compensation and pension
cases; active compensation cases, by degree of impairment and type

of major disability; and age groups of veterans receiving compensation or pension benefits. Educational data concern educational assistance for veterans and vocational rehabilitation training. Housing assistance data concern guaranteed or insured loans, and data on expenditures concern Veterans Administration expenditures from appropriated funds, Vietnam era.

320. Prolonged separation; the prisoner of war and his family,
edited by Edna J. Hunter. San Diego, CA, Naval Health Research Center, 1977. 40p. ED 153167.
        This collection of articles was produced by the Center for Prisoner of War Studies, whose purpose is fourfold: (1) to provide information useful for planning the long-term health care of prisoners of war (POW's); (2) to evaluate the prison experience so that military survival training programs may be effectively planned; (3) to enumerate the factors characterizing the health and adjustment of families of POW's, in order to meet their needs in the future; and (4) to compile a variety of reference materials useful for health professionals who deal with POW's and their families. To this end, four articles are presented, one giving a longitudinal study of POW's and their families, the others analyzing various aspects of stress and the captivity experience. The POW's relation to his family receives special attention; it is recognized that POW's spouses and children also experience strains whose resolution is essential to successful post-imprisonment adjustment.

321. Changing families in a changing military system, edited by
Edna J. Hunter. San Diego, CA, Naval Health Research Center, 1977. 91p. ED 153168.
        Recently, the military system has begun to feel the impact of the military family. Whenever sudden dramatic changes or transitions occur, crises may result either for the individual or for the institution. At present both the military system and the military system and the military family are in a period of rapid transition. Perhaps one of the most important changes that has occurred within the military since World War II has been the change from a single-man's Army to a married-man's Army, Navy, or Air Force. A more recent change is the growing acceptance of women service personnel as an integral part of the military structure. With the increasing numbers of women affiliated with the military, including servicewomen and wives of servicemen, their importance to the military and their impact upon the military organization increases. Perhaps this change may be even more than proportional, when the ingredient of the changing role of women in society in general is added to the equation for change. The papers included as part of this symposium focus on: (1) the various pressures and transitions which have been occurring from within and without the military system; (2) the impact of these transitions on individuals, institutions, and policies; and (3) the changing relationships between individuals, families, and the military system. Effects of the transitions now in process are discussed, and an attempt is made to show how events outside the system (wars, depression, legislation, and court decisions) often adumbrate these effects.

322. <u>Divorce counseling</u>, by Sheila Kessler. Ann Arbor, MI, ERIC
      Clearinghouse on Counseling and Personnel Services,
      1977. 107p. ED 150534.
      This paper offers an overview of existing services for
divorcing individuals and their children, and focuses specifically on
one model of divorce counseling. Emerging trends are identified
as the monograph addresses the practical, financial, emotional and
social services now offered in the U.S. The bulk of the document
is devoted to the format, dynamics and techniques of a specific
model for conducting a divorce adjustment group. The model allows
unstructured time for divorcing individuals to release and discuss
feelings, and describes preventive exercises which foster individual
growth. A brief discussion of counseling services for children comprises the last section of the monograph.

323. <u>The Social readjustment for the remaining partner</u>, by Lynn
      D. Lomen. March 1975. 59p. ED 109555.
      This study is a compilation of some of the published
material on the social readjustment of widows and widowers plus a
sampling (26) of personal interviews which the researcher conducted.
The loss of a spouse is a traumatic experience. The emotional tur-
moil that follows, caused by the personal mode of living, circumstances of the death, treatment by friends, job situation, and other
factors influence the recovery from grief. The completeness of
recovery bears directly on the remaining partner's entry or re-entry
into the social world, dating, and remarriage. Anticipated grief
during a spouse's long illness, continuing friendships, and the remaining partner's own determination to gain self-confidence in the
new "singles" world, were found to be important factors in the remaining partner's re-entry into the social world.

324. <u>Toward a true marriage partnership</u>. Madison, Wisconsin
      Governor's Commission on the Status of Women, Novem-
      ber 1976. 108p. ED 161779.
      The booklet examines economic handicaps faced by home-
makers and outlines a program for marital property reform. The
document is presented in three chapters. Chapter I stresses the
need for marital property reform by presenting case studies of situations in which a wife's contributions to a marriage were unrecom-
pensed. Chapter II presents underlying assumptions of community
property laws in various states. Topics discussed include problems
in classifying property as community or separate; management and
control of property; credits and debts; interpersonal contracts; dis-
solution of the community; problems encountered when couples move
from state to state; and federal tax treatment of community property.
Chapter III offers recommendations for classification of property in
a model marital property system. Recommendations are that: (1)
marital property should include all property, rents, and profits acquired by either or both spouses during marriage--except property
designated as separate; (2) separate property must be formally declared; (3) all property is presumed to be marital property unless
proven to be separate property; and (4) all expenditures from separate assets for family use are to be considered as gifts.

325. Inmate involvement in prison legal services; roles and training options for the inmate as paralegal, by William P. Statsky. Washington, DC, American Bar Association, March 1974. 105p. ED 163894.

An introduction to the role of the paralegal in the free world, the inmate as paralegal, legal service needs, and program planning are included along with guidelines for the training of inmates as paralegals. Paralegal services, legal problems, and legal services are extensively defined. The legal problems of inmates and methods of providing legal services other than through paralegal inmates are discussed. A number of models of inmate paralegal programs as well as descriptions of some major programs in this country are presented, and resources necessary for setting up training programs are discussed. Guidelines for trainers in the design of training programs for paralegals are included, emphasizing legal vocabulary, question and answer-anecdotal, and skills development. Trainee recruitment and techniques for teaching inmate paralegals how to state a claim, basic mechanical procedures, and constitutional law governing institutional life are also covered. Major curriculum issues that need to be explored in designing any training program are also discussed.

326. Immigration 1975-2001; report of the National Conference on Immigration Policy. Toronto, Canadian Association for Adult Education, 1975. 90p. ED 117399.

Canadians experienced in the field of immigration and representing the academic community, government, and community-based organizations discussed major policy issues regarding the Canadian Federal Green Paper on Immigration Policy and the possibility of a national council on immigration and migration at the conference. A variety of topics were considered and condensations of each discussion and who was involved are presented in the 41-page report for the following areas: immigration and population growth, immigration and provincial responsibilities, immigrants and cities, immigration and Francophone Canada, refugee policy, the case for National Immigration and Migration Council, Canada's selection policy, immigration and the labor force, the illegal immigrant, the brain drain, Canada as a multiracial society, and immigration policy forum. The text is in both French and English, with tables supplementing the discussions. A proposal to create a National Immigration and Migration Council is appended, along with the conference program and a list of participants. It is stated that more can be done to facilitate the economic and social integration of immigrants into Canadian society, with institutions cooperating in their integration and the alleviation of discrimination.

327. The Terminology of machismo, by Marcela T. Gaitan. Paper presented at the annual conference of the Western Social Science Association, May 1976. 14p. ED 130803.

The term "macho" has been increasingly incorporated into the English language with various connotations and definitions, i.e., male chauvinist, superman, and hyper-manliness. Yet these words are not substitutions for "macho" which has an intrinsic value of its own. For English speakers, the most prevalent definition is "virile". While this is a correct definition, it is not the only meaning the concept has for Mexicans and Chicanos. To Chicanos, "machismo" has both positive and negative aspects. Positive aspects include: bravery, loyalty, pride in self, leadership responsibility, respect for religion and elders, modesty, and good manners. Negative aspects include: absolute power in the form of exploitation, self-centeredness, violence used to maintain power through fear, and closed aloofness; women seen as subordinate creatures, created to make man's lot more comfortable and pleasurable; too much pride; and too modest and reserved for survival in today's society. While some positive and negative aspects seem to cancel each other, it is generally the individual who defines "macho" in the Chicano community. As the word "macho" has taken on many and varied definitions, the word "hembra", which is its female counterpart, must also acquire many positive definitions besides "fertile". This paper discusses the various definitions of "macho"; its historical background; how writers such as Bernice Rincon, Samuel Ramos, Octavio Paz, Anna Mayo, and Aniceto Aramoni have used it; and means whereby Chicanas can begin to assert themselves.

328. Turtle manual, by Marlene Schneider and Arthur Robin. Sponsored by Office of Education, DHEW, 1974. 42p. ED 128680.
   This manual describes the Turtle Technique which was developed to help children with behavior problems control their own disruptive behavior. The technique differs from other behavior modification techniques in that it is based upon self-control rather than external control of disruptive behavior. The Turtle Technique first teaches the child how to respond when he feels threatened by uncontrollable emotions or external events which make him feel like lashing out. The learning of the turtle-like withdrawing response is then followed by relaxation training, generalization training and problem solving. Suggestions for maintenance of this system of self-control and other possible applications of it are provided in the concluding section.

329. Halfway houses; a selected bibliography, compiled by Carolyn Johnson and Marjorie Kravitz. Germantown, MD, Aspen Systems Corp., March 1978. 46p. ED 155350.
   This bibliography on halfway houses contains seventy-two entries (includes books, journals, films, technical reports, and government publications) which address the critical issues in halfway house operations, evaluations, and innovations. Each entry includes an annotation preceded by the appropriate bibliographic information, such as author, title, journal, publisher, publication date, pages (or length), color, and source. Listed alphabetically by author or title, the entries are grouped into three sections as follows: (1) "Development, Standards, and Program Descriptions," which contains thirty-five entries covering the concept underlying halfway houses and their development in specific communities, and includes guidelines and standards for halfway houses and descriptions of specific programs; (2) "Evaluation," comprised of thirty-four entries,

focuses on halfway house evaluations (both fiscal and program) utilizing varied measures of evaluation, including cost-benefit analyses,
recidivism rates, and the effect of halfway houses on crime; and (3)
"Directories," which furnishes information on three published listings
of halfway facilities.   Information on ways to obtain listed documents
precedes the bibliography, and sources and resource agencies are
listed in the appendix.

330.   Obscenity law since Miller; another troublesome balancing
          formula, by David H. Haan.   Paper presented at the
          annual meeting of the Association for Education in Journal-
          ism, August 1978.   53p.   ED 165161.
          A 1973 Supreme Court decision ("Miller v. California")
established the system of defining obscenity on the local level according to the following criteria: first, prurient appeal and patent
offensiveness are to be determined by a community rather than by
a national standard; second, sexually explicit materials are judged
obscene only if specified as such by state or federal law; and, finally,
sexually explicit communications are protected only when they are
judged to be of serious literary, artistic, political, or scientific
value.   During the past five years, each criterion has created problems and aroused controversies involving the definition of a relevant
community, the subjective attitudes of jurors, the development of
state guidelines on obscenity, and valid judgments regarding the
quality of questioned material.   In addition to the confusion it has
produced, the shift to local standards in obscenity prosecution has
required repeated appeals to higher courts and has thereby established
a process similar to the original national standard that governed
judgments on obscenity.

331.   Smokers vs. nonsmokers; toward an understanding of their
          differences, by Joanne M. Buhl and Roger A. Bell.
          Louisville, KY, School of Medicine, Louisville University,
          April 1976.   20p.   ED 123217.
          This research was conducted to contribute to the general
knowledge concerning differences between smokers and nonsmokers.
The data were obtained from a major epidemiologic study conducted
in 1973 in the southeastern United States.   A survey instrument
composed of 403 questions and administered to 2029 randomly selected
adults was designed to elicit mental and physical health information
as well as sociodemographic and service utilization data.   Significant
differences have been found between smokers and nonsmokers.   The
highest percentage of smokers was found among males, those aged
30-44, the less educated, the divorced or separated, the middle
socioeconomic class, those experiencing larger numbers of stressful
life events, those who did not grow up with both their real parents,
and those who had unhappy childhoods.   Smokers as a group tended
to score higher on psychological scales measuring anxiety and de-
pressive symptomatology.   The findings support that smoking is a
compensatory form of behavior, a symptom of other problems of
emotional health.   Until it becomes possible to identify individuals
who are biologically cancer-prone and to therefore direct educational
efforts toward specific target groups who will suffer the most de-

bilitating consequences of smoking, intervention must be persistent, individualized, and socially reinforced.   (Charts and graphs are included in the report.)

11.
EMPLOYMENT,
LABOR,
CAREERS

332. Quality of work life; the issues in the debate, by Al Nash.
        Chicago, Illinois Labor History Society, 1977. 36p.
        ED 171907.
        Diverse opinions are held by workers, union officials,
and labor researchers about the importance of the quality of working life to workers. Major issues in this debate focus on the following questions: (1) Is there a workers' movement to improve the
quality of working life? (2) Do workers seek meaning and self-
fulfillment in their jobs? (3) Can work be redesigned and humanized
without affecting profits and efficiency? (4) To what extent are employees alienated or dissatisfied? (5) How reliable are the findings of
studies on these issues? and (6) Why are experiments in job enrichment and restructuring considered successful in Europe, but not
in the United States? The quality of working life is influenced by
such factors as the application of technology to the work, economic
structure of an industry, division of labor, private ownership and
management, and society's emphasis on material success. Proposals for improving working conditions range from the utopian solutions of left-wing critics and sociologists which require vast changes
in technology and social structure to the practical methods of union
leaders which focus on the work environment, safety and health
standards, and grievance procedures. While some experts contend
job enrichment will not ultimately work, others feel it has already
proven itself: both conclusions are premature as more time is
needed before passing judgment.

333. The Labor market consequences of dropping out of high school,
          by Randall H. King. Columbus, Center for Human Re-
          source Research, Ohio State University, 1978. 116p.
          ED 158034.
          A study, growing out of human capital theory, examined
the economic consequences of dropping out of high school. Effect
of schooling over time on labor market success (hourly pay rate,
occupational prestige, and employment incidence and duration) was
measured. Data on young men and women was obtained from the
National Longitudinal Surveys of Labor Market Experience and per-

sonal interviews. The study universe consisted of respondents who
left school between 1958-70 (males) and 1960-72 (females), completed nine-to-twelve years of schooling, and were not enrolled at
the time of the survey. A three-equation recursive model was used
to determine schooling contribution to success measures. Findings
demonstrated substantial labor market benefits for all groups during
the first decade of labor market experience. Earnings differences
between graduates and dropouts were not pronounced immediately
upon leaving school, but became significant over time. Graduates'
age-earnings profiles were steeper than those of dropouts. The
difference in occupational status between black graduates and dropouts shrank over time. All graduates, except black females, enjoyed greater immunity to unemployment than dropouts. In employment duration the advantage of black males and black and white females deteriorated over time; little difference was demonstrated between white male graduates and dropouts.

334. The National apprenticeship program. Washington, DC, Em-
      ployment and Training Administration, Department of
      Labor, 1976. 46p. ED 138730.
         A brief explanation of the national apprenticeship pro-
gram is presented primarily in terms of the more important policies
and the role of government in this system of training. Eleven sections are included: (1) What is Apprenticeship? (2) Why Is Apprenticeship Important? (3) What can Apprenticeship Do? (4) How the
National Apprenticeship Program Operates, (5) Basic Standards of
an Apprenticeship Program, (6) Information on Laws and Regulations
Affecting Apprenticeship, (7) Veterans' Training Allowances, (8)
Where Apprentices Are Employed, (9) Where to Apply, (10) Apprenticeable Occupations, and (11) List of Apprenticeable Occupations.
The section on apprenticeable occupations constitutes the majority
of the booklet. Ninety-four basic trade classifications are presented,
with related occupations grouped under them. Although not final or
all inclusive, the list of occupations are those that meet the criteria
for apprenticeable occupations and which are included in programs
registered with State apprenticeship agencies or the Bureau of Apprenticeship and Training. Each basic trade classification includes
the customary term of apprenticeship, in years, and a code number(s)
from the "Dictionary of Occupational Titles." Appended are lists
of Bureau of Apprenticeship and Training regional offices and State
and territorial apprenticeship agencies, and The National Apprenticeship Act, (as amended).

335. Discrimination in employment, by Irving Kovarsky. Iowa
      City, Center for Labor and Management, University of
      Iowa, 1976. 248p. ED 141636.
         Intended as a guide on discrimination problems and
issues for students and practitioners in the area of employment re-.
lations, this book interrelates historical, religious, economic, medical, and sociological factors surrounding racial, religious, national,
sex, age, and physical and mental discrimination to explain discrimination in employment. The chapters in the first half of the book on

racial and religious discrimination develop the background related to
the roots of discrimination; discuss the relationship between traditional economic theory and discrimination issues; analyze Court
interpretations of the Constitution; and examine the development and
application of Federal policy related to discrimination through a discussion of Federal labor laws and executive orders, and State and
Federal fair employment legislation. The remainder of the book
focuses on sex, age, health, and other specific types of discrimination such as experienced by homosexuals and ex-convicts, each
in turn being discussed in terms of history and applicable legislation.
Supreme Court decisions in six cases, a bibliography, and publications of the Center for Labor and Management are appended.

336. Last hired, first fired; layoffs and civil rights. Washington,
     DC, Commission on Civil Rights, February 1977. 98p.
     ED 137503.
          The effects of the 1974-75 economic recession on the
effort to ensure equal employment opportunity for the Nation's minority groups and women are examined in the first section of this
report, which documents the layoff of disproportionately large numbers of minority and female workers during the recession, generally
resulting from the fact that many were only recently hired and thus
had earned little seniority. It is concluded that the recession seriously eroded affirmative action gains of recent years, frustrating
the intent of Title VII of the Civil Rights Act of 1964. Executive
Order 11246, as amended and other programs enacted to help minority and female workers narrow the historic economic gap between them and white male workers. The likelihood of continuing
high unemployment and future economic slowdowns, which threaten
not only vulnerable minority and women workers with low seniority,
but many white males, particularly youths, as well, is analyzed.
The social costs of such employment, particularly that involving job
losers and discouraged workers are described. Two sections of the
report discuss layoffs and seniority and review the legality of layoffs
by seniority when disproportionate numbers of minorities or women
are affected. Alternatives to layoffs are explored in the fourth
section, some of them already widely practiced in Western Europe
and by some industries in the U.S. (e.g., reduction of hours, early
retirement, rotation of layoffs, cuts in cost other than wages). In
the concluding section suggestions are made for explicit Federal
guidelines by the Equal Employment Opportunity Commission with
regard to the "last hired, first fired" conflict based on the principle
that all seniority-based layoff policies should be invalid as they apply to any work force that does not mirror the relevant labor market and the composition of which cannot be explained successfully
by the employer.

337. The Role of prison industries now and in the future; a plan-
     ning study. Washington, DC, Law Center, Georgetown
     University, August 1975. 66p. ED 117441.
          The Institute of Criminal Law and Procedure analyzes
the merits, limitations, and problems of various approaches to prison industry and recommends measures and programs to improve

industries. Federal and State legislation affecting prison industries
were examined, several prison industries were visited, and the literature of prison industries was reviewed. The study's findings are
these: Prison industries exist in the context of correctional systems
whose future dimensions are unknown and whose purposes are un-
clear. Therefore, before effective prison industry planning can take
place, agreement must be reached as to underlying correctional
philosophy and as to the expected numbers and distribution of offenders in the correctional system. Prison industries today do not
achieve their traditional goals and should be modified (possibly eliminated). Intelligent modification will be possible only with better
information on the true costs of prison industries as determined
through standardized accounting procedures. Prison industries should
provide a real work experience, including full work days, job compensation, minimum wage, and merit increases in pay. New and
closer relationships with private industry can benefit prison industry.
Finally, laws restricting prison production and marketing should be
repealed.

338. The Challenge of preparing an urban population for full employment, compiled by Daniel Koble, Jr., and Bruce
Shylo. Columbus, National Center for Research in
Vocational Education, Ohio State University, May 1978.
148p. ED 159406.

Twenty-one conference presentations are included in this
report of a national conference for large city vocational education
administrators. Section 1 includes one presentation entitled "The
Challenge of Youth Unemployment in Urban Areas" and three on
"Changing Vocational Education to Impact on Youth Unemployment
in Urban Areas." Each of the three papers in section 2 is entitled
"Coordinating Vocational and Manpower Training Activities in a Large
Urban Area." Section 3 contains two presentations on "Practices to
Assure Sexual Equality in Vocational-Technical Programs," three on
"Practices to Assure Racial Equality in Employment of Graduates of
Vocational Education," and two on "Techniques for Orienting Vo-
cational Education Personnel to the Needs of Minority and Female
Clients." In section 4 two papers deal with "Strategies for Coordi-
nating Secondary and Post-Secondary Vocational-Technical Education
in Urban Areas," two with "The Future of Part-Time Adult Voca-
tional Education in Urban Areas," and one with "Changes Needed in
Vocational-Technical Education to Better Serve the Needs of Post-
Secondary and Part Time Adult Clients in Urban Areas." "The
Role of Career Education in Desegregating Schools in Large Cities"
is contained in section 5 and "Providing Inservice Education to Meet
the Training Needs of Building Level Vocational Administrators in
Urban Areas" makes up section 6. Appended are simulation exercises used at the conferences, the conference program, and the
names and addresses of program participants, presenters, and pre-
siders.

339. Employment services for older job seekers; final report, by
Thurlow R. Wilson. Alexandria, VA, Human Resources
Research Organization, June 1978. 247p. ED 159458.

Results are presented of a project to analyze employment assistance given to persons fifty-five or older and to recommend improvements in older job seekers' employment services. (The project evolved from income security concerns expressed in the Older Americans Act.) The report, divided into seven chapters, reviews employment characteristics and needs of older job seekers in chapter 1. This chapter also examines the job market, employment services, and legislation relative to the older worker. Chapter 2 presents the methodology used in the job seeker survey and the studies of senior nonprofit employment offices and state and regional aging offices. Chapter 3 reports on the older job seekers' survey and interview results. Chapter 4 includes findings related to senior nonprofit employment offices. Chapter 5 examines how state employment security agencies might augment services to aid older job seekers. In chapter 6 the role of regional and state offices on aging in employment programs is considered. The final chapter summarizes and discusses older job seekers' problems and needs. State Employment Office assistance, the State Office on Aging's employment role, and recommendations. References, three appendixes (data collection instruments, New York training workshop report, and job seeker survey responses), and forty-five tables are included.

340. Poverty and public policy; final draft, by Irving Leveson.
       Croton-on-Hudson, NY, Hudson Institute, July 1975.
       342p. ED 145035.
       This comprehensive document studies poverty in the
U. S. and develops a set of recommendations for dealing with the
problems. It examines poverty from the perspectives of both the
national economy and local areas. It considers circumstances in
both labor and consumer markets and looks at public and private
activities, at revenue and spending decisions, at earned and un-
earned income and at population groups and problem areas. Chapters are devoted to the following areas: (1) poverty concepts and
measures, (2) revision of poverty standards over time, (3) poverty
and the national economy, (4) problems and progress in a growing
economy, (5) racial differences in the mobility of males, (6) restructuring income maintenance, (7) issues in income maintenance and
social insurance, and aspects of urban development. It is concluded
that the long prospects for poverty reduction are very optimistic.
Both the natural course of the economy and deliberate public efforts
have had and can continue to have a substantial impact. The problems which remain, however, will be the ones that do not respond
readily to economic growth and with which public policy has not yet
been effectively able to deal.

341. Poverty profile USA, by Mariellen Procopio and Frederick
       Perella. New York, Missionary Society of St. Paul the
       Apostle, 1976. 93p. ED 137421.
       This second edition of "Poverty Profile", published by
the Missionary Society of St. Paul the Apostle as part of their
Campaign for Human Development, updates the data examined in the
earlier (1972) edition and examines some of the current social welfare programs designed to alleviate the effects of poverty. The

extent to which poverty affects millions of Americans is discussed and specific groups such as the elderly poor, children, the rural poor, the urban poor, and the working poor, along with the racial-ethnic distribution of poverty are addressed. Various standards that are used to measure poverty, such as the poverty index and the one half of the median income index are defined and explained. A variety of government sponsored programs such as the U.S. Department of Agriculture's Food Assistance Programs, Title VII and Title XX for the elderly are discussed. Also included is an explanation of myths and facts about welfare programs and welfare recipients. A short bibliography on poverty, hunger, the elderly, employment, housing, health, social welfare programs, and other poverty related issues is included.

342. Handbook for preparing job classifications, by John C. Thomas. Iowa City, Institute of Public Affairs, University of Iowa. 121p. ED 099590.

To assist local governments in their responsibility for eliminating and preventing discrimination in employment based on race, color, religion, sex, or national origin as specified by the Equal Employment Opportunity Act of 1972, the handbook provides guidelines for analyzing jobs and preparing job classifications (defining; listing duties performed; listing related knowledges, abilities, skills; employment qualifications). The main portion of the document (110 pages) consists of sample job classifications for approximately 50 positions commonly found in municipal government. Each classification description contains the four parts of job classification mentioned above. All or most of the major and typical duties of a city's class should be expected to be contained in the sample class. To further aid in the construction of a municipal classification plan, a comprehensive outline of common clerical job duties has been included. An outline of job responsibility and difficulty and explanation of types of supervision is also included.

343. Early perceptions of the Comprehensive Employment and Training Act. Washington, DC, National Academy of Sciences, 1974. 39p. ED 110822.

A Committee on Evaluation of Employment and Training Programs was established by the National Academy of Sciences to assess the impact of the passage of the Comprehensive Employment and Training Act (CETA), which created a shift of control of manpower programs from Federal to State and local officials. At the first committee meeting a panel of five participants, representing Congress; the Department of Labor; and State, county, and city governments, presented its perceptions and expectations of CETA. The document contains the five presentations of panel members (Daniel Krivit, William Kolberg, George Basich, Jon Weintraub, and Thomas Nagle) which deal with the issues and problems of decentralization, decategorization, Federal role, State and local role, capabilities of local government, political leadership and ramifications, program coordination and cooperation, public employment provisions, management decisions, training needs, and funding.

344. This union cause; an illustrated history of labor unions in
      America. Revised edition. Detroit, United Automobile,
      Aerospace, and Agricultural Implement Workers of
      America, October 1974. 33p. ED 130974.
      This pamphlet on labor history highlights some of labor's
economic and political actions during the past 200 years. The purpose is to provide inspiration and motivation for greater participation in union work. The introduction explains the purpose of unions--
to pursue economic independence and social stature for all individuals
--for defenseless people, minorities, aged, and youth. The booklet
contains short historical descriptions of labor topics, each accompanied by an illustrative picture. Topics include descriptions of colonial indentured servants; early factory conditions; the first strike
by Cordwainers; workingmen's political parties; Negro slave labor;
the end to slavery after the Civil War; the melting pot; higher education as a union cause; the squalid life of miners; the Haymarket
Riot; birth of the AFL; the Pullman strike; working women; the seamen's fight; the Wobblies; steel unions; political friends of organized
labor; economic depression of 1930s; formation of CIO; the Reuther
brothers; battles between labor and industry; Labor's Magna Charta;
collective bargaining; and the slogan "Bread, Freedom, and Peace."
An accompanying film and set of posters can be obtained for rent
or purchase from the UAW Education Department, 8000 E. Jefferson
Ave., Detroit, Michigan 48214.

345. The History of the labor movement in the United States; a
      bibliography, by Luvenia Compton. 1976. 120p. ED
      139732.
      The bibliography covers the history of the labor move-
ment in the United States from Colonial times through the 1970s.
It has been compiled almost entirely from books and periodicals
available in the California Polytechnic State University Library at
San Luis Obispo, California. Most of the entries have been published since the 1930s, with almost one-half published since the
1960s. The sources range from scholarly journals to short articles
in popular magazines. The bibliography contains listed works about
significant individuals such as William H. Taft, Joe Hill, and Henry
Ford. Citations are given for books and articles focusing on collective bargaining, American Federation of Labor, New Deal, steel,
and strikes. The 1,560 entries are numbered consecutively in alphabetical order by author. A subject index of 296 terms is provided
as a reference to various aspects of the labor movement. Format
includes author, source, pages, and date. A journal source list
concludes the bibliography.

346. The Characteristics and role of illegal aliens in the U.S.
      labor market; an exploratory study, by David S. North
      and Marion F. Houstoun. Washington, DC, Linton and
      Company, March 1976. 330p. ED 133420.
      Data on the characteristics and labor market experiences
of illegal aliens in the U.S. work force were collected by voluntary
interviews with 793 apprehended illegal immigrants who had worked
at least two weeks in the U.S. From the resulting diverse col-

lection of case histories, it was concluded that (1) illegal workers in the U.S. are likely to be disadvantaged persons with little education and few skills and employed in low-level jobs. (Most reported employment as the primary motive for migration and sent an average of $105 a month to their homeland to help support an average of 4.6 people); and (2) since illegal workers are successful in finding low-level jobs due to work experience in their own countries, and appear to be highly motivated and productive, an increasing supply of illegal aliens is likely to depress the educational and skill level of the workforce, depress labor standards in the secondary sector, cause displacement of low-skill legal resident workers, and create a new class of disadvantaged workers. Data are provided for the survey respondents on demographic characteristics, work experience, backhome socioeconomic conditions, reasons for migration, and on their contact with various governmental systems. U.S. immigration policy and practices are discussed, as well as the role and impact of illegals on the U.S. labor market. Appended to the report are results of another survey of illegal immigrants and the interview schedule.

347. Youth labor markets and the military, by Richard Cooper. Santa Monica, CA, Rand Corporation, March 1978. 52p. ED 163199.

This paper argues that the military plays an extremely important role in youth labor markets by providing not only jobs but also experience and training which can later be transferred to the civilian labor market. Following the introduction, section II examines the military's demand for labor; its fluctuations due to secular, cyclical, and seasonal variables; and its impact on the youth labor market. The military is an important factor in the youth labor market, and it is becoming an important one also in the minorities and women's labor markets. Section III considers the supply side effects of military service by discussing the flow between the military and civilian youth labor markets, the variables that affect the decisions of enlisting or leaving the military, and the human capital accumulation gained through military work experience that can then be used in the civilian manpower pool. Sections IV and V explore the military's impact on youth unemployment, focusing on demographic trends over time and the black unemployment problem. In section VI it is concluded that the paper's findings have several implications for the measurement and collection of data on the youth labor market, specifically in the areas of (1) youth unemployment rates which should include military as well as civilian labor, (2) aggregate labor force statistics which should be subdivided to reflect factors such as age and race, and (3) special labor force data which should acknowledge an individual's military experience.

348. Peak use of peak years; an examination of mid-career potential, edited by Forbes Bottomly. Washington, DC, Council of Chief State School Officers, 1975. 133p. ED 132117.

The report examines the needs and methods for administrative self-renewal from several viewpoints--Forbes Bottomly,

Terrel Bell, Ralph Nader, Price Cobbs, Malcolm Knowles, Philip
Swain, and Edward Brainard. The introduction notes that rates of
change in all fields of education are increasing, but the infusion of
techniques and ideas via new personnel is slowing. Average age
and service time of administrators is increasing and in order to
retain and improve the competence of administrators, techniques of
adult learning are needed. A critical examination of our consumer
society is tied into examining the educational system itself as a
product, one which should be consumer oriented and accountable.
From a psychiatric view, mid-career is a time of crises--in motivation, outlook, confidence, and morale. Recognizing these problems
and finding methods to deal with them are of top priority. Basic to
this is the need to view education as a lifelong process of developing
roles for coping with life. Another report examines the dynamics
of implementing training programs in a business firm. Recognizing
that industry has its particular problems with management renewal,
it stresses that the receptiveness of the administrator is basic to
the success of the program. The concluding report examines the
experience of the Colorado state school system in setting up a program, describing the administrator renewal concept, the characteristics of effective district programs, and how the Department of
Education is helping the districts set up their programs. The balance of the report deals with a presentation and panel discussion of
the United States-OECD Forum of Educational Leaders 1975 retreat,
a roster of conference speakers and biography.

349. How to get a job; it's your move. Columbus, Ohio State
        Bureau of Employment Services, 1976. 26p. ED
        152976.
        Providing helpful hints for the job seeker, this booklet
is designed to increase the reader's chances for getting a good job.
The contents are divided into four sections. Section one presents
the following forms to help the job seeker identify possible choices:
personal checklist, skills learned in everyday life, and list of possible jobs. The second section provides instructions on how and where
to look for a job. The third section discusses how to apply for the
job, including the job application and interview. The final section
presents tips for evaluating a job-search plan. The following materials are attached: instructions for writing a resume, a sample
resume, a sample covering letter, and a sample job application
form.

350. Leisure; perspectives on education and policy, by Max Kaplan.
        1978. 124p. ED 155154.
        This compilation of essays presents a broad introduction
to substantive issues entering into leisure studies, placing emphasis
on the matters of values, goals, and lifestyles. Specific educational
perspectives are discussed through such aspects as language, futurology, the arts and recreation, and human values and religion. Related social policy issues considered include aging, the urban framework, business, labor and new work patterns, and the design profession. The twelve essays, appearing either as first publications
or revisions of previously presented material, are grouped into three

categories--introduction to concepts of leisure, educational perspectives, and policy perspectives. The essay titles follow: (1) "Origins of the New Leisure: Four Mini-Revolutions"; (2) "New Concepts of Leisure Today"; (3) "Leisure Education--For Whom, With Whom, By Whom"; (4) "A New Language for a New Leisure"; (5) "Personal Tensions, Leisure, and Futurology"; (6) "The Arts and Recreation"; (7) "Leisure, Human Values, and Religion"; (8) "The Urban Framework for New Work and Leisure"; (9) "The Implications of Leisure Theory for Gerontology"; (10) "Leisure and the Design Profession"; (11) "Business, Labor, and the Four-Day Work Week"; and (12) "Leisure and the General Process of Theory/Policy."

351. Leisure and career development at mid-life, by Carl McDaniels. 1976. 58p. ED 155577.

This collection of papers represents the thoughts of five faculty members from three different divisions in the College of Education at Virginia Polytechnic Institute and State University, who have been working together on the topic over the past 12 months. The papers represent an attempt to think through the entire interrelationship between leisure and career development at mid-life. The first paper articulates the basic issues in this relationship, setting the stage for the papers to follow. The remaining papers deal with the contributions of Adult Education, Vocational-Technical Education, recreation, and the special problems of minorities and women, all as they relate to the leisure-career development process at mid-life.

352. Mid-life career change, by Leon Bramson and Lisa Kohn. 1975. 128p. ED 156826.

This report deals primarily with the literature involving mid-career changes within the paid labor force. Changes from unpaid to paid employment and the career shift of the housewife who joins or rejoins the labor force are considered, but shifts to unpaid work, volunteer jobs, and early retirement without a second career are not included. The focus of this examination of career change emphasizes a shift in the occupational field to a new career pattern. The information based on a literature review is organized in the following manner: definitions of mid-career change and other related terms; potential interest in mid-career change; historical, sociological perspectives on work; theories of adult development and mid-life crisis; policy and reform; and programs to facilitate career change. Research recommendations conclude the report. Annotated bibliographies from several sources are included in the appendixes.

12.
RURAL
AND
REGIONAL
TOPICS

353. Poverty in Mississippi; a statistical analysis, by Tommy W.
Rogers. Jackson, Office of Human Resources and Community Services, June 1977. 469p. ED 151456.
This study addresses major identifying characteristics
of the poor in Mississippi. These include problems which are apparent from a study of census data and other secondary materials,
such as family composition, family size and occupation, and socioeconomic and demographic attributes. Mississippi has changed from
a one crop economy to a diversified economy. Mississippi has the
largest proportion of poor families and persons of any State and
poverty is more frequent among persons over the age of 65, persons
living alone, black families, female headed families, and rural residents. Mississippi also has the largest proportion of school age
children in poverty. Poverty is more severe among blacks than
whites. Mississippi has the lowest per capita income, but it has
been increasing in both relative and absolute terms. Levels of
formal education attained by the population have rapidly improved
except for blacks. Much remains to be accomplished in the provision of adequate housing. Ameliorative steps suggested include
policies relating to migration, selective placement programs, tax-
ation, educational opportunity, employment opportunities, retirement
plans, and minimum wage legislation. Three analytical models are
presented as a means of assisting action agencies to identify and interpret data in terms of the role of particular agencies and what this
means with respect to their resources.

354. Rural White poverty in the Mid-South, by Lewis H. Smith and
Brian Rungeling. Austin, TX, Center for the Study of
Human Resources, December 1973. 176p. ED 149948.
In an effort to present a descriptive verbal picture of
white nonmetropolitan poverty in the Mid-South and to identify those
factors contributing to white rural poverty, 1970 census figures were
analyzed in conjunction with survey results derived from responses
to an 83-item questionnaire made by a random sample of 106 poverty
families living in three counties. General characteristics of the

white population of the Mid-South were identified as well as poverty-specific characteristics of the Mid-South population. Differential poverty in the Mid-South was analyzed in terms of white and black and metropolitan and rural populations. White poverty in three randomly selected non-metropolitan counties was analyzed in terms of county poverty variations and population attitudes. Correlates of poverty in the Mid-South were assessed in terms of intercounty variations in the poverty rate. Results indicated that in the rural Mid-South: the percent of the white population on an income below the generally accepted poverty cutoff exceeded that of other white populations; poverty of the aged was significant; health problems were significant among the unemployed in the surveyed population; low levels of educational quality/quantity attainment were associated with poverty; underemployment of males and females was comparatively severe, associated with the "discouraged worker" phenomenon, and the industrial structure; a relationship existed between the absolute and/or relative size of the black population and white poverty and between relative isolation, absolute county size, and white poverty.

355.   The Extent and distribution of poverty in Mississippi, by
          Tommy W. Rogers. Jackson, Office of Human Resources
          and Community Services, June 1976. 335p. ED 133415.
          Statistical and descriptive data are used to analyze the
location, incidence, characteristics and general dimensions of poverty
in Mississippi. The following areas are examined: Mississippi's
population structure, the development of public concern with anti-
poverty measures and the State's economic structure in terms of its
income sources and its labor force. The paper identifies major
characteristics and problems of the poor which are apparent from
the study of the census data and other available materials. These
include family composition, family size, nutrition, health, income,
and education. Extensive statistical detail is found in the two appendices.

356.   Poverty in the lower Rio Grande Valley of Texas; historical
          and contemporary dimensions, by Michael V. Miller and
          Robert Lee Maril. Texas Agricultural Experiment Sta-
          tion, Texas A & M University, August 1978. 90p. ED
          158911.
          Relative to other urbanized areas, the Lower Rio Grande
Valley of Texas consistently ranks at the bottom in regard to almost
every objective indicator of socioeconomic welfare: per capita income, educational attainment, employment, and health and housing
conditions. The 1970 census discovered that approximately one-half
of its population, comprised primarily of Mexican Americans, fell
below government designated poverty thresholds. Based on a multidimensional approach, including assessment of the region and population in dynamic and longitudinal terms rather than as static en-
tities, this paper provides a broad overview of the region's poverty
through the synthesis of existing literature and data. The paper
provides a brief sketch of the Valley; addresses the nature and extent of real poverty (the poverty status accorded on the basis of in-

come below government established criteria) in the region by reference to data on income, education, employment, housing and health;
addresses the question of regulated poverty (the differential distribution of real poverty across ethnic or racial groups) via a historical
discussion of the region as an ethnically stratified social system;
and, stimulated by the relative poverty concept (calls attention to
cultural definitions and individual subjective evaluations of poverty
status), establishes the hypothesis that the region may be sociologi-
cally approached as a "staging area", characterized by five on-going
and interrelated mobility patterns.

357. Poor, rural, and Southern, by Robert E. Anderson, Jr.
     New York, Ford Foundation, December 1978.   25p.
     ED 165943.
          Despite political gains and the lowering of social barriers,
most Southern blacks still face formidable economic obstacles.   More
than half of rural Southern black families are living at or below
poverty level.   Efforts to improve their lot have included a number
of cooperative and self-help community programs.   The Southern
Cooperative Development Fund, the Mississippi Action for Community
Education, and the Southeast Alabama Self-Help Association are
among those receiving large scale assistance from the Ford Foundation.   The common goal of the three organizations is to enable those
who wish to remain in the South to do so by providing a social and
economic environment in which people can live and work with dignity
and security.   Their combined efforts include: funding to establish
consumer, agricultural marketing and fishing cooperatives and credit
unions; scholarships and other types of educational assistance; lobbying efforts; advancement of civil rights; demands for equalization of
community services; creation of ombudsman agencies for the rural
poor; establishment of health care services; and economic development of manufacturing, housing, construction, and financial services.
This document reports on the growth of each of the three organizations and describes specific projects undertaken to provide opportunities and a better life for the South's rural poor.

358. Toward a platform for rural America; report of the National
     Conference on Rural America.   Washington, DC, Rural
     America, Inc., May 1975.   65p.   ED 110256.
          A distillation of hundreds of speeches, working papers,
panel sessions, informal discussions, and formal resolutions, this
report is derived from the First National Conference on Rural
America (April 1975) and reflects emergence of a rural political
platform.   Attended by approximately 1,500 people from 49 States,
Puerto Rico, and Canada, the conference was divided into 12 basic
subject areas, which constitute the following major report divisions:
(1) Self-Government in Rural America; (2) Rural Poverty; (3) Land,
Resources, and People; (4) Rural Health; (5) Agricultural Production;
(6) Employment, Jobs, and Training; (7) Housing and Community
Development; (8) Energy and Rural People; (9) Public Education; (10)
Rural Economic Development; (11) Rural Public Transportation; (12)
Rural Justice and Legal Assistance.   Major themes found interwoven
among these 12 areas of concern are identified as follows: (1) the

belief that sooner or later everyone will move to the cities and live
happily ever after is "factually false and morally offensive"; (2) a
new national policy is needed which recognizes the right of people to
live where they choose and is sensitive to the survival of rural
America; (3) Congress must redress long-standing rural inequities;
(4) solutions to rural problems must be "rural" solutions; (5) to
avoid the urban emphasis in national planning rural "desks" should
be established in appropriate Federal agencies.

359. The Small town in America; a guide for study and community
        development, by Bert E. Swanson and Richard A. Cohen.
        Rensselaerville, NY, Institute on Man and Science, 1977.
        235p. ED 171440.
        Small town community improvement planning is often
subjected to urban type analysis. When concepts applicable to the
largest cities are grafted onto small towns, a misunderstanding of
small town problems and prospects is often the result. Social ecology offers a framework for understanding what a small town is, how
it functions, and what is uniquely important about it. It focuses on
four dimensions: (1) social structure; (2) the local economy; (3) influence patterns; and (4) cultural norms. These dimensions are
highly interrelated and to understand a small town (population less
than 10,000) without coming to grips with them is "impossible, inadequate, and seriously misleading". In this manual the basic elements of social ecology are explored. Chapter II discusses the
social structure of a small town--the characteristics and dynamics
of grouping small towners according to indicators of status and prestige. Chapter III presents the local economy as an essential analytic component, and Chapter IV explores the patterns of influence--
who shapes opinions, where decisions are made, and how government is implemented. Chapter V's discussion of cultural norms
involves both the kinds of beliefs and values and the institutions
that generate and preserve them. In each chapter a discussion guide
lists tasks to assist the reader in applying the concepts toward his
own community. The final chapter integrates the four dimensions
and discusses their meaning for small town problem solving.

360. Small towns in rural America; a study of the problems of
        small towns in Idaho, by J.R. Hamilton. Moscow,
        Agricultural Experiment Station, University of Idaho,
        April 1976. 160p. ED 139573.
        Using aggregate data from several Idaho counties and
towns, the study examined the economic forces which pressure small
town people and merchants--pressures which ultimately shape and
will shape small towns in areas like Idaho. Six towns chosen for
intensive study were Priest River, Cottonwood, Riggins, Shoshone,
Oakley, and Malad. Focusing on small towns and their businesses,
the study examined the: regional economic theory (location and
regional economics) by providing a spatial model of small towns;
relationship between the range of goods and services and the town
size; and relation between community size, migration, and the expenditure patterns of local governments by using cross-section
county data. It was found that: costs of providing public services

was related to population changes, and local access to commercial goods and services was also closely related to population. The evidence on public services seemed to support the contention that small communities suffer from significant diseconomies of small scale and that outmigration imposes an additional burden of increased cost on those people who remain. Transportation improvements have allowed residents of a small town-based community to have better access to the goods and services of nearby larger towns. The elimination of jobs in the countryside has reduced the role of some small towns in line with the reduced population to be served.

361.   Regional planning and development; organization and strategies,
            by Anne S. Williams and William R. Lassey. Bozeman,
            Agricultural Experiment Station, Montana State University,
            June 1974. 135p. ED 124361.
            Illustrating components of multi-county organization and
emphasizing the rewards of area organization when carefully used as
a tool to close the gaps between local, state, and Federal governments, this monograph presents the following five chapters: (1)
"Key Factors in Area or Regional Boundary Delineation" (natural
physical, biological, and human processes; spatial, social, political,
and government organization; economic criteria); (2) Federal, State,
and Local Programs Emphasizing Regions" (dispensing the Federal
dollar; coordination of planning/development programs; planning
grants; rural areas; economic development areas/districts; resource
conservation and development projects; community action programs;
state-created or supported multi-county areas; councils of government; privately sponsored development organizations); (3) "-Processes,
Problems, and Requirements of Regional Organization and Planning";
(4) "Organization and Action Strategies" (degrees of citizen participation; identification with the new area; maximizing effective involvement; formal planning process; a planning process model; the action-
planning concept; the role of professional staff as advocates; single-
purpose and comprehensive planning; change strategies; resistance to
change; living with conflict); (5) "Regional Multi-County Areas as a
Tool for Planning and Development.

362.   Reasons and underlying philosophies for living in the country,
            by Herbert Lionberger. August 1978. 59p. ED 158932.
            Six ideological types of rural residents were defined
to represent empirically determined reasons and underlying philosophies for living in the country, addressing a need to look at aspects
of the growing nonfarm contingent of rural population, especially
as it concerns extension program needs. The types were descrip-
tively named Committed Farmers, Reluctant Residents, Nature Lov-
ers, Guests of the Country, Child "Raisers", and Agrarian Corner-
stones. Rural residents Q-sorted 90 items representing diverse
reasons (farming as individual achievement, business, cornerstone
of society, escape release, child raising, naturist) and philosophies
(Protestant ethic, consumerism, new naturalism, agrarianism, human-
ism) and rated reasons for rural living to provide a congruency test
for factored types. Net results showed high congruency between

types and rated reasons. No type was primarily committed to farming either as a business or to make money--even committed farmers rated quality of life issues and importance of farming to society over making money. No retirement-oriented type emerged, despite many retired and semiretired respondents--retirement concerns came after basic ideologies and quality of life reasons. Commitment to country living varied from Reluctant Residents longing for urban culture to those who saw farming as a cornerstone of society. There were no highly rated consensus items among types.

363. <u>Mountain Heritage.</u> Revised edition by B.B. Maurer. Ripley, WV, Mountain State Art and Craft Fair, October 1975. 341p. ED 135543.

Written by West Virginia scholars, this resource book consists of 12 chapters and is designed to: (1) produce understanding and appreciation of West Virginians' cultural heritage, and (2) aid in developing cultural educational programs. Beginning with man's entry into the mountain wilderness, the contents progressively move through his cultural development, arts and crafts, use of language, folklore and literature, folk music, family and home, religion, Black culture, and a cultural overview of the Mountain State on the eve of the Bicentennial. These are followed by sections on folk and religious songs (with guitar chords) and folk and square dances (complete with calls and instructions) of the region. Biographical sketches of the authors are included.

364. <u>Appalachia; a reference book</u>, by Jonathan Linkous. Washington, DC, Appalachian Regional Commission, June 1977. 84p. ED 143474.

With a total area of 197,116 square miles, the Appalachian Region has an uneven distribution of population, income, wealth, and natural resources. The Region's 19 million people live in 397 counties and 5 independent cities in Virginia, which range in population size from 2.6 thousand to 1.5 million. Under 50% of the population live in metropolitan counties while only 25% live in rural counties. Economic productivity varies from one-sixth above the national average in Allegheny County, Pennsylvania, to less than one-fourth of the U.S. level in the poorest county in eastern Kentucky. Huge reserves of good coal are found in some counties, while others are without economically significant mineral resources. Appalachia also varies in the population's age structure, racial and ethnic composition, educational attainment, labor force participation, poverty levels, health conditions and services, and other facets of economic life and socioeconomic well-being. This reference book presents information on the Region's topography; population change; population concentration and dispersal; population growth trends by county groups; population ethnicity; population 65 years of age and older; labor force, employment, and unemployment trends; employment by industry; personal income; poverty status of families; educational attainment and school enrollment; nonfederal physicians; infant mortality trends; housing; coal production; mineral industry establishments; agricultural and farm land; and local governments.

365. Appalachia; goals, objectives, and development strategies.
     Washington, DC, Appalachian Regional Commission,
     December 1977. 85p. ED 156375.
          Goals, objectives, and strategies for development in
the 13 states involved in the Appalachian Regional Commission (ARC)
are detailed in this document adopted by ARC in 1977. The regional
development plan incorporates earlier evaluation and program design
efforts, discussion from an issues report, state comments and development plans, and public meetings results. A section on Appalachia today records conditions (geography, population, jobs, incomes,
housing and community facilities, health and education, energy,
natural resources, government) and issues (growth, human services,
natural resources, cooperation between governments and government
and the private sector). Regional goals are discussed in terms of:
economic development and institutional demonstration of this Federal
multistate mechanism for improved performance of government. The
last half of the document covers development policies (aimed at
achieving the most return from limited funds allocated to help the
region solve its special problems and promote its economic development) and development strategies, under which objectives for seven
major functional areas are outlined: transportation, community development (in rural, suburban, and urban areas), human services
(health, education, child development), energy, natural resources,
and government.

13.
SPORTS
AND
RECREATION

366. <u>Violence in Sports,</u> by Donald L. Cooper. 1978. 14p. ED
174596.
Increasing violence in sports is deplored, and a warning
is issued on an apparent trend toward antisocial behavior. Contact
sports such as hockey and football are cited as typically engendering
aggression among athletes, but spectator sports (boxing, car racing,
basketball, and baseball) are also singled out as eliciting increasing
violence on the part of the fans attending these events. Several specific incidents are described.

367. <u>Pearl Harbor; a failure for baseball?</u> by Richard C. Crepeau.
Paper presented at the annual convention of the North
American Society for Sport History, June 1976. 17p.
ED 130993.
The history of sports is closely tied to the larger history
of the society in which they are played. Baseball in the United
States in the 1920's and 1930's assumed a major role in spreading
the ideals of fair play, sportsmanship, and democracy to the Far
East, with tours by amateur athletes and professionals such as Lou
Gehrig and Babe Ruth. Even after the passage of the Immigration
Act of 1924, it was felt that Baseball Diplomacy should continue in
order to lessen Japanese resentment at American racial prejudice.
The ideals of the early thirties, both in sports and diplomacy, were
slowly dispelled by activities in the European sphere, where nations
were preparing for war. The major baseball-related news from
Japan, after successful tours in 1934, 1935, and 1936, came in
1940, when radio broadcasting of professional games ceased, and
English playing terms and team names were replaced by Japanese
words. In August of 1940, baseball was abolished in Japan, and on
December seventh, Pearl Harbor was attacked. The sports world
tried to explain the deed as a weakness in the Japanese national
character, rather than as a failure of the civilizing role of baseball,
and threw itself fully into the war effort. A period of idealism and
naivete was coming to an end, and, sports slowly came to recognize
the fact, just as did the rest of society.

368. The Soviet physical fitness tests; an essential aspect of the
     Soviet organizational plan, by Reet Howell. Paper pre-
     sented at the annual meeting of the American Alliance
     for Health, Physical Education and Recreation, April
     1976. 27p. ED 124500.
          This study analyzes the Soviet award system, in par-
ticular the Prepared for Word and Defense (PWD) program. The
PWD program is composed of five stages and embraces people from
ages 10 to 60. Each stage has a section of requirements and a
section of norms, which take into consideration age variations. The
norms section, which is the most important part of the total complex, deals with items that test physical fitness and motor skill-
abilities. Upon completion of both the requirements and norms at
each level, silver or gold badges are awarded as well as a badge
with honors at stage four. The requirements section deals with
basic principles of physical culture, personal and social hygiene
habits, morning exercises, and fundamentals of civil defense. The
five stages of the PWD program are: (1) brave and agile (boys and
girls 10-13 years); (2) the rising sports generation (boys and girls
14-15 years); (3) physical perfection (men 19-39 years, women 19-
34 years); and (5) vigor and health (men 40-60 years, women 35-55
years). The PWD system is an essential part of the Soviet organizational plan, which is concerned with mass participation and the
development of the elite, super-athlete. (The requirements, exercises, and norms for each stage are presented in tables.)

369. The Health Spa industry and the profession, by Glenn Swengros.
     Paper presented at the annual convention of American
     Association for Health, Physical Education and Recre-
     ation, April 1976. 17p. ED 124522.
          During the past three decades, the health spa industry
has grown to become a viable component of our society. Many
people, however, still have reservations about the sincerity of health
spa proprietors. This is a result of non-professional management
in the first years of business. Today the health spa industry finds
itself with changed perspectives, modified objectives, restructured
priorities, and redefined responsibilities. To meet these vicissitudes
and challenges, the industry is undergoing a transformation defined by
the following criteria: professional management; long range profit maxi-
mization objectives; large capital investments and permanent facilities;
extensive advertising and promotion covering large geographic areas and
encompassing all media; establishment of a structured pricing policy;
permanent and professional programs of instruction and supervision;
regulation of activities at the federal, state, and local levels; and institutions of a total recreational concept. Recently, Health Industries, Inc.,
operators of European Health Spas, formed the Association of Physical
Fitness Centers. The primary objective of the organization is to provide
a vehicle for its members to police its own industry. Through this
association and the hiring of staff with professional backgrounds, the
health spa industry is seeking to provide professional, reliable
service to the consumer.

370. The Effect of New York's elite athletic clubs on American

amateur athletic governance, 1870-1915, by Richard
Wettan and Joe Willis. 1975. 28p. ED 110429.
During the early history of amateur athletics, the large
and affluent athletic clubs--mostly in New York City--took the initiative in the formation of the first associations of amateur clubs, the
National Association of Amateur Athletes of America (NAAAA), and
its successor, the Amateur Athletic Union (AAU). Athletic clubs
in New York City in the nineteenth century were stratified along
religious, ethnic, occupational, political, and social class lines.
These factors had a significant impact on the athletic associations
and sport governing bodies. Although the NAAAA maintained that
it was the national governing body for amateur sport, it was never
capable of controlling professionalism and gambling, and never, in
reality, a national organization. In 1888 the New York Athletic Club
withdrew from the NAAAA to form the AAU. The AAU was then
the dominant association until these two organizations merged in
1890. During the next twenty-five years the power of the New York
clubs in the AAU declined. However, they still maintained their
influence on the AAU governing board through the hard work of
several of their representatives. The New York clubs were thus
able to hold positions of power in athletic club associations disproportionate with their numbers. The decisions and policies that
were made therefore may have favored these larger, upper middle
class male clubs. These affluent athletic clubs, however, gained a
respectability for sport which it otherwise would never have achieved.

371. Sport in the People's Republic of China; selected issues, by
Donald Chu. Paper presented at the convention of the
American Alliance for Health, Physical Education and
Recreation, April 1978. 27p. ED 161855.
Marxist/Maoist interpretations of sport in China differ
significantly from the functional and meritocratic perspectives in
the West which emphasize competition and personal reward. The
latter school stresses the ability of the upwardly mobile aspirant
to prove ability through competition. Individuals with talent are
placed in valued positions in society. Proponents of the Marxist/
Maoist school, however, view sport as traditionally a repressive
vehicle that legitimizes the already stratified society. Sport need
not, however, be repressive and can be consciously used to reshape
society and avoid anomie; the means and methods of sport can be
directed to avoid normlessness by emphasizing the cooperative spirit
in sport. It is clear that the image of sport in China is crucial; it
must conform to the image of cooperation rather than competition.
Historical analysis of the development of sport in China shows that
despite a long tradition against needless exertion, larger forces for
change (from the young and from women) may have contributed to
the rapid growth of sport. Sport has, in turn, been used by the
Communists to resocialize the masses in the modes of thought
deemed proper for a China capable of modernization and self-defense.

372. Physical Education and recreation in Europe, by M. L. Howell
and M. L. Van Vliet. Ottawa, Department of National

Health and Welfare, 1972. 72p. ED 127298.

Physical education and research programs, and recreational and athletic facilities, in Yugoslavia, Sweden, Denmark, Germany, England, and the U.S.S.R. are examined by two faculty members from the University of Alberta. This publication is an abridgement of their report on European approaches to physical education and recreation, giving their observations and the philosophy behind physical education in the countries visited, and listing practices and policies that could benefit Canadians. Each country visited is discussed in terms of general background, philosophy of physical education, recreational and sports organizations, research, teacher training, organization of sports, facilities, and general recommendations. Following are some of the features that have met with success in Europe and are summarized as recommendations for Canadians: (1) Establishment of a national training center for recreation leaders and coaches; a federal training camp for athletes and representative teams; a national research institute in physical education and sports medicine; and a national research institute to study present facilities. (2) Creation of a sports secretariat for all of Canada. (3) Initiation of an awards system for all adults and children, and greater promotion of provincial and national competitions for all age categories. (4) Development of a system of coaches paid by the federal government and working on a nationwide basis. (5) The introduction of two European sports--orienteering and European handball--to Canadians, and active promotion of both activities. (6) The provision of extensive playing fields for school and community use. (7) The launching of a national study aimed at the development of outdoor facilities that would encourage Canadians to make use of their scenic terrain. (8) Several features apply particularly to schools: encouragement of provincial and national sports schools; realistic provincial standards for facilities; greater emphasis on elementary school physical education; and development of small, inexpensive swimming pools for elementary school use.

373. The Historical aspects of the Pan American games, by Curtis R. Emery. Paper presented at the annual meeting of the American Alliance for Health, Physical Education and Recreation, 1975. 10p. ED 106290.

The purpose of this study was to produce an accurate account of the origin and development of the Pan American Games. A further purpose was to collect, organize, and systematically compile the results of competition for each festival, and to identify some noteworthy incidents in each series of games. The document first explains that the idea of the games originated when the Olympic Games schedule for Tokyo in 1940 could not be held. It states that the games were modeled after the Olympic Games and, in general, Olympic competition rules and regulations were to be followed. The 33 countries eligible to participate in the games are listed, and it is explained why the first series of games was not held until 1951. Since then, the games have been held every four years, the year before the Olympics. The document looks at each of the series of games individually in terms of location, number of participants, number of spectators, records set and broken, and other noteworthy incidents.

374. President's Commission on Olympic Sports; first report to the
President. Washington, DC, 1976. 141p. ED 121756.
Initial findings, conclusions, and recommendations, based
on studies during the commission's first five months of existence
concerning the current structure of amateur sports in the United
States, are presented in this document. It is shown that there is
no truly effective system for amateur athletics in this country, that
the system is influenced by the International Olympic Committee and
the international sports federations, and that the role of American
governing bodies differs from sport to sport. Significant differences
in systems in other countries are described in the areas of organization and management, mass participation, development programs,
financing, facilities, and competition. The need for reorganization
of amateur sports in the United States is emphasized, and ways are
suggested for accomplishing the reforms. A potential solution is
presented in the concept of a higher sports authority, which is
conceived as a permanent organization of national scope with responsibility for handling those essential functions not currently being
carried out by existing organizations and for mobilizing existing
financial, technical, and organizational resources in support of a
comprehensive national amateur sports effort. The goals and means
of implementation of a highest sports authority are discussed.

375. The Appalachian Trail; guidelines for preservation. University
Park, Department of Landscape Architecture, Pennsylvania State University, May 1977. 229p. ED 139592.
With increasing developmental pressure being asserted
on land resources, there is a need for identifying unique areas that,
once destroyed, may never be recouped. Many of the areas suffer-
ing from developmental encroachment are located on or along the
Appalachian Trail, which is a continuous footpath about 2,000 miles
long that follows the Appalachian mountain chain from Maine to
Georgia. The Appalachian Trail Study Group has studied four areas
of the Trail (Michaux State Forest, Cumberland Valley, Saint Anthony's Wilderness, and Kittatinny Mountain) and has attempted to
provide a workable trail protection strategy for use by local planners and others concerned with protecting the Trail. In studying
the four areas, the Study Group examined the site, alternative routes,
soils, geology, vegetation, wildlife, and the amenities of the area.
The strategy devised consists of five steps from the pre-development
planning of land use to better design solutions for those segments
passing through various land developments. Emphasizing physical
design solutions, this guide recommends corridor widths for various
landform vegetation and land use situations; suggests possible design solutions to specific problems that may arise; describes various legal and planning devices that may be used as part of a future
overall trail protection strategy; and discusses the role of the Federal, state, and local governments. A map showing the land ownership and areas with a high potential for access is included.

376. Elementary map and compass instruction, by Elston F. Larson. 1974. 15p. ED 087577.
The purpose of this booklet is to help teachers, scout-
masters, and other group leaders give elementary map and com-

pass instructions in a manner that is both simple and fun. It is intended to be a guide for a training course on this subject. Much of the text is taken directly from an actual training course and is written in the manner of a teacher talking to his students. The teacher, therefore, can give a part of his presentation by reading directly from this guide. Necessary materials and a setup of the instruction area are given. The instructor's presentation includes: The Map; The Compass; Directions; Orienting a Compass; Measurement; Competitive Compass Game; Combining Use of Map, Compass and Measurements; Method of Getting the Compass Degree Reading from the Map; and Practice Course Using Map and Compass.

377. Exercise and the knee joint, by H. H. Clarke. Washington, DC, President's Council on Physical Fitness and Sports, January 1976. 18p. ED 132149.
         This report by the President's Council on Physical Fitness and Sports examines the effects of various forms of physical exercise on the knee joint which, because of its vulnerability, is especially subject to injury. Discussion centers around the physical characteristics of the joint, commonly used measurements for determining knee stability, muscular and ligament strength. The deep knee bend, an exercise of highly questionable value in conditioning regimens, is criticized on the grounds that it contributes to chronic synovitis, promotes early arthritic onset, and produces gross knee instability. Exercise regimens are proposed and discussed for the treatment and prevention of knee injuries. Practical advice for the development of physical education and athletic programs justifiable from this review of knee joint exercise is given, and includes: (1) Exercises that unduly stretch or damage the ligaments of the knee should be avoided; (2) The deep knee bend should be used sparingly, if at all, in physical education and athletic conditioning, and substitutes should be developed such as bench stepping and weight training routines; (3) In performing knee bends for developing and maintaining the strength and endurance of the quadriceps muscles, a half knee bend is recommended; (4) Progressive resistance exercises of the muscles activating the knee joint should be routinely employed for the prevention of knee injuries and for the rehabilitation of the knee during postinjury or postsurgical rehabilitation. A bibliography of 37 citations is appended.

14.
BOOKS
AND
LIBRARIES

378.   What is this thing called book? a BARC workshop on the topic
        of the book, its materials, its manufacture, its care
        and treatment in libraries, its repair, and a word about
        fine printing and fine bindings, edited by Thomas S.
        Fowler. San Francisco, Bay Area Reference Center,
        San Francisco Public Library, March 1978. 36p. ED
        158736.
        Five speeches from a one-day workshop are concerned
with book manufacture, marketing decisions, preservation of books,
and binding techniques. Librarian Bonnie Jo Dopp defined terminology used in describing books and book manufacture, and mentioned the destructive action of acid in paper and the increasing use
by book publishers of perfect binding methods. Roger Levenson,
lecturer on the history of the book at University of California Berkeley and publisher, maintained that handsomely made books need not
come from fine presses or in limited editions--well-made, attractive books are entirely possible from the trade press, even when
employing computerized production techniques. Design, production,
life expectancy, quality of materials, and pricing practice in book
manufacture were discussed by publisher Frederick Murphy. Donald
Etherington reported on activities at the Library of Congress Preservation Office and described some of Library of Congress' very sophisticated restoration techniques together with advice for small in-
house operations to help and preserve materials in library collections. Susan Wilson, a Fellow of the Design Binders, briefly described several methods of binding books and outlined some of the
steps in hand binding.

379.   Handbook of reference sources. Second edition, by Margaret
        I. Nichols. Austin, Department of Library Development,
        Texas State Library, 1979. 341p. ED 174256.
        Designed to serve as a selection aid for small public
libraries and to list important sources available through the major
resource centers of the Texas Library System, this bibliography
lists 804 annotated reference sources with 126 additional works
named within the annotations. The books are grouped into 18 major

areas, each of which is broken down into smaller subsets: (1) Bibliographies, (2) General Reference Tools, (3) Encyclopedias, (4) Dictionaries, (5) General Bibliography and Genealogy; (6) Literature, (7) Visual Arts, (8) Performing Arts, (9) Philosophy and Religion, (10) Social Sciences, (11) Geography and Archaeology, (12) Education, (13) Political Science and Law, (14) Business and Economics, (15) History, (16) Sports, Hobbies, and Recreation, (17) Science, and (18) Applied Sciences. Of the total number of references (930), 310 are starred as most suitable for selection by a small library, and prices and International Standard Book Numbers are provided for most items. An index is included.

380. A Banquet of books; an assortment of engrossing books for all ages and reading levels. Winnipeg, Manitoba Department of Education, 1975. 216p. ED 117681.
     The books listed in this annotated bibliography have been selected to assist teachers, librarians, and other interested persons in choosing books for reluctant readers. The books present a wide range of high interest material which is not always at a low reading level. Books are listed in three categories: picture books, intended mostly for use with primary grade children; fiction--adventure and mystery, animal stories, fantasy and science fiction, sports stories, miscellaneous fiction, and story collections; and nonfiction--biography, haunted houses, monsters and UFO's, hobbies and crafts, the world of entertainment, Indians of North America, science, sports, wild animals and pets, wings and wheels, and the world at war. Annotations for each entry include bibliographic data, a brief description, print size, vocabulary range, and reading and interest levels.

381. Canadiana; Canada's National Bibliography; description and guide. Ottawa, National Library of Canada, 1978. 53p. ED 169891.
     This guide to the national bibliography of Canada includes works published in and about Canada, works by Canadian authors, and federal, provincial, and municipal government publications. "Canadiana" became operational in 1951 when bibliographic citations to monographs and serials were listed. As resources became available, more information and more types of materials were listed. Most recently, automation has been instituted. Brief discussions are provided of the purpose of the bibliography and its content, exclusions, and arrangement, including treatment and inclusions by material type-monographs, theses in microform, serials and monographic series, pamphlets, sound recordings, films, filmstrips, and videotapes, and Canadian government publications. Classification and cataloging procedures and a discussion of future directions are included, as well as a chronology of Canadiana inclusions since its inception in 1950 through 1978. Both English and the French versions are provided.

382. Volunteer assistance in the library, by Christine Kuras. Inglewood, CA, Public Library, 1975. 37p. ED 111399.
     Procedures for dealing with library volunteers developed by the staff of the Inglewood Public Library are presented. The

need for volunteer programs is discussed, as well as volunteer recruitment, selection and orientation, training and supervision, evaluation, recognition, and some problem areas. Forms, schedules,
publicity materials, and a short annotated bibliography are included.

383. Friends' organizations; the supportive element essential to
      libraries, by Dorothy Progar. 1975. 25p. ED 127998.
      Reviewed are the history and public relations, financial
and service roles of lay "Friends of the Library" groups. Programs and techniques useful in the pursuit of these roles are suggested. Guidelines for a constitution, fee schedule, and administrative structure plus a bibliography give potential friends organizations
help in establishing themselves as useful adjuncts to their community
library.

384. The National Library of Canada; twenty-five years after, by
      Ian Wees. Ottawa, National Library of Canada, 1978.
      59p. ED 168591.
      Although calls for a National Library began as early as
1883, the cornerstone of the future national library was the Canadian
Bibliographic Centre, established in 1950, which began work on the
national bibliography and national union catalog. When the National
Library of Canada was established in 1953 under the direction of
W. Kaye Lamb, the National Library Act became effective and
Canadian publishers were required by law to deposit two copies of
each new book they published at the National Library. From 1956
to 1966, the library moved to a different building, the staff began
cataloging the collections and organizing material transferred from
the Library of Parliament, and the organizational structure took
shape. In 1968, after another move to the National Library and
Archives Building, the Office of Library Resources was created
and Guy Sylvestre was appointed National Librarian. Since that
time, various new divisions have been created to deal with changing
needs, including the automation of library service.

385. The Public Library talks to you, by Alice Hagemeyer. Wash-
      ington, DC, Gallaudet College, 1975. 40p. ED 125221.
      Intended for deaf individuals, the booklet provides infor-
mation on services provided by the public library. Covered, in
question and answer format, are the following areas: definition of
library, what kind of people use the library, library services for
children, reference books, location of books using the catalog, newspapers, audiovisual materials, and deaf interpreters. Appended are
a sample catalog card, added entry cards, the Dewey decimal classification outline, Library of Congress classification outline, sample
reference questions, a message from the "Deaf Awareness Handbook
for Public Librarians," and suggestions for further reading on using
the library.

386. United States Information Service Libraries, by Jody Sussman.
      Urbana, Graduate School of Library Science, University
      of Illinois, 1973. 24p. ED 088440.
      Since the establishment of the pioneer USIS library in

Mexico City in 1942, the nature of The United States Information Service (USIS) libraries has been subject to political disputes. The question of whether or not they should function as propaganda arms or information centers still remains a polemical issue. The USIA became an independent agency of the executive branch of government in 1953. Since then, the number of U.S. Information centers has grown to its present level of 133. Each Center tailors its programs to meet the special needs of its own community. Generally, the Information Center Service maintains four types of programs: 1) libraries or cultural centers for the study of the U.S.; 2) a commercial book program to place more American-written books in bookstores and classrooms; 3) teaching English; and 4) exhibits of American achievement. Moreover, the Centers assist the Informational Media Guaranty Program and Binational Centers around the world. Since 1961, a policy has been made to withdraw funds from Western Europe and to use them in the developing nations. Funds are appropriated each year by Congress. The future of USIS libraries is as uncertain as ever-changing world politics, the availability of funds, and the predispositions of the current administration.

387.   Bibliotherapy; an overview and the librarian's role, by Sherry
         P. Chadbourne. September 1976. 42p.   ED 131426
         This document describes a literature search on bibliotherapy, discusses historical development and current trends in bibliotherapy, details the educational aims of bibliotherapy, and explores the part librarians should play in bibliotherapy, particularly when working with children and adolescents. Also included are a selected, annotated bibliography of bibliotherapy, a list of bibliographies of bibliotherapy, under the following categories: ethnic groups, family relations, peer relationships, accepting oneself, adoption, adjusting to change, broken home, death, lacking confidence, overcoming fear, plumpness, poverty, positive self-image, recognizing one's abilities, and religion.

388.   An Outline of how to plan a workshop, by Anne Roughton and
         Audrey Powers.   San Francisco, Bay Area Reference
         Center, San Francisco Public Library, August 1976.
         26p.   ED 136792.
         This is a revision of a guide (IR 003 265) for planning a library workshop. It is presented in five parts: (1) the workshop planners, (2) planning the program, (3) the day of the workshop, (4) evaluation and followup, and (5) information sources. The major part of the guide is concerned with program planning and covers needs assessment, objectives, audience definition, selection of time and place, equipment and materials, presentation techniques, speakers, budgeting, kit materials, display plans, announcements, and agenda. Most of the instructions are given in outline form as check lists, questions, or brief directions.

389.   Workshops; the educator's manual for coordinating the com-
         plete conference, by Alvin L. Taylor. Berkeley, Far
         West Laboratory for Educational Research and Develop-
         ment, May 1976. 27p.   ED 137426.

This document is an educator's manual for coordinating a complete conference. It was developed under contract for a General Assistance Center under Public Law 88-352 Civil Rights Act of 1964 Title IV "Desegregation of Public Education" Section 403 "Technical Assistance". The manual discusses the mechanics of planning a workshop and includes the following topics: objectives of the workshop, budget, attendance, convention bureaus, facility selection, content and scheduling, audio-visual equipment, and agenda. The mechanics of conducting the workshop are also discussed. These include the following topics: registration, the workshop, evaluation, adjournment, and follow-up activities. A list of characteristics of successful workshops is provided.

390. Library programs worth knowing about, by Ann Erteschik. Washington, DC, Bureau of School Systems, DHEW/OE, September 1977. 108p. ED 145858.
This publication highlights sixty-two outstanding projects originally funded under the Library Services and Construction Act. Designed as a descriptive, annotated guide, the catalog shares information about library programs selected from 34 states and territories to exemplify some of the diverse services stimulated by Federal funds. These innovative approaches to library services are successfully meeting the challenges presented by today's varied library constituencies, and are suggested in this source book as worthy of further investigation by other libraries. Librarians are encouraged to examine the entire book to identify program strategies, service delivery methods, evaluation techniques, and other project components.

391. Library community services, by Therese Correy. Inglewood, CA, Public Library, 1977. 99p. ED 157548.
Services to the elderly, institutionalized, and physically and mentally exceptional, who are unable to use the public library in its traditional form, are described in this guide to programs at the Inglewood (California) Public Library. Topics include: (1) overall library goals and activities; (2) functional and organizational structure of community services, internal relationships, and job descriptions; (3) Talking Book Service for the visually and/or physically handicapped--history, eligibility, registration procedures, sample forms, book selection, processing and circulation, service evaluation, and plans for additional service; (4) Braille book collection--history, selection, ordering, and circulation; (5) history of the brailler writing machine, charge out procedures, and users; (6) large print collection--selection, publishers, ordering and cataloging, shelving, circulation and the large print book catalog at the library; (7) extramural services (collections housed outside the library for those unable to visit)--collections, selection, processing and routing, audio materials, maintenance, and problems; (8) proposed service to shut-ins--organization, volunteers, shut-in eligibility, equipment and materials, procedures and reports, sample forms, and a booklet on guidelines to service; (9) additional programs for special patrons and publicity for them; and (10) plans for future development. Also included is a list of resources--books, periodicals, circulars, and films--of interest to others serving the community.

392. <u>Popular culture and the library</u>, edited by Wayne Wiegand.
Proceedings of the Current Issues Symposium II, School
of Library Science, University of Kentucky, October
1977. 70p. ED 158711.
This collection of four speeches given at a symposium
in October 1977 all deal with a particular aspect of popular culture--
reflecting the values, convictions, and patterns of thought generally
dispersed through and approved by society. The terms popular and
culture are defined separately and two definitions for the complete
term are considered--one dealing with products, the other with activities. The study of popular culture can bring people to a deeper
understanding of today's society, therefore the use of popular culture
materials, i.e., music, in the classroom, and in libraries is advocated. Guidelines for their acquisition and utilization are presented. Although there are problems connected with both, and these
are discussed, there is a trend in this country toward the utilization
of such materials. A popular culture librarian discusses this trend
and his education and role in building such a collection at Bowling
Green University.

393. <u>The Role of libraries in America</u>. Princeton, NJ, Gallup
Organization Inc., October 1975. 384p. ED 163950.
At the request of the Chief Officers of the State Library
Agencies, the Gallup Organization, Inc. studied attitudes and behavior
concerning the use of public libraries in America and reported their
findings. In the first phase of this national survey, 1,561 adult men
and women were asked their sources of information; the extent to
which the library served as a resource; their readership of books,
magazines, and newspapers; purpose for which books are read; the
type of books read; where books and magazines are obtained; their
incidence of library use; their encouragement of their children's library use; suggestions for library improvement; their awareness of
library funding; and their ownership of a library card. Based on
their replies to these questions, respondents were partitioned into
user and non-user groups and questioned regarding their particular
circumstances. The demographic information taken for crosstabular
analysis included sex, age, education, occupation, region of residence, and stage in life. Data are presented in 155 tables and a
summary of key findings is included.

394. <u>Procedures for salvage of water-damaged library materials</u>,
by Peter Waters. Washington, DC, Library of Congress,
1975. 40p. ED 108657.
Procedures for salvaging water-damaged books, film,
archives, and other library materials are outlined, from assessment
of damage to final returning books to shelves. Advice is given on
removing the materials, packing, freezing, drying, treating for
mold, sterilizing, removing mud, forming a salvage team, evaluating
losses, salvaging the catalog, keeping records, controlling humidity
and temperatures in work and storage areas, and handling the chemicals necessary in the process. Initial emergency procedures are
summarized. Appendixes list sources of assistance, services, supplies, and equipment.

395. An Index to the Caricatures in the "New York Review of Books" from its inception through the fifteenth anniversary issue (1963-1978), by Joseph G. Drazan and Phyllis Sanguine. 1978. 32p. ED 171264.

This index identifies caricatures drawn by David Levine which are found in the "New York Review of Books" from its first issue in 1963 through the special fifteenth anniversary issue dated October 12, 1978. The index is arranged alphabetically by surname for each personality caricatured, with some cross references. The numbering system used refers to the volume, issue number, and page on which that drawing can be located.

396. The Copyright revision act of 1976, by Earl W. Kintner. Washington, DC, Arent, Fox, Kintner, Plotkin & Kahn, December 1976. 57p. ED 165758.

Though not exhaustive, this report explains the substantive aspects of the Copyright Revision Act of 1976 that would be of interest to copyright proprietors and/or users of copyrightable works. The major part of the report deals with the subject matter and scope of copyright; topics discussed include fair use, reproduction by libraries and archives, ownership rights "in lawfully" made copies, exempt performances, cable television-secondary transmission, ephemeral recordings, sound recordings, recording rights in music, jukebox exemption, and public broadcasting. Other areas covered are the new scheme of statutory copyright, copyright ownership and transfer, the formalities necessary for enjoying the rights of copyright ownership, copyright infringement and remedies, manufacturing requirements in importation, the Copyright Royalty Tribunal, criminal offenses, and supplemental considerations. For quick reference, a summary of highlights from the Act is provided at the beginning.

397. Coping with copyright, by Elizabeth B. Merriam. Madison, Wisconsin State Department of Public Instruction, 1978. 25p. ED 172829.

Intended to help librarians, administrators, and trustees better understand the ramifications of the new copyright law, Public Law 94-553, this brief document asks and answers some of the basic questions concerning compliance with it. Questions answered include: What is the new copyright law? What are the implications for libraries? What is fair use? What are the copyright guidelines? What are the minimum requirements which a library should meet for compliance? Should your library adopt a copyright policy? What are the guidelines of the National Commission on New Technological Uses of Copyrighted Works (CONTU) relating to Subsection 108 (g)(2) (interlibrary arrangements for photocopying)? What record maintenance is necessary? What is copyright clearance? How will copyright law affect contractual arrangements for purchase of serials or other materials? What effect does the law have on local archives? and Who is liable under what circumstances? Appendices provide the minimum guidelines for classroom copying of books and periodicals in nonprofit educational institutions, guidelines under fair use for music, and CONTU guidelines for interlibrary loans: a bibliography of primary and secondary sources is also included.

398. Chinese folktales for children, Irene Kwok. San Francisco,
     Unified School District, 1976. 528p. ED 139258.
          This bilingual text contains ten traditional Chinese folk-
tales which have been rewritten for children.   Each story deals with
interpersonal relationships and/or stresses the Chinese way of life.
Each page of text is given first in English and then in Chinese and
is illustrated with a full-page drawing.   The titles of the folktales
are: (1) "One Winter Night"; (2) "The Story of a Tiger"; (3) "The
Greedy Fly"; (4) "The Little Brother"; (5) "The Man Who Shot the
Sun"; (6) "The Old Woman and the Chimpanzee"; (7) "The Stolen
Duck"; (8) "The Story of a Smart Boy"; (9) "The Story of Ng Fung";
and (10) "The Story of the Sword."

399. Notable Canadian children's books, by Irene Aubrey. Ottawa,
     National Library of Canada, 1974. 103p. ED 136815.
          This annotated bibliography dealing with Canadian child-
ren's books aims to show the historical development of the literature.
Included within the bibliography are: (1) notable Canadian books from
the eighteenth century to the modern period, (2) lists of books which
were awarded a bronze medal for the years 1947-1975, and (3) a
list of fiction for the young French Canadian.   Although historically
Canadian children's literature has been sparse, the notable improvement of late in the quality of writing, illustration, and overall design and production is encouraging.   Introductory materials are in
both French and English; parts 1 and 2 of the bibliography are in
English, and part 3 is in French.

400. Child and tale; the origins of interest, by Andre Favat. Ur-
     bana, IL, National Council of Teachers of English, 1977.
     112p. ED 137830.
          The purposes of this study were to investigate the phe-
nomenon of children's interest in fairy tales, to identify the point at
which the reader's interest corresponds most highly with the nature
of a book or story, and to analyze the sources of data that lead to
common characteristics between reader and tale.   Chapters include
discussions of analytic methodologies for gauging children's interest
in fairy tales, psychological and literary sources of information, the
establishment of correspondences between children and fairy tales,
explanations of children's interest in fairy tales, and implications
for parents, teachers, and researchers.   It was concluded that,
generally, fairy tales embody an accurate representation of the child's
conception of the world.   Children are attracted by the predictability
of fairy tales; those younger than eight years are attracted to the
form because, through their form and content, the tales reaffirm
assumptions which characterize the world as a stable and gratifying
universe.

401. The Traveling plays of Clara Tree Major, by Michael W.
     Gamble.   Paper presented at the annual meeting of the
     American Theatre Association, August 1976. 21p. ED
     126545.
          Clara Tree Major, the first producer to provide pro-
fessional touring plays exclusively for children's audiences (from

1925 until 1954), not only produced these plays but also wrote the scripts by adapting children's stories for the theatre. This paper investigates Major's playwriting principles and techniques, examines Major's philosophy in play selection, provides an overview of all the titles chosen for presentation, and analyzes the script of "Little Women" to discover Major's use of dramatic form in her adaptations. Two tables illustrate the text: one diagrams the doubling of actors for "Toby Tyler" and the other charts the number of productions of each play title.

402. Directory of United Nations Information systems and services.
      Geneva, Inter-Organization Board for Information Systems, 1978. 265p. ED 168498.
      This directory brings together in summary form the functions of the various members of the United Nations Organization and the information systems and services they provide. It is intended to show the reader what exists and where to obtain further details. The contents are divided into four parts. The first part lists the organizations of the United Nations whose functions or programs involve the collection, dissemination, or analysis of information; organizations of an administrative nature are not included. The second part gives individual descriptions of the information systems belonging to the organizations listed in the preceding section. The third part presents addresses by country to facilitate contact between users and organizations, systems, and services. The last section is a subject index designed to assist users in identifying the systems and services which deal with information in a given field.

15.
READING,
LANGUAGE,
COMMUNICATION

403. How can I help my child get ready to read? by Norma Rogers.
      Newark, DE, International Reading Assoc., 1972. 25p.
      ED 112359.
      This micromonograph describes reading readiness and
offers suggestions for parents to help their children develop skills
and abilities useful for reading. The six sections discuss the following topics: parents' roles and how children learn, toys which build
reading readiness, the importance of encouraging children to talk
and listen, ways in which to help children develop social and emotional
balance, ways to provide a broad intellectual experience for children,
and the importance of reading frequently to children. A brief annotated list of books on readiness is included.

404. Reader expectations and the poetic line, by James C. Stalker.
      Paper presented at the annual Interdisciplinary Confer-
      ence on Linguistics, April 1978. 18p. ED 161054.
      The form of the print poetic line is partially determined
by the expectations of the potential readers since authors, as participants in the common literary heritage of their culture, make use
of the common expectations of that literary heritage. As a test of
this hypothesis, one poem by James Dickey and one by Ted Olson
were printed as prose, and 25 readers were asked to divide them
into lines. Their expectations were then compared to the linear
organization of the poems. Analysis of the results suggests that
readers end lines at major syntactic breaks and that reader expectations and author practice show definite patterns of congruence.
Dickey and his readers agree on the number of lines for the poem
but disagree on where the lines should end; his line end choices,
however, are predictable from the readers' expectations. Olson
and his readers expect far more lines than he produces. His lines
too are predictable from the readers' responses. The results, while
not discounting rhythm as a significant feature in defining the poetic
line, suggest that lines are definable, as poets generally agree; that
poets' "energy" is the play between syntactic expectation and linear
fulfillment; and that the reader takes part indirectly in poets' line
end decisions.

405. Daily newspaper non-readers; why they don't read, by Paula
      M. Poindexter. Paper presented at the annual meeting
      of the Association for Education in Journalism, August
      1978. 32p. ED 159683.
      In an attempt to understand nonreader attitudes toward
the daily newspaper, 576 non-newspaper reading adults were queried
in three waves about their reasons for avoiding newspapers. In the
first wave, the major findings were that nonreaders avoid newspapers
because of lack of time, preference for another news medium, newspaper cost, and lack of interest. In the second wave, typical nonreaders (those low in income and education, the young and the elderly)
and atypical nonreaders (those high in income and education, and
the middle-aged) were queried about a checklist of 15 avoidances
developed from the first wave of interviews. Responses fo the checklist were factor analyzed and reduced to five significant reasons nonreaders avoid newspapers: newspaper content, poor eyesight, lack
of time, use of other media, and perceived newspaper bias. It was
found that typical nonreaders avoid newspapers because of poor eyesight, while atypical nonreaders do not read because of lack of time
and newspaper content. In the third wave, nonreaders were defined
as those avoiding both daily and weekly newspapers. Four major
factors were found to cause this group's avoidance of newspapers:
perceived newspaper bias, avoidance of print, use of broadcast
media, and lack of time.

406. Reading for parents, by Peter Winograd. 1979. 19p. ED
      170715.
      Designed to give parents an overview of reading and
some suggestions on how they can help their children, this guide
has been used in parent classes and workshops throughout Illinois
since 1976. The nine sections of the guide cover the following areas:
a general definition of reading, some causes of reading difficulty,
various techniques used in the teaching of reading, ways in which
parents can help teach reading, how to read aloud, informal reading
games, commercially prepared games, a list of books for parents,
and suggestions for choosing books for children.

407. Teaching children to read; a parent's guide. Springfield, IL,
      State Office of Education, 1977. 26p. ED 149280.
      This report is an educational guide for parents of young
children with reading problems. It explains the prereading skills,
such as sitting quietly, paying attention, and listening, that must be
mastered before a child can learn to read and then describes nine
approaches used by public schools for teaching reading. The report
offers practical ways in which a parent can be involved in the child's
reading development and stresses the importance of home atmosphere
and parental example. Two types of games that relate specifically
to reading are suggested: those used primarily to interest a child
in reading and those that teach specific reading skills. Examples
of each type and suggested applications are provided. Appendixes
include books for additional study on this topic, an annotated list of
children's books designed to improve reading skills, and a list of
games that help children learn and enjoy reading. A source book for
designing games at home is described in detail.

408. How to help your child grow in reading, by Neil J. Vail and
      and Nancy R. Neill. Racine, WI, Unified School Dis-
      trict #1, May 1975. 83p. ED 157012.
      The purpose of this publication is to show parents how
they can facilitate their children's growth in reading. Section one
suggests numerous parental activities to aid children's reading
growth, such as reading to children, talking and listening to them,
giving them responsibilities, and building a reading atmosphere at
home. Sections two and three present a pyramid of reading skills
and a summary of consonant and vowel sounds. Section four discusses games and activities that pertain to the following areas:
visual and auditory discrimination, sight and meaning vocabulary,
word attack skills, library and study skills, and comprehension.
Section five describes recommended books for parents of children
in the primary grades, and section six presents a core vocabulary
list, a list of Dolch basic sight words, and a handwriting model.

409. Black American English; a survey of its origins and develop-
      ment and its use in teaching of composition, by Edward
      Anderson. 43p. ED 130726.
      Although some educators have advocated eradication of
Black American English and other non-standard American English
dialects in formal school training, it is recognized that many dialects are effectively used to a great degree by many Americans.
Black American English, like other dialects, is a legitimate linguistic system that has logic, coherence, and grammaticality. A
survey of its development shows it to be the result of a pidginization-
creolization process that started with the West African slave trade,
progressed through the development of the Gullah dialect, to Black
American English. Notable contributors to this dialect have been
West African and peasant English influences. A review of the literature indicates that there are desirable and advantageous features
associated with use of Black American English; in certain situations
it enhances the individual's ability to communicate effectively. Further, great value can be derived by both blacks and whites from use
of this dialect. The Black American Code-Switching Technique is a
strategy for teaching the utility of both standard and non-standard
English forms and of enhancing student facility with each. Its use
in the English composition classroom is discussed and a suggested
curriculum outline is presented. An extensive bibliography is attached.

410. Black English goes to school, by Jane W. Torrey. New Lon-
      don, CT, Department of Psychology, Connecticut College,
      1977. 141p. ED 158275.
      To test the effects of black English on school perform-
ance, 27 second graders in a Harlem school were interviewed and
tested for competence in spontaneous speech, comprehension of oral
and written materials, and oral reading, as well as for explicit
grammatical knowledge of standard English morphemes often missing
in black English. The data show large individual differences in
ability to use standard forms and low but significant correlations
between speech and reading performance. Instruction in use of

standard forms significantly influenced several performances. The speech patterns and grammatical knowledge of the Harlem children were compared with those of second graders in a predominantly white middle-class school in Connecticut. High school students in Connecticut were also tested for their use and comprehension of standard verb inflections and negatives. Data from developmental English classes showed white students better able than blacks to do grammatical exercises involving standard English. An attempt to improve use of standard verb inflections and negatives through systematic instruction proved unsuccessful with the high school students. It is concluded on the basis of this study that command of standard English is related to school performance.

411. Baby talk as a simplified register; papers and reports on child language development, no. 9, by Charles A. Ferguson. Stanford University, Committee on Linguistics, April 1975. 31p. ED 159904.
Every speech community has a baby talk register (BT) of phonological, grammatical, and lexical features regarded as primarily appropriate for addressing young children and also for other displaced or extended uses. Much BT is analyzable as derived from normal adult speech (AS) by such simplifying processes as reduction, substitution, assimilation, and generalization. Not all BT features are simplified: some manifest clarifying processes (and redundancy), diminutivizing or hypocoristic processes (add effect), identifying processes. The BT register also has independent material not derivble from AS. BT is variable in degree of deviance from the AS norm, and the variability tends to neglect the speaker's assessment of the hearer's language development as well as other factors in the communication situation. The use of BT is neither a necessary nor a sufficient condition for the acquisition of AS but assists in the child's language development. BT is universal because of its effectiveness in language socialization and in the transmission of social roles such as age, sex and kin, and cultural values of objects and actions (good, bad, sweet, dirty, dangerous, etc.).

412. Sexism and language, by Alleen Pace Nilsen. Urbana, IL, National Council of Teachers of English, 1977. 206p. ED 136260.
The book contains the following essays regarding sexism and language: "Linguistic Sexism as a Social Issue," "Sexism as Shown through the English Vocabulary," "Sexism in the Language of Marriage," and "Sexism in Children's Books and Elementary Teaching Materials" by Alleen Pace Nilsen; "Gender-Marking in American English: Usage and Reference" by Julia P. Stanley; "Sexism in the Language of Legislatures and Courts" by Haig Bosmajian; "Sexism in the Language of Literature" and "Sexism in Dictionaries and Texts: Omissions and Commissions" by H. Lee Gershuny. The National Council of Teachers of English Guidelines for Nonsexist Use of Language are appended.

413. Expletive deleted; a study of language usage, by Nick Nykodym and John A. Boyd. Paper presented at the annual

meeting of the International Communication Association,
April 1975. 16p. ED 108267.

The research findings of profane language usage need to
be extended so that more may be learned about human communication. In order to establish profane language usage norms, eighty-
six university students were asked to estimate their profane language usage in each of three categories (excretory, religious, and
sexual) in reference to three general social situations (sex relationships, friendships, and public-private situations) and three specific
categories (same or opposite sex; alone, close friends, and strangers;
and private, semipublic, and public). Results of the tests showed
that excretory profanity is used more than religious or sexual, that
profanity occurs at a higher frequency when a person is alone, and
that less profanity is used in the presence of strangers than in other
situations. (Tables of findings and a list of references are included.)

414. Appalachian speech, by Walt Wolfram and Donna Christian.
Arlington, VA, Center for Applied Linguistics, 1976.
195p. ED 130511.

This description of Appalachian speech, derived from
one part of the final report of a research project on Appalachian
Dialects, is intended as a reference work for educators, particularly
reading specialists, English teachers, language arts specialists, and
speech pathologists. Chapters deal with the following main topics:
(1) a sociolinguistic framework for the study of Appalachian English;
(2) phonological aspects of Appalachian speech; (3) grammatical features of Appalachian speech; and (4) educational implications of dialect diversity, with particular reference to language attitudes, testing, language arts, and reading. Appendices contain interview questionnaires, a sample informant interview, and a complete list of in-
formants.

415. Gesticulation; a plan of classification, by Francis Hayes.
Paper presented at the meeting of the American Association of Teachers of Spanish and Portuguese, December
1975. 15p. ED 122617.

People take their folk gestures seriously, which is illustrated in the fact that several folk gestures, such as raising the
right hand and kissing the Bible, are used in religious and legal
ceremonies. These and other gestures, such as making the sign
of the cross and knocking on wood, are folk gestures used today
which have their roots in early religion and tradition. Gestures
include "official" types used by the deaf and dumb, American Indians
or sports referees; military salutes; and gestures communicating fear,
anger, friendship, scorn, etc. Nervous or autistic gestures are
widespread. Ethnographers, sociologists, psychologists and others
study gestures to determine their origins and significance. Tribal
or political gestures and salutes can unite people or create enemies.
The picture writing of American Indians, Egyptian hieroglyphics and
Chinese written characters may have their origins in gestures. Numerous English words and metaphoric idioms reflect gestures: "high-
brow, bootlicker, holding one's head high, pricking up one's ears,
keeping a stiff upper lip," etc. A practical classification of ges-

tures might include: (1) fold gestures - shaking the head for a negative, pointing, shaking a fist in defiance, etc.; (2) technical gestures - sign language of the deaf or of North American Indians, umpire signalling, etc.; (3) autistic or nervous gestures, such as doodling, fiddling with an object in the hand, etc. A few resource works are recommended for those interested in studying gestures.

416. <u>The Doublespeak of sexism</u>, by H. Lee Gershuny. Paper presented at the annual meeting of the Modern Language Association of America, December 1978. 20p. ED 172221.

The depth and pervasiveness of linguistic symbols of sexual identity, difference, and hierarchy are discussed in this paper. After noting that the language of sexism begins at birth and is recognized and used by preschool children, the paper points to patterns of linguistic sexism in the semantics and syntax of the English language, in written and spoken language about women and men, and in women's and men's use of verbal and nonverbal aspects of language. Among the topics dealt with are the following: the way female-associated language is defined not only by men but in terms of women's sexual relationship with men: frequent descriptions of nature and the land in images and metaphors of female sexuality and submission; the linguistic invisibility and pejoration of the female as reflected in the use of so-called "generics" and the adding of female markers (poet "ess") to distinguish women's achievement as deviant from the male norm; the way the English language teaches a prescriptive sociopolitical grammar that perpetuates the symbol systems of patriarchy; and differences in women's and men's language that reflect expectations of male dominance and female submission. The paper concludes by noting the penalties and risks encountered by those who attempt to change the restricted codes of thinking, speaking, and behaving.

417. <u>Communication and sexuality; an annotated bibliography</u>, compiled by Jerry Buley. 1978. 53p. ED 168105.

The entries in this annotated bibliography represent books, educational journals, dissertations, popular magazines, and research studies that deal with the topic of communication and sexuality. Arranged alphabetically by author and also indexed according to subject matter, the titles span a variety of topics, including the following: sex and morality, marital communication and sexism, birth order and its sequence, career choices of married women, sex differences in expressiveness, sexual permissiveness, research in homosexuality, cross-culture sexual attitudes, fatherhood, the influence of parental attitudes on the child's sexual attitudes, women in a sexist society, sex and nonverbal communication, dating adjustment, the influence of television on sex role stereotypes, family planning motivations, alternative styles of marriage, wife dependency as related to marital adjustment, self-definition and role definition in women, changing sex ethics, childhood and sexual attraction, and intrafamily patterns of conflict resolution.

418. <u>A Monograph on interpersonal communications</u>, by Richard

Gemmet. Redwood City, CA, San Mateo County Office of Education, October 1977. 48p. ED 153323.

Intended for use by managers, this guide is meant to focus attention on communication skills and to provide a new approach to improving interpersonal communications. The authors divide these skills into two categories--listening and speaking. Effective listening entails skillful use of paraphrasing (any method of showing the speaker what his or her idea or statement conveys) and perception checking (a process describing the listener's perceptions of the speaker's feelings). Effective speaking necessitates describing feelings and behavior, using constructive confrontation, and giving and receiving feedback. Exercises are appended that are intended to give the reader opportunity to practice these skills.

16.
MEDIA:
TELEVISION,
NEWSPAPERS,
RADIO,
ADVERTISING

419. Censorship and the media, by Daniel M. Rohrer. 1979. 33p.
        ED 162373.
        This review of current legal practices with respect to
censorship in the areas of obscenity and pornography contains a
history of anti-obscenity legislation; a review of the efforts of the
United States Supreme Court and lower courts to define obscenity;
a discussion of publisher Larry Flynt's battle against the "community standards" criterion for defining obscenity; a discussion of
the self-regulation efforts of the radio and television media; a consideration of the problems of obscenity and pornography on billboards;
and an examination of child pornography laws.

420. Adult individual criminal records and the news media; inherent
        problems for access and privacy, by Jay B. Wright.
        Paper presented at the annual meeting of the Association
        for Education in Journalism, August 1978. 46p. ED
        161043.
        Public access to criminal records, facilitated by the use
of computerized information storage and retrieval systems, sometimes appears to infringe on individual rights of privacy. Examples
may be cited to show that the records compiled on individuals do
not always present an accurate picture, due to factual inaccuracies,
incomplete information, or problems created by examining information out of context. Policies regarding access to criminal records
may be affected by whether the record is formal or informal, separate or mixed with confidential information, current or noncurrent,
original or secondary, related to convictions or nonconvictions,
sealed or open, or expunged by court order or still in existence.
Government officials' behavior in granting or denying access may
be affected by how well they know the journalist seeking access, the
absence of clear directives on the matter, or a natural resistance
to instructions to expunge records. The behavior of both government officials and journalists may be affected by bureaucratic in-
efficiency, perceptions of the effects on individuals of having crimi-

nal records published, and public adoption of extreme positions for bargaining purposes. Differences in viewpoint exist among journalists, government officials, and privacy advocates regarding the conflict between open access to criminal records and limited access that would protect privacy.

421. Journalists and terrorism; captives of the libertarian tradition, by Walter B. Jaehnig. Paper presented at the annual meeting of the Association for Education in Journalism, August 1978. 46p. ED 161070.

Because modern terrorism threatens democratic values such as personal liberty, free expression, and the limitation of institutional authority, it raises ethical problems for journalists who are drawn into a symbiotic relationship with those who threaten or use violence against a community. Recent terrorist incidents in the United States involving the Hanafi Muslims in Washington, D.C., Anthony Kiritsis in Indianapolis, and Corey Moore in Cleveland have caused a public reconsideration of the role and purpose of journalism in issues that threaten a free society. The responses from the news industry on this issue are libertarian in nature, upholding classical concepts such as free market of ideas, individualism, the self-righting nature of truth, and antigovernmental sentiment. Such a notion of objective journalism exempts the journalists from any moral or ethical response to the issue of terrorism. This lack of concern with values promotes a moral neutrality that evades the issue and determines the journalists' coverage of terrorism according to the economic and organizational imperative of the new media.

422. International news and the new information order, by Tapio Varis. Finland, Institute of Journalism and Mass Communication, Tampere University, 1977. 154p. ED 159680.

The international research project, "Transnational Communication," has concentrated mainly on the role and impact of transnational corporations in international communications, and the effects of creating a new international information order; this report presents papers summarizing three particular aspects of the world information order that were produced as by-products of the research project. The first paper describes the international broadcast system in Europe and its relation to the developing countries and their broadcast news sources. An analysis of Associated Press coverage of the first Intergovernmental Conference in Communication Policies held in Costa Rica in 1976 is covered in the second paper. The third paper, which deals with the Inter Press Service (IPS) as a source for alternative news, is a description of a particular type of news agency which is mainly operating in the third world countries. Appended tables present the newspapers which have published IPS materials and how much material they published in 1976, the subject areas IPS reports and analyses have dealt with, and the subject countries of IPS reporting published by various newspapers.

423. The Press and the Lincoln-Douglas debates of 1858, by Tom Reilly. Paper presented at the annual meeting of the

Association for Education in Journalism, August 1978.
31p.   ED 159708.
   The Lincoln-Douglas debates were significant in the
history of political journalism in that new ground was broken by
reporters traveling extensively with candidates, making extensive
use of shorthand to record campaign speeches, and fighting for
the press rights to cover the events.   Also, the press coverage
preserved the candidates' debates on the crucial issues of the day
which became part of the presidential campaign of 1860.   The performance of the press in such key campaigns helped refine its role
in modern political coverage.   For the most part, political reporters
and their papers reflected a particular political bias.   Innovative
exceptions in debate coverage were the objective reporting of entire
debates and the reporting of both candidates' activities by one newspaper.   The growing influence of press coverage is indicated by the
fact that at least one speech was delayed by waiting for a reporter
to get to his place.   The coverage gave the relatively unknown Lincoln national exposure which partially allowed his presidential victory two years later over the previously better-known Douglas.

424.   Mass communication and voter volatility, by Jack M. McLeod.
        Paper presented at the annual meeting of the Association
        for Education in Journalism, August 1978.   33p.   ED
        158320.
   Personal interviews were conducted with 353 eligible
voters in Madison, Wisconsin, in October 1976, and repeated with
all but 30 after election day to examine the correlation between
voters' age, paper reading (especially public affairs), and television
watching (especially public affairs), and the amount of behavioral
volatility (voter abstention, unstable party affiliation, and openness
to alternatives) and subjective volatility (contingent voting, antiparty
sentiment, conflict and indecision, and compromise).   The study
specifically measured the contribution of media (especially television)
to voter volatility, the unidimensionality of volatility, and the various normative aspects of volatility (single subjective dimension or
several dimensions).   Results indicated that both behavioral and
subjective volatility are multidimensional rather than unidimensional.
Education did not predict either kind of volatility very well; political
interest had more consistent nonvolatile effects, except as reflected
in conflict and indecision; and both television viewing time and public affairs viewing had little effect on volatility.   Among the younger
respondents there was a stronger correlation between public affairs
viewing time and volatility than among the older subjects.

425.   Here is our Ernie Pyle, by Gretchen Letterman.   Paper pre-
        sented at the annual meeting of the Association for Edu-
        cation in Journalism, August 1974.   44p.   ED 098573.
   This document contains a biographical sketch of Ernie
Pyle, the Pulitzer Prize winning journalist from Indiana who gained
fame during World War II as a nationally syndicated correspondent
for the Associated Press.   The story of Pyle's life is traced from
his birth in Dana, Indiana, through his college years and his early
years as a roving reporter for the "Washington Daily News, " and

concludes with his experiences as a war correspondent and his death while covering an invasion in the Pacific.

426. Veiled news sources; who and what are they? by Hugh M.
        Culbertson. Washington, DC, American Newspaper
        Publishers Association, May 1975. 24p. ED 130266.
        In recent years, increasing concern with newspaper accuracy and credibility has led some people to question whether newspapers should use veiled, non-specific, attributions in news reporting. This study contains a content analysis of a sample of newspapers to determine the frequency and nature of veiled attributions as they are now employed. The newspapers selected for this study were located in the East and Midwest. One of the major findings of the study was that 36 percent of the 5182 stories examined in this investigation contained at least one attribution to unnamed sources. Additional findings of this study are reported in both narrative and table format.

427. The CIA-media connection, by Eugenia Zerbinos. Paper presented at the annual meeting of the Association for Education in Journalism, August 1978. 23p. ED 163458.
        The Central Intelligence Agency (CIA) has paid journalists, used information from unpaid journalists, owned foreign media outlets, planted stories, and put the lid on other stories throughout its 30-year history. Journalism makes a good cover for agents because journalists can ask questions without arousing suspicion. It has been estimated that between 40 and 400 overseas journalists from all media have been on the CIA payroll at least part time. They have written stories, cut them, or not printed them at all at the request of the CIA. On at least some occasions, false stories have been planted in the foreign press, have been reprinted in the United States, and have misled the American public. The use of journalists as agents has met opposition from the owners and publishers of the various news media and has raised questions about the ability of a journalist to serve the purposes of the intelligence community and retain integrity as a newsperson.

428. Press opinion in the Eagleton affair, by Donald S. Kreger.
        Association for Education in Journalism, August 1974.
        57p. ED 097692.
        This monograph discusses the role of the press in reporting the nomination of Senator Thomas Eagleton for Vice President of the United States, the revelation of his hospitalization for mental illness six years prior to the nomination, and his eventual resignation as George McGovern's running mate in the 1972 Presidential elections. Four sections of the booklet consist of a discussion of the nomination, a description of the disclosure of Eagleton's history, an examination of the public reaction, and a review of the resignation based on reports and editorials gleaned from the news media. The final section of this document attempts to place the Eagleton affair in perspective, concluding that most elements of the news media acted responsibly during the controversy.

429. Developing world and mass media. Papers presented at the
International Scientific Conference of the International
Association for Mass Communication Research, Leipzig,
September 1974. 128p. ED 136276.
This volume presents six keynote papers submitted by
noted scholars to the Working Group on Mass Media and Developing
Nations at the International Scientific Conference of the International
Association for Mass Communication Research held at Leipzig,
Germany, in September 1974. The following titles are included:
"Mass Media and Developing Nations: A Global Perspective of Mass
Communication and Its Research" (Kaarle Nordenstreng), "The Press
in the Developing Countries of Asia and Africa: Its Social and Class
Character and Function" (Azad Khadian Talivaya Ibragimov), "Mass
Media in the Developing World: Four Conundrums" (John A. Lent),
"Tasks and Problems of Mass Media in the Political, Ideological,
Economic, and Cultural Process of Transformations in the Countries
of Sub-Saharan Africa" (Werner Ullrich), "Communication Research
in Latin America: The Blindfolded Inquiry?" (Luis Ramiro Baltran
S.), and "The Foundation and Development of National Languages
and Their Importance for the Creation of Indigenous Mass Media in
Africa" (Siegmund Brauner).

430. Newsmen's privilege, by Daniel M. Rohrer. 1978. 31p.
ED 166695.
In response to recent court decisions limiting reporters'
rights to confidentiality, this paper considers whether a shield law
would increase or decrease the flow of information desired in the
investigation of a crime and what constitutes the public's right to
know. It argues that since many reporters obtain stories by rely-
ing on the confidentiality of sources, the threat of forced disclosure
thwarts access to information. Without such assurances of confidentiality, many important stories might not have been written.
Among the stories mentioned in this regard are Lincoln Steffens'
report on big city corruption, Ida Tarbell's report on oil trusts,
and the reports about Watergate. The paper quotes a number of
sources, among them the "London Times," the United States Senate
Judiciary Committee, and Theodore H. White, concerning the problems of not protecting reporter confidentiality, and it discusses the
implications of several court decisions. It also explores the possible
conflict between Sixth Amendment guarantees to a fair trial and
First Amendment guarantees of a free press.

431. John Milton's place in journalism history; champion or turn-
coat? by Paul M. Fackler and Clifford G. Christians.
Paper presented at the annual meeting of the Association
for Education in Journalism, August 1979. 22p. ED
172219.
Historians of journalism cite John Milton's speech
"Areopagitica" as the first major English-language document to ar-
ticulate the ideas of free speech and freedom of the press. Milton's
reputation as spokesman for freedom to publish is sullied, however,
by his having served as Cromwell's press licenser. Historians of
journalism have attacked Milton's "censorship" as evidence of con-

tradiction and compromise of his ideals. An examination of the
nature of his responsibility as licenser within his social, political,
and personal situation leads to a different conclusion, however;
that his commitment to the ideal of just and virtuous government
gave him warrant for direct involvement in the political life of
the Commonwealth, and that in his role as licenser, he merely
played the role of senior editor rather than authoritarian censor,
and contributed little aside from his bureaucratic imprimatur.

432. John Thomson; photojournalist in Asia, 1862-1872, by Elliott
     S. Parker. Paper presented at the annual meeting of
     the Midwest Conference on Asian Affairs, October 1977.
     26p. ED 153213.
          John Thomson was a nineteenth-century British photo-
journalist who used the wet-plate process to illustrate his explora-
tions of eastern and Southeast Asia. His travels from 1862 to 1872
took him to the following places, among others: Ceylon, Cambodia,
Singapore, Thailand, Saigon, Siam, mainland China, and Taiwan.
Thomson chose to use the wet-plate process, despite its problems
and demands, because of the quality of negative possible. As one
of the earliest European photojournalists to work in Asia, Thomson
produced work that goes beyond mere documentation; it presents
the grandeur of the Asian landscapes and gives probing images of
living people that together convey a full sense of the land. He also
experienced many difficulties with malaria, hostile people, and harsh
climates. He was especially interested in the "small trades" and
in anonymous individuals who could not pay for their portraits and
who are thus underrepresented in the works of most Victorian photo-
graphers. A bibliography of Thomson's work is included.

433. The Telegraph and the news report, by James W. Carey and
     Norman Sims. Paper presented at the annual meeting
     of the Association for Education in Journalism, August
     1976. 37p. ED 150591.
          This paper describes an episode in the history of jour-
nalism that reveals a continuing tension in news reporting. Dating
from the invention of the telegraph in the late nineteenth century,
news reports have been increasingly patterned after either a "scientific" or a "literary" model. The scientific report is based on
irreducible facts, high-speed national communication networks, the
professionalization of the journalist, and an integrated social foundation for the newspaper. The literary perspective is a more conservative approach to news writing, based on the integrity of feelings, personal observations, interpretations, and opinions, with an
essentially local and individualistic organization of society. Although
no resolution to the conflicting perspectives has been reached, a
few scholars, such as Robert Ezra Park and John Dewey, attempted
to find a balance between the two perspectives. The debate continues today, in similar terms, between proponents of new journalism and precision journalism. A bibliography is included.

434. An Evening with Walter Cronkite. Transcript of an interview,
     July 1975. 16p. ED 157128.

In an interview at a Speech Communication Association conference in 1975, Walter Cronkite of CBS news was asked a number of questions on the role and characteristics of television news. Among the items discussed with Mr. Cronkite were the following: the degree to which events are shaped by their being reported on national news programs; the news media as a free-enterprise open market; television coverage of the International Women's Year conference; the process of deciding what will be included in an evening's broadcast; the perception of Mr. Cronkite in national polls as an optimally credible individual; interviews (including Cronkite's impressions of people he has interviewed), the Lyndon Johnson interviews, and Cronkite's position on the practice of paying individuals for interviews ("checkbook interviewing"); the use of women as anchor persons; ratings; network pressure on news production; the first amendment in broadcasting, especially with reference to the fairness doctrine and other FCC regulations; personal preparation for interviews; Watergate and the media; the 1976 election; the burden of responsibility placed on television news by its being most people's primary source of news information; personal bias and subjectivity in reporting; provision of free time to political candidates; and television coverage of the Vietnam war.

435. Public participation in public broadcasting. Washington, DC, Corporation for Public Broadcasting, August 1978. 44p. ED 166743.

The task force that compiled this report was created to identify ways to improve citizen involvement within all sectors of the public broadcasting system and to offer recommendations for change. The report presents a brief history of the Corporation for Public Broadcasting, offers six general recommendations for advancing public involvement, and identifies areas of public participation that include governance and policy, research, programing audience building, and employment. Appendixes contain comments by the individual task force members, a list of guest speakers, a bibliography of resource materials, a working definition of public participation, a glossary of terms, and the task force resolutions.

436. Beyond the wasteland; the criticism of broadcasting, by Robert R. Smith. Falls Church, VA, Speech Communication Association, 1976. 112p. ED 120838.

This book on television and radio criticism is intended to encourage viewers to listen and view the broadcast media more critically. The first part of the book is concerned with the process of criticizing broadcast programs. This part of the book considers criticism as a way of knowing, the varieties of criticism, two critical approaches--the mythological and the public policy oriented-- and looks at criteria that have been used by some critics in the past. The second part of the book deals with issues in the broadcast industry. Among these are broadcast journalism, the planning and evaluation of cable and pay-cable television services, and the social effects of broadcasting.

437. Cameras in the courtroom; from Hauptmann to Wisconsin,

by James L. Hoyt. Paper presented at the annual meeting of the Association for Education in Journalism, August 1978. 22p. ED 158307.

After questionable behavior was exhibited by photojournalists at the Bruno Richard Hauptmann trial in 1935, many states adopted a recommendation of the American Bar Association (Canon 35) and totally banned film and electronic coverage of courtroom proceedings. The ban of media became almost complete in this country after the Supreme Court overturned the guilty verdict of Billie Sol Estes in Texas in 1965 because of television coverage of this trial. However, as a result of intensive media lobbying, states such as Washington, Alabama, Florida, Georgia, and Wisconsin now have some type of policy permitting media access to the courtroom. The guidelines released by the Wisconsin Supreme Court in March 1978 to govern a one-year experimental period empowered the media in each district to designate a media coordinator to work with the judges, established a committee to monitor and assess the experiment, rigidly restricted the amount of video equipment allowed in the courtroom, and authorized the presiding judge to decide the rules for media behavior in the courtroom. A possible change in the earlier decision of the American Bar Association is indicated by the cautious testing of media coverage in other states.

438. Television in the courtroom; an Ohio experiment, by Edna F. Einsiedel. Paper presented at the annual meeting of the Association for Education in Journalism, August 1978. 27p. ED 158326.

As a result of the Bruno Richard Hauptmann trial in 1935, the American Bar Association enacted Canon 35 (amended in 1952 and 1963 to incorporate stricter standards) that recommended the banning of certain media coverage in the courtroom. Subsequent surveys conducted among the legal community in Oklahoma, Illinois, and Florida regarding Canon 35 have produced mixed reactions. In March 1978, a study examined the effects of controlled audiovisual coverage (with participants and spectators unaware of what was being recorded) of the second trial of a person convicted in 1973 for murder and rape. The study included a tabulation and filing of all newspaper stories and pictures, evaluation of television coverage by four stations, interviews with trial participants, and a telephone survey of a random sample of lawyers and judges in Summit County (Ohio), where the trial took place. It was concluded that the news reporting was fairly straightforward; the televised coverage did not sway the surveyed lawyers in their attitudes toward media coverage of trials; the attorneys, presiding judge, and witnesses felt that the coverage had been fair and responsible; most respondents and participants approved of the manner of coverage; and attitudes toward the issue correlated with age, experience, knowledge of videotaping, and type of practice. (Tables are included and the Ohio rules governing media access are appended.)

439. The myth of television news, by Robert L. Stevenson and Kathryn P. White. Paper presented at the annual meeting of the Association for Education in Journalism,

August 1977.   26p.   ED 149334.

After critiquing the usual estimates of the importance
of television as a source of news, the national audience for television
news over a two-week period is identified from the 1974-1975 W.R.
Simmons study (which uses a diary technique for gathering data).
Analysis showed that, in the two-week period, 49% of the adult population did not watch a single evening network-television news program; only one adult in four watched more than four network news
programs.   On the average weekday, about one adult in five watched
network-television news, while four out of five read a newspaper.
The audience for network-television news is described demographically
and is compared to the national audience for newspapers.   People
who use both media and those who use neither are also identified
and described.

440.   TV and kids.   Washington, DC, National Public Radio, Au-
        gust 1978.   38p.   ED 165776.

        In this series of National Public Radio interviews, indi-
viduals from education and television broadcasting discuss the use
and abuse of television by schools and the influence of television
on children in home viewing.   It is asserted that television is and
will continue to be watched, and therefore it is necessary to learn
how to deal with it.   By having children view programs, create
programs, and read scripts, schools do use television to help teach
organizational, creative, writing, and reading skills, in addition to
critical viewing skills.   These interviews noted that: (1) teachers
feel that television produces unrealistic competition between the
teacher and entertainer; (2) children are able to learn at varying
rates from instructional television; (3) children are influenced by
television; (4) violence in the media has been replaced by sex; which
has proved to be difficult to define; (5) broadcasting networks argue
that television productions and stereotypical characters merely reflect social issues; (6) the Parent Teachers Association has issued
viewing guides to help parents select productions; and (7) despite
discriminate selection, too much television viewing has an effect
on children's ability to develop cognitively or develop complex skills.

441.   On meeting real people; an evaluation report on "Vegetable
        Soup"; the effects of a multi-ethnic children's television
        series on intergroup attitudes of children, by Luberta
        Mays.   Albany, New York State Education Department,
        August 1975.   227p.   ED 123319.

        A summative evaluation of a unique television experience
for children is presented in this document.   Vegetable Soup, a multiethnic television series, is designed to reduce the adverse effects
of racial prejudice.   A major focus of the program is to assist
elementary school children in the development of genuine appreciation of members of all ethnic groups.   The purpose of this research is to test the objectives of the program in order to determine the effect on attitudes of those children who viewed the programs compared to children who did not.   A posttest-only design
is used to examine the differences between the two groups.   Sixteen programs are shown only to the experimental group and re-

sults are based on information gathered from spontaneous responses made by children while viewing the program and by responses to the instrument designed to test the objectives of the series. In conducting the evaluation, the focus is on four specific questions which encompass most of the stated objectives of the program. It is generally concluded that the program succeeds in affecting inter-group attitudes of children who view the show, but that this does not apply consistently over all of the racial/ethnic groups on which the study focuses. An interpretation of the results as well as a discussion of reactions to major segments of the shows and recommendations with reference to content and presentation for future T.V. productions for children, are included.

442. Five years of the "Electric Company"; television and reading, 1971-1976, by Joan Ganz Cooney. New York, Children's Television Workshop, October 1975. 28p. ED 122805.
      "The Electric Company" was created by the Children's Television Workshop (CTW) as an experiment in using television to teach reading skills to children in grades 2-4 who were having difficulty learning to read in school. With more than 500 shows completed and four seasons behind it, the series continues to be an experiment. The methods of presenting the curricula via television are still being tested, altered and refined to build on the show's experience and to attain optimum effect. There has been a gradual shifting in emphasis from a show to be viewed at home to one to be used in a classroom. The series was initially conceived as primarily an after-school program, but research during the first season of 1971-72 made it clear that the series had dramatically found its way into schools and was being incorporated into the classroom routine.

443. The Electric Company; television and reading, 1971-1980; a mid-experiment appraisal, by Joan Ganz Cooney. New York, Children's Television Workshop, September 1976. 36p. ED 130635.
      "The Electric Company" was created by the Children's Television Workshop as an experiment to teach reading to 2nd, 3rd, and 4th grade children having difficulty learning to read. Solidly based on research in the teaching of reading, the curriculum emphasizes decoding skills. The production process included several phases: (1) assembling the repertory company, (2) graphic innovation, (3) research on appeal factors, (4) training of writers in teaching methods, (5) evolution of characters, (6) editing, (7) filming, and (8) informing the public. Each season of productions has been evaluated, and results have been used as formative input in the following year's productions. Research efforts have measured attention, comprehension, attitudes, and national impact. The program has been viewed extensively, and it has received wide acclaim.

444. Sesame Street; 1000 hours of a perpetual television experiment, by Joan Ganz Cooney. New York, Children's Television Workshop, September 1976. 28p. ED 130634.
      During its seven year history, "Sesame Street" has

maintained high popularity, while introducing such innovations as new cognitive curricula, new characters, bilingual elements, and affective and social education. Early goals emphasized 40 predominantly cognitive objectives aimed at helping the disadvantaged child. Additions have included location-based programs, specially designed segments for the mentally retarded, the Muppets, original music, and guest stars. Both formative and summative research have been conducted. Though attracting an audience was initially a problem, the program now has an extensive global audience. A chart of curriculum innovations is included.

445. The Effects of television advertising on children; survey of children's and mothers' responses to television commercials: final report, by Charles K. Atkin. East Lansing, College of Communication Arts, Michigan State University, 1975. 108p. ED 123675.

This research assesses reactions to Saturday morning television advertising by four to twelve year old children and their mothers and examines young viewers' naturalistic learning of facts, attitudes, and behavior from commercials. An omnibus questionnaire was administered to 738 children. Interviews were conducted with 301 randomly selected mothers of these children to provide parallel and supplementary information. Some of the major findings are that children express generally positive evaluations of specific TV commercials, but tend to be bothered by commercial interruptions; that mothers are more favorable than hostile toward children's advertising; that amount of exposure to television is not related to knowledge of brand names, substantive qualities, or promotional characters featured in Saturday commercials, with age and school performance the strongest predictors of knowledge; that children's responses to TV commercials become increasingly skeptical as they mature; that from one-third to one-half of the children talk about specific commercials with mother and peers; that a large majority of children are stimulated by TV advertising to ask for toys and cereals; and that two-thirds of the mothers feel that commercials produce materialistic orientations in their children.

446. Edible TV; your child and food commercials, compiled by Robert B. Choate and Pamela Engle. Washington, DC, Council on Children, Media, and Merchandising, June 1977. 105p. ED 143420.

This document reports on the impact of television food commercials on children under 12, focusing specifically on how commercials influence children's food preferences and concepts, how they affect children's knowledge of nutrition, and how they contribute to obesity. Part I is a compilation of short excerpts from relevant testimony before the Federal Trade Commission (FTC), 1976-77. Included are witnesses' remarks on the above issues and comments concerning ways to make television a more educational medium in matters pertaining to food selection. Part II contains (1) a synopsis of the 1976 testimony of Robert B. Choate dealing with the frequency and content of food commercials directed toward children, and (2) a report on a developmental study of the use of graphics to convey nutritional information to children aged 4 to 10.

447. <u>Effects of television on children; what is the evidence?</u> by
George Comstock.   Santa Monica, CA, Rand Corporation,
April 1975.   20p.   ED 111348.
Studies and writings on the effects of television on children are reviewed and summarized.   Topics are the young people's
pattern of exposure to television, the nature of their viewing experience, the way they respond to television, and the direct effects
on their values, attitudes and behavior.   Research on the influence
of television violence on aggressive and anti-social behavior is discussed at length; it is concluded that violent television entertainment
increases the probability of subsequent aggressive behavior on the
part of children and youth.   The question of what, if any, action
should be based on these findings is also discussed.

448. <u>Television and its effects on children</u>, by Lewis Miller.
Toronto, Ontario Educational Communications Authority,
June 1978.   23p.   ED 164138.
This paper presents a redefinition of the term "television,"
examines problems of determining the effects of television on children, reviews research on possible effects of TV on children, and
concludes by focusing on prosocial, educational programing.   The
argument is made that because we are immersed in the phenomenon
of television, we can not obtain an accurate assessment of the macro-
effects of the medium.   Such assessments are best made by a social historian perhaps a century or two from now.   The characteri-
zation of TV as an exploitative and manipulative medium which builds
passive information processing habits among viewers is viewed as
one-sided and incomplete.   Television's potential for prosocial programming is emerging in popular educational programs for children
which, in conjunction with adult direction, stimulate active learning
orientations.   While the influence of programs on children is still
a controversial issue, agreement on the influence of advertisements
exists.   Children do learn from commercials and also learn to evaluate them.   Agency attempts to limit exploitative practices are indicated.   More parent involvement in their children's use of TV is
recommended.

449. <u>Through the tube darkly</u>, by John F. LeBaron.   1975.   30p.
ED 168578.
The research literature on the effects of television on
the behavior and attitudes of children shows that most television
programs and commercials present a highly distorted view of life
and society and show discrimination in character roles with regard
to sex and race.   Above everything, American commercial television
is violent and children represent an extremely large viewing population.   Research indicates that television viewing strongly affects
children in such areas as creativity, role models, cognitive development, and aggressive-violent behavior.   Attitudes toward commercials tend to become more negative as children become older, but
tolerance increases with the amount of television watched.   The
purchasing patterns of families with younger children appear to be
affected by commercials.   Much publicly-supported children's television programming is cognitively focused, but, despite its apparent

success, public commitment to children's television shows little improvement. Child-care television, in which children produce their
own programming, provides an alternative model to present practices
and allows children's television to program "real" problem situations
while controlling for anti-social behavior models.

450. Comprehension; the challenge for children's television, by
     Susan R. Storm. Paper presented at the annual meet-
     ing of the Association of Educational Communications
     and Technology, April 1977. 23p. ED 142197.
        The purpose of this research was to determine young
children's comprehension of selected TV program content. The
subjects were 210 children in grades K-2. All subjects in groups
of five, were shown segments from four TV programs: a scalloped
potatoes commercial, a "Batman" and Robin episode, a news story
on the MIG-25 and a segment of the "Electric Company." Testing
was a one-to-one interview. The percentage of correct responses
in the four segments was: the news (75%), "Electric Company"
(72.1%), "Batman" (70.9%), the commercial (54.8%). Tentative
conclusions were: (1) children understand most of what they see
and hear on TV, (2) children don't understand what they say (and
appear) to like more than what they appear to dislike, (3) children
cognitively understand fairly sophisticated information, and (4) TV
research must concentrate on comprehension in conjunction with
other variables to explain and identify TV's effects.

451. Children's television programming; some prior considerations
     and research designs for Canadian broadcasts, by Janet
     Solberg. Ottawa, Canadian Radio-Television Commission,
     1977. 102p. ED 153647.
        This handbook was produced to address some of the
questions raised at a workshop for producers, programmers, performers, researchers, and writers in the field of Canadian children's television. Three main areas are covered. The first section
provides an indication of some of the information that research can
supply for the improvement of children's programming, and offers
some before, during, and after research designs. The second section offers a general description of the growing child with age profiles of children from two to eleven years. The last section shares
some of the more important insights into elements of appeal, attention, comprehensibility, and learning which Canadian broadcasters
have acquired from their experience with producing children's programming. Not intended to be definitive, this handbook was developed as a selective and descriptive collection of material which
may encourage improvements in the creation, production, and evaluation of children's programming.

452. Movie and TV nostalgia, by Diana Elsas. Washington, DC,
     American Film Institute, November 1977. 27p. ED
     153612.
        This guide to movie and TV nostalgia lists organizations
and events, both with descriptive information. Sources include U.S.
stores and outlets which carry publications, stills, posters, and other

memorabilia related to movies and TV, as well as a selected list
of sources of 8mm and 16mm films in the public domain. The annotated bibliography lists general reference guides to movies and
TV, selected publications of movie and TV nostalgia, movie and TV
quiz books, and books on collecting. An annotated list of periodicals
and publishers specializing in film scripts is included.

453. Changing public attitudes toward television and other mass
        media, 1959-1976. New York, Roper Organization, Inc.,
        1977. 30p. ED 142218.
        This national survey attempted to discover the feelings,
and perceptions of American viewers--about the roles of the media,
about the degree of success broadcasters have as journalists and en-
tertainers, about the appropriate relationship between government
and broadcast programming, and about the acceptability of the commercial television systems. The first four chapters focus on: (1)
trends in attitudes toward media between 1959 and 1976, (2) media
in election years, (3) media compared to schools and government
during social change, and (4) attitudes toward programs and commercials. The final chapter describes how the study was conducted.

454. Television and terrorism; professionalism not quite the answer,
        by Herbert A. Terry. Paper presented at the annual
        meeting of the Association for Education in Journalism,
        August 1978. 70p. ED 158309.
        The responsibilities and role of the broadcast media in
reporting acts of terrorism are examined in this paper. The paper
first discusses such topics as new types of television equipment that
permit easy and instantaneous coverage of fast-breaking news; television coverage of two 1977 cases in which persons were held hos-
tage by terrorists; and discussions among broadcast journalists of
such issues as whether terrorist strategy should be reported in detail, whether terrorist events should be covered live, and whether
reporters should become intermediaries. It then lists CBS and UPI
(United Press International) guidelines for coverage of terrorist acts
and discusses the issue of the professionalism of journalists, as explored in research studies and in cases involving newspaper employees' right to form bargaining units. The paper also reports results of a survey of television station news directors' attitudes toward and experiences with self-regulatory codes, attitudes toward
statements related to the controversy, professionalism and professional autonomy, and probable behavior in terrorist/hostage situations.
Finally, suggestions are presented for dealing with the controversial
issues. The questionnaire mailed to television news directors, and
tables of their responses, are included.

455. The Social effects of cable television, by Leland L. Johnson.
        Santa Monica, CA, Rand Corporation, March 1975. 15p.
        ED 161447.
        Cable television illustrates the problems that can arise
in exploiting a promising new technology to meet social needs. Cable
operators' marketing procedures have emphasized improvement of
the quality of reception from local broadcasting stations, increased

programming choice by introduction of distant signals, and introduction of special pay channels for movies and sports. Programming and operating costs are so high that mass appeal broadcasting is economically more attractive than cable. Using cable as a polling device, or burglar alarm, or for meter reading, are other applications which are accompanied by a variety of problems, the greatest of which is cost. The extent to which new socially significant services develop on cable in the future will depend on a number of factors including federal regulatory policy, interconnection of cable systems, social experimentation, and technological developments.

456. A Qualitative study; the effect of television on people's lives.
      Washington, DC, Corporation for Public Broadcasting,
      October 1978. 88p. ED 162370.
         A total of eight focused group discussions, each with 12 participants, were held in Philadelphia, Minneapolis, Denver, and Houston to examine participants' television viewing habits, attitudes toward television, and perceptions of public versus commercial programs. Analysis of the results revealed a similar breakdown of response to television among all the groups. Among the major findings were that television played a number of roles for respondents, including those of entertainment source, escape mechanism, causal companion, educational tool, and filler for unstructured time; that those who believed television was worthwhile were more likely than others to plan their viewing; that the problem of choice of programs did not arise frequently because of multiple television sets in homes; that many of the women enjoyed soap operas but not sports, while the opposite was true for many of the men; that shows most often disliked were those considered superficial, ridiculous, or racy; that "Roots" and "Holocaust" were valued greatly by almost all respondents; that public television was seen as educational but was also perceived to be humorless, unexciting, and repetitious, while commercial television programs were seen as having more interest and variety; and that a more important role for public television was predicted for the future.

457. The Exportation of U.S. television abroad; a review, by
      Josephine Annino and Deborah Burghardt. Paper presented at the annual meeting of the Eastern Communication Association, May 1979. 26p. ED 172300.
         An estimated 100,000 to 200,000 hours of television programing per year are exported by the United States and the effects of this programing on other cultures, particularly those in developing nations, have generated concern. The appeal of this programing can be explained by its intended universality: it is produced within a multiethnic culture, is escapist in nature, and is designed for the "lowest common denominator." It is also being exported to nations for whom the cost of producing original programing is prohibitive. A frequently expressed conviction is that invasive United States programing causes "Americanization" of other cultures; however, this concept is undefined and research has not presented any conclusive evidence about it. While television is clearly active in the modernization of developing cultures, it is not clear whether the values and artistic traditions of a society will necessarily make way for Western popular culture.

458. The Sunny South; a gilded age publishing phenomenon, by Alan
       Bussel. Paper presented at the annual meeting of the
       Association for Education in Journalism, August 1973.
       37p. ED 088065.
       This document analyzes the South's most successful ver-
sion of a Gilded Age reading favorite, the "Sunny South" story magazine, published by John Henry Seals and edited by Mary Edwards
Bryan, in terms of its economic growth and development, article
and short story content, and editorial policy. The history of the
magazine is traced over a period of years from its inception in
1874 to its eventual sale to the "Atlanta Constitution" in 1893, and
the development of the "Sunny South" is examined in terms of national,
regional, and local contexts. This document also examines the
personalities of the editor and publisher as they reflect editorial and
content policies, specifically analyzing the magazine's conservative
editorial remarks about Mormonism in contrast to a progressive approach toward women's rights and liberties. The document concludes with a brief summary about the editor and publisher.

459. The Mass communication "theories" of the muckrakers, by
       Warren T. Francke. Paper presented at the annual
       meeting of the Association for Education in Journalism,
       August 1978. 24p. ED 161030.
       While muckrakers such as Upton Sinclair, Ernest Poole,
Thomas Lawson, and others chose individual approaches for their
investigative reporting to the public, they shared some common assumptions about mass communication that influenced the operative
impact of their views. In addition to adhering to a simplistic belief in the power of bare facts, these writers calculated the recep-
tivity of their audiences, searched for the prime conditions to present their messages, and measured reader response according to
indexes they devised themselves. Effective strategies included
sarcasm in praising those who voted for dishonest politicians, pre-
tended innocence in conveying startling facts, a tombstone photograph for a patent medicine fraud expose, and emotion-packed descriptions and insinuations. The muckraker studied public opinion,
frequently commenting on its power and abuses, on how to predict
it and how to measure it; the ultimate goal in investigative reporting was effecting a change in American society. Response was
solicited directly, through requests for letters of complaint to the
company or government agency responsible for the problem and
through the endorsements of readers by increased circulation of the
magazine or newspaper that printed the report.

460. "Out of sorts and out of cash"; problems of newspaper pub-
       lishing in Wisconsin Territory, 1833-1848, by Alfred
       L. Lorenz. Paper presented at the annual meeting of
       the Association for Education in Journalism, August
       1976. 23p. ED 158298.
       The problems faced by the printer-editors in Wisconsin
Territory were financial want, dependence on slow and unreliable
transportation and mail systems, and a lack of reliable journeyman
compositors and printers. Sources of income regularly included

backers who were community promoters of politicians and who frequently withdrew their support with little notice. Other sources of
income were equally unreliable and included advertising (very cheap
and infrequent), subscriptions (often not paid for), public printing
(not very profitable), and job printing (rare). Getting supplies was
difficult, and the mails could not be counted on for delivery of news
from the East or for delivery of papers to subscribers. Equipment
was seldom adequate and was often second or third hand. Journeyman printers and compositors of the time were difficult to find and
moved often. Nevertheless, the newspaper business flourished and
by 1850 the combined circulation of Wisconsin Territory newspapers
was more than two million.

461. Chinese newspapers in the United States; background notes and
      descriptive analysis, by Elliott S. Parker. Paper pre-
      sented at the annual meeting of the Association for Edu-
      cation in Journalism, August 1978. 31p. ED 165178.
         The background and the current status of Chinese news-
papers in the United States are examined in this paper. The first
section considers early immigration patterns of Chinese people, their
immigration to the West Coast of the United States beginning in the
mid-nineteenth century, laws passed to exclude Chinese from legally
entering the U.S., and the recent liberalization of U.S. immigration quotas for Chinese. Among the topics discussed in the second
section are the early history of Chinese newspapers in the U.S., the
way in which the Chinese press in the U.S. has been linked with
events in China, current readership for Chinese newspapers, problems involved in setting type for Chinese characters, and the trend
toward use of a colloquial newspaper style. The third section describes ten currently published Chinese newspapers and presents
tables of data about them that show the amount of newspaper space
devoted to news, non-fiction, fiction and literature, and advertising;
the space devoted to specified geographic areas in China and the
U.S.; and the space devoted to the inauguration of Chiang Ching-kuo
as President of the Republic of China and to Zbigniew Brzezinski's
visit to Peking. A brief concluding section notes problems peculiar
to the Chinese press in the United States.

462. Ethnic newspapers in the United States, by Rosanne Singer.
      Paper presented at the annual meeting of the Association
      for Education in Journalism, August 1978. 30p. ED
      165186.
         Defining ethnic newspapers as those published in a for-
eign language or in English that address themselves to a national
group, this paper presents an overview of such papers currently
published in the United States. The paper is organized into three
sections. The first deals with the function served by ethnic papers,
including aiding in assimilation, helping to preserve ethnicity, filling
news gaps, serving as watchdogs of foreign governments, and contributing to the diversity of political and social thought in the United
States. The second section covers the drawbacks of ethnic papers,
specifically their high mortality rate, increasing financial difficulties,
and the problem they face of incurring criticisms that they are

anti-American if they attempt to be outspoken organs in their communities. The third section discusses the future of the ethnic press and concludes that the current emphasis on exploring cultural roots and learning second languages will affect its role.

463. Audiences for contemporary radio formats, by James T. Lull. Paper presented at the annual meeting of the International Communication Association, April 1978. 27p. ED 159755.

A radio audience survey of 110 sample geographic clusters in the Santa Barbara, California, area served a twofold purpose: the construction of a demographic profile of audience types according to radio format choices, and the identification and analysis of various audience subgroups. A skip interval technique of these geographic clusters resulted in 523 in-home interviews where participants were asked their preferences of six radio formats: top forty, beautiful music, middle of the road (light rock, ballads, and news), live progressive rock, automated rock, and all news. Format choices were then analyzed according to the demographic variables sex, age, marital status, education, geographic stability, dwelling type, and residence ownership. Results indicated that persuaders and informers who use radio can use demographic distinctness to select an appropriate format for the target audience and stations with distinct audiences can predict that their programing is reaching a selected subgroup, that many subjects who named a top forty station as their favorite were past their teenage years, that nearly half of those with a four year college education indicated a preference for beautiful music and news, and that listeners of rock stations were more likely to call the station.

464. A Question of interference; FM radio's early struggle for survival 1934-1945, by Jayne W. Zenaty. Paper presented at the annual meeting of the Association for Education in Journalism, August 1978. 34p. ED 166688.

This paper explores FM radio's struggle for survival in the 1940s, focusing primarily on the impact of Federal Communications Commission (FCC) decision making and on the influence and activities of the well-established radio corporations, primarily the Radio Corporation of America (RCA). It describes the invention of FM radio by Edwin H. Armstrong and his early demonstrations of it to RCA. The paper next explores some of the early FCC considerations on allocating unoccupied radio channels and notes the reaction of the AM radio industry and of those who were developing television in the 1930s. An FCC decision to allow commercial FM broadcasting is discussed, and then the paper considers post-World War II planning by the broadcast industry, including the industry's efforts to move the band on which FM could be broadcast and the effects that move had on FM radio and on television. The final FCC decision reallocating FM Channels is reported and a series of questions asked of the FCC by FM industry proponents and not responded to are appended.

465. Gasps, Guffaws, and tears; an apology for melodrama, by
     John R. Clark and Anna L. Motto. Paper presented at
     the annual meeting of the Popular Culture Association
     in the South, October 1977. 26p. ED 150619.
     This paper traces the historical development of melo-
drama in the theatre and discusses its influence on twentieth century
drama. Melodrama is a responsible literary mode based on romance
and allegory, and its deliberate exaggeration of external actions
represents figuratively the interior or psychological dimensions of
imagination. Good melodrama portrays life experienced at its moral
and emotional peak and arranges action into one of these basic patterns: love-threat-survival or love-threat-demise-repose. The
paper discusses the specific use of melodrama in dramatically significant plays by Tennessee Williams, Luigi Pirandello, Anton
Chekhov, Bertolt Brecht, and other modern playwrights.

466. Patterns of propaganda and persuasion, by Hugh Rank. Paper
     presented at the annual meeting of the Conference on
     College Composition and Communication, April 1978.
     20p. ED 158322.
     Because children are exposed to highly professional sales
pitches on television and because the old material produced by the
Institute of Propaganda Analysis is outdated and in error, a new
tool for the analysis of propaganda and persuasion is called for.
Such a tool is the intensify/downplay pattern analysis chart, which
includes the basic intensify/downplay pattern and paragraphs discussing propaganda, persuasion, and advertising. The chart has
received considerable favorable comment from scholars and from
respondents outside the academic community, including the National
Council of Teachers of English Committee on Public Doublespeak.
As a simplified tool for analyzing any human communication (verbal,
nonverbal, and symbolic), it has the virtue of making clear not only
what has been emphasized in a particular pitch but also what has
been deemphasized. It can be used by children as well as by such
groups as Nader's Raiders and Congressional committees. (A copy
of the pattern accompanies the paper.)

467. Advertising and defamation of character, by Daniel M. Rohrer.
     1978. 22p. ED 159741.
     Defamation of character, as applied to libel and slander
legal decisions, is the subject of this paper. After briefly describing the basis of liability, the author discusses "libels per quod."
He then cites numerous court decisions in commenting on mitigating
circumstances in action for libel or slander, including absolute privilege, fair comment, matters of public interest, the effect of being
a public figure, good faith, reliance on government information, and
lack of malicious intent. In discussing retraction as a defense, the
author indicates that retraction does not eliminate liability but may
reduce penalties. He cites and discusses several cases relating to
defamation by radio, television, and cable television. In an extensive concluding section, the author considers cases and points
referred to elsewhere in the paper and adds more case illustrations

in describing the parameters of defamation of character in legal
decisions in cases of libel and slander.

468. Deception in advertising; a receiver oriented approach to un-
        derstanding, by David M. Gardner. Paper presented
        at the annual meeting of the American Psychological
        Association, August 1975. 21p. ED 117738.
        The purpose of this paper is to examine deception in
advertising from a behavioral perspective, and to attempt to formulate a definition that can guide both research and governmental regulation. Whether or not an advertisement is said to be "-deceptive"
depends on the definition of deception being used. The position
advocated here is that the focus of any definition must be the receiver of the message. Based on the analysis of veridical preception, a definition of deception in advertising is offered. An approach to measuring deception is also offered. The techniques are
all seen as screening techniques, although by their regular use, ad-
vertisers should improve the ability of their advertisements to reach
their stated objectives as well as reduce the amount of deception.

469. The Emergence of ethics and professionalism in the early ad-
        vertising business, by Quentin J. Schultze. Paper pre-
        sented at the annual meeting of the Association for Edu-
        cation in Journalism, August 1979. 30p. ED 172233.
        In the pre-World War I era, advertising practitioners
attempted to make their craft a profession. Generally agreeing that
the creation of ethical codes was the most important step toward
professionalism, practitioners organized the Associated Advertising
Clubs of America (AACA). Early journal articles and AACA proceedings indicate that practitioners were motivated by social status
and economic self-interest in their quest for professionalism. The
development of advertising ethics was tied to interconnected political,
economic, and cultural motivations. Practitioners formed political
groups to influence other political groups and various government
bodies, and created economic groups to protect and solidify their
financial relationships with clients and publishers. Practitioners
thus hoped that professional ethics would enhance their collective
power and improve their potential for gain and social respectability.

470. Volney B. Palmer, 1799-1864; the nation's first advertising
        agency man, by Donald R. Holland. Minneapolis, As-
        sociation for Education in Journalism, May 1976. 44p.
        ED 124940.
        This monograph examines the life of Volney B. Palmer,
who was the prototype of the modern advertising person. The first
section discusses his background and early experience in Pennsylvania. The second section discusses the American Newspaper Agency, established as the first advertising agency in 1842. The third
section examines the kind of man Palmer was and concludes that,
among his many accomplishments, he was the first advertising agent
in the country; he promoted the concept of advertising to change
marketing techniques; he sold a "system of advertising" instead of

simply offering newspaper space for sale; and he wrote, produced and delivered advertisements to newspapers for advertising.

471.　Advertising and invasion of privacy, by Daniel M. Rohrer.
　　　　1978.　66p.　ED 168069
　　　　The right of privacy as it relates to advertising and the use of a person's name or likeness is discussed in this paper. After an introduction that traces some of the history of invasion of privacy in court decisions, the paper examines cases involving issues such as public figures and newsworthy items, right of privacy waived, right of privacy precluded by consent, limits of consent, termination of employment, revocation, malice, sufficiency of identification, incidental use of name, and who may bring action against whom.　A second section of the paper discusses usage of name or likeness as an invasion of privacy as it relates to endorsement of products or services, usage of name on a product, and recovery allowed and denied.　A section is included on use of pictures for display purposes, in newspapers or other printed publications, in television or motion pictures, and mistaken use of pictures.　A final section discusses usage of name or likeness in false light including misrepresenting of authorship or statements and alteration of pictures.　Each section includes numerous references to court decisions.

472.　The National Advertising Review Board, by Eric J. Zanot.
　　　　Minneapolis, Association for Education in Journalism,
　　　　1979.　50p.　ED 170745.
　　　　The creation in 1971 of the National Advertising Review Board (NARB) and its investigative arm, the National Advertising Division, was a response by the advertising industry to the pressures and criticisms of consumerism that had mounted during the previous decade and peaked as the 1970s began.　In contrast to previous periods, the 1960s and 1970s posed a greater threat to advertising because of government actions; in turn, the industry responded with a mechanism of self-regulation far surpassing any previous efforts, and including methods of detection, methods of adjudication; and sanction procedures that were meaningful reforms in the area, although somewhat weaker modifications were adopted.　This effort at self-regulation serves the trade both as a means of eradicating deception and as a means of dealing with public criticism and its attendant threat of government regulation; indeed, there appears to be an inverse correlation between the rise of NARB and the diminution of criticism and government interest in advertising.

473.　Computer art; a new tool in advertising graphics, by Brigit L.
　　　　Wassmuth.　Paper presented at the annual meeting of the
　　　　Association for Education in Journalism, August 1978.
　　　　16p.　ED 159712.
　　　　Using computers to produce art began with scientists, mathematicians, and individuals with strong technical backgrounds who used the graphic material as visualizations of data in technical fields.　People are using computer art in advertising, as well as in painting; sculpture; music; textile, product, industrial, and interior

design; architecture; city planning; concrete poetry; dance; theatre lighting; and animation and cartooning. Several computer output devices produce different kinds of visuals, some of the most common of which are the line printer (prints letters, dots, lines, and so forth in various shades and densities), the CalComp plotter (computer-driven vertically moving drum), the cathode-ray tube (electric beam deflected across a screen which allows for interaction in real time), and Dicomed Image Recorder (digitizes transparencies so that sections can be manipulated separately). There is great potential for computer graphics in advertising; computer animation is highly flexible for commercial purposes and cuts the time for conventional animation from several weeks to a couple of days.

17.
MISCELLANEOUS
DOCUMENTS

474. The Third try at world order; U.S. policy for an independent
      world, by Harlan Cleveland. New York, Aspen Institute
      for Humanistic Studies, 1977. 143p. ED 155092.
          The booklet discusses America's changing role in world
affairs. The ideas, concepts, and theories were developed by participants in a workshop on American leadership held at the Aspen
Institute for Humanistic Studies in August, 1976. The document is
presented in ten chapters. The first chapter identifies new cooperative attitudes as the basis for the third try at world order. Reasons
are offered for the failure of the first try, the League of Nations,
and the second try, the United Nations. Chapter II characterizes
the modern world as a leaderless entity which is no longer managed
from Washington, and is not managed from anywhere else. Chapter
III examines international interdependence in technology, economics,
politics, and morals. Chapter IV outlines attitudes toward interdependence in third world nations and in the United States, followed
by a call to Americans to translate interdependence into an agenda
for action in Chapter V. This action agenda, discussed in Chapters
VI through IX, consists of moderating weapons races; staying inside
ecological limits; handling international problems; and coping effectively with interdependence within the United States. The final chapter examines attitude changes in the United States toward consumerism, family planning, the status of women, and environmental protection. The conclusion is that the third try at world order may
succeed where previous attempts have failed because of more advanced technology, an increased awareness of the need for restraint,
and a new sense of economic and technological cooperation.

475. Argumentation in the Canadian House of Commons on the issue
      of nuclear weapons for Canada, by John Alfred Jones.
      1976. 37p. ED 137889.
          The Cuban missile crisis of October 1962 forced the
Canadian House of Commons to consider whether Canadian forces
in NORAD and NATO were effective without nuclear warheads on
special weapons systems. This paper provides an overview of the
debates and their milieu, identifies the issues involved, and analyzes
the effects of the argumentation. The shifting and reformulating of
opinions by the nation's press as the debate progressed demonstrated

that oral arguments were a means of challenging and informing opinion-making groups such as newspaper editors and reporters. The debate resulted in the defeat of the Conservative party, the return of the Liberal party to power, and a change in Canada's nuclear weapons policy.

476. A Teaching and learning guide for organ instruction, by Mallory W. Bransford. PhD dissertation, Walden University, 1975. 150p. ED 130973.
The principles, rules, and directions needed for an introduction to learning the art of organ playing are presented in this guide. It is directed toward the needs of volunteer, part-time organists, such as church organists, who might not have had the opportunity for concentrated study. A series of ministudies is included which enables the teacher and student to evaluate progress promptly, eliminate bad habits, and establish new procedures quickly, in order that specific skills can be developed. The guide stresses absolute accuracy in all technical details and suggests perfecting pedal techniques before combining hands and feet. Various musical styles are explored, ornamental trills are explained, and construction of the organ itself is discussed. If the work is completed under the guidance of a competent teacher, the student should be able to pass the American Guild of Organists examination for the service playing certificate or go on for further study. An appendix lists addresses of 66 American music publishers. A selected bibliography of 36 books and essays is included.

477. Teaching woodwinds. Albany, New York State Education Department, 1976. 160p. ED 139704.
The guide contains suggestions for the selection, repair, and care of woodwind instruments and equipment; goals and procedures for beginning, intermediate, and advanced levels of study; and specific annotated reference lists. The book is arranged into five major sections by type of instrument: flute, oboe, clarinet, saxophone and bassoon. Each section contains (1) an introduction discussing historical background of the instrument, selection, care, repair and tuning procedures; (2) method criteria; (3) teaching and learning techniques for beginning, intermediate, and advanced levels; and (4) annotated bibliographies of relevant books, methods, periodicals, recordings, and films and filmstrips. The longest section on teaching techniques focuses on breath control, fingering, tone quality, articulation, range, and style. All sections emphasize the need for students to clean instruments regularly and properly, and to practice in groups as well as alone. A final section contains a bibliography of 59 general resources such as instrument repair manuals, other teaching guides, and indexes of musical wind instrument makers.

478. Dance; a catalyst of religion, by Ida F. Chadwick. 1976. 69p. ED 129815.
This paper traces the history of the dance as a religious expression. Dance rituals identifying with a deity predate written history and have persisted in all cultures up to modern times. Individual and group ecstasy induced by dancing enacted man's relation-

ship to God as well as interpreting God to people of widely different cultural backgrounds. The ancient pagan rite of dancing as a religious expression was so deeply ingrained in the human need for vivid and enthusiastic experience that it was carried into the very early Christian church. Gradually, as church organization and authority grew, it became formalized and at length repressed. While spontaneous dancing remains a part of ritualized religion in primitive cultures, with the exception of a few minor cults it is no longer a feature of western religions. Recently, however, interest in the dance incorporated into liturgical worship has revived. It presently takes the form of structured religious interpretation by professional dancers.

479. Idea exchange; volunteerism, edited by Jamice Ryan. Durham, Learning Institute of North Carolina, 1974. 58p. ED 114185.
        This issue of "Idea Exchange" which focuses on the volunteer in education programs includes a variety of materials related to volunteer experiences and viewpoints: (1) a handbook for volunteer coordinators which discusses the coordinator's role, the recruiting and interviewing of volunteers, and the essentials of volunteer placement and evaluation; (2) a sample volunteer job description form, and application, placement and evaluation forms used by one organization; (3) tax benefits for volunteers; (4) a bill of rights for volunteers; (5) selected bibliography on volunteerism; and (6) several short articles for volunteers and volunteer coordinators concerning such topics as the definitions of roles, pre-service training, and recruitment.

480. Voluntarism: the real and emerging power. A report of the International Conference on Volunteer Service, by Colin Ball. Washington, DC, ACTION, 1976. 191p. ED 135993.
        The principal objective of the international conference reported here was to bring together people involved with the promotion, development, support, coordination, and funding of volunteer programs to exchange ideas and experiences. Part I is a short paper on the historical perspective of voluntarism. Part II, a summary of conference proceedings, synthesizes conference discussions on several specific themes: Voluntarism in the context of the development process; approaches to volunteer work, organization, and mobilization; international voluntarism; domestic development schemes including study-service schemes, training and employment schemes, social and technical development service schemes, and short-term services; and forward strategies (international, regional, and general). Part III contains six conference speeches and case study presentations from Africa, Asia, North America, and Latin America. The conference program and a list of participants with their addresses are also included.

481. Because they care; a resource manual for volunteer programs. Springfield, IL, State Office of Education, 1976. 85p. ED 130250.

Beginning in 1973, meetings of 12 regional education advisory councils (composed of students, teachers, parents, administrators, board members, superintendents, and other citizens) studied volunteer programs in Illinois to determine their drawbacks and to formulate recommendations for expanding the concept of volunteers in education. This publication is the first attempt to disseminate information about volunteer programs in Illinois and to help local school districts interchange resources about their programs. Chapters focus on a rationale for using volunteers, potential problem areas and recommended solutions, orientation and evaluation, volunteer resource people, volunteers in career education programs, senior citizens as volunteers, the volunteer tutor, and specific volunteer programs in Illinois. An appendix contains material relevant to the state's volunteer programs.

482. New places for the arts; a report. New York, Educational Facilities Labs, Inc., 1976. 79p. ED 125078.
This catalogue of facilities and centers built specifically for the arts within the last decade dramatizes the commitment to facilities made by arts organizations and agencies all over the country--a commitment that is having a significant impact on the quality of life and the physical environment of many neighborhoods and urban centers. The purpose of the catalogue is to gather basic information on 49 new arts facilities as a resource for arts organizations and planners interested in similar kinds of facilities. Photographs and a floor plan, a brief listing of the major spaces provided, the cost, area, and date completed describe each building. Architects and other consultants responsible for design of the facility are also given. The buildings have been divided into three categories: museums, performing arts, and arts centers. For each type, a wide variety of examples was sought--in size, geographic distribution, function, and architectural style.

483. The Arts in found places; a report. New York, Educational Facilities Labs, Inc., 1976. 137p. ED 125077.
The experiences of several hundred arts projects across the country are distilled and illustrated in a report that communicates the variety and importance of the arts activities and how their use of found space has helped to stabilize and upgrade many communities. A mix of building types, a variety of arts activity, and broad geographic representation are included in an attempt to illuminate problems and creative solutions. The arts projects described and photographed are housed in facilities that formerly were (1) storefronts and other small-scale commercial spaces, (2) industrial and farm buildings, (3) specialized buildings in the private sector, (4) public buildings, (5) residential properties, and (6) whole neighborhoods. The last section of the report offers advice on planning, working out program budgets, phase development, obtaining professional assistance, and special aspects of housing the arts. The names and addresses of the organizations mentioned or described in the text are listed.

484. Landmarks of the American Revolution in New York State; a guide to the historic sites open to the public, 3d edition, by David C. Thurheimer. Albany, New York State American Revolution Bicentennial Commission, 1974. 65p. ED 115524.

Forty historic sites around the state of New York are listed in this guide to landmarks of the American Revolution. Each entry includes a photograph of the site, a map showing where it is located, a description of its history, and visitation facts. Most of the landmarks are buildings containing artifacts and displays, which visitors can enter and browse through; but some are monuments and parks.

485. New York's signers of the Declaration of Independence, by Paul J. Scudiere. Albany, New York State American Revolution Bicentennial Commission, 1975. 32p. ED 115523.

The purpose of this booklet is to bring New York state's four signers of the Declaration of Independence back into the mainstream of American Revolutionary history. Brief biographical sketches are presented about four patriots--Philip Livingston, Lewis Morris, William Floyd, and Francis Lewis. After providing a short history of New York during the years surrounding the signing of the Declaration, the booklet illuminates the involvement of each of the signers in the Continental Congress. The document concludes with a reading list on the four men and the Declaration of Independence.

486. The Discovery of the future; the ways science fiction developed. Texas A & M University Library, 1975. 19p. ED 117726.

This booklet discusses the development of science fiction, tracing its origins to the time of the industrial revolution. Many of the people of this time realized that life was changing and would continue to change, that there were new forces at work in the world, and that humankind should exercise some forethought about the direction in which change was going. Mary Shelley's "Frankenstein" is often thought of as the first science fiction novel. Other writers discussed include Edgar Allan Poe, Nathaniel Hawthorne, Fitz-James O'Brien, Jules Verne, and H.G. Wells. In 1926, Hugo Gernsback founded the first science fiction magazine, called "Amazing Stories." The state of science fiction today is also discussed, as well as science fiction and the movies, the possibilities of science fiction, the readers of science fiction, and the different perspectives of science fiction.

487. Guide to sensible surveys, by Donald C. Orlich. Olympia, Washington Research Coordinating Unit for Vocational Education, July 1975. 162p. ED 112017.

The manual provides vocational educators with information and guidelines regarding the design and use of questionnaires and interviews for gathering data and the construction, tabulation, and analysis of both open ended and forced response survey instruments. The first of nine chapters deals with surveys as a data collection technique, discusses the use of printed instruments, other information collecting techniques, and additional guidelines to determine the selection of survey type. Chapter 2, writing questions, covers plans for question building and response modes. Chapter 3, forced response questions, deals with establishing appropriate scales and includes self-practice items. Chapter 4, coding survey items, discusses forced response and open response codes. Chapter 5, preventing biased results, deals with wording the questions, sampling considerations, and selecting the appropriate response type. Chapter 6, conducting the survey, discusses knowing the target population, protecting the participants, using inclusionary language, and communicating with the target population. Chapter 7, tabulation of data, discusses methods of tabulation, especially electronic tabulation. Chapter 8, statistical analysis of data, discusses descriptive techniques and the use of statistical tests. The last chapter, the research report, covers planning and constructing the report. An appendix includes three model questionnaire formats. The document is indexed.

488. The Principles of leadership, by Gerald P. Burns. San Antonio, TX, Our Lady of the Lake University, April 1978. 72p. ED 154700.
    The primary but not exclusive concern in this monograph is the principles and qualities of dynamic leaders of people rather than of ideas or cultural and artistic pursuits. Theories of leadership in the past, present, and future are discussed, as are the principles, rewards, exercise, and philosophy of leadership. A bibliography is included.

489. Your chance to live. San Francisco, Far West Laboratory for Educational Research and Development, 1972. 107p. ED 154298.
    Disaster is a fact of life. More than 68 disasters occur every day in the United States. These catastrophes range from hurricanes, tornadoes and earthquakes to train wrecks and neighborhood fires. All people face these and many other kinds of disasters, both natural and man-made. Air and water pollution, industrial accidents, and the possibility of attack on this country are other hazards that are constantly with us. This book is an attempt to help the reader live safely in this increasingly complex, cluttered and dangerous world. Personal safety is the first objective. As more people become knowledgeable about civil preparedness, there will be more safety for all.

490. Taga the Great, by Frances S. Baker. Los Angeles, National Dissemination and Assessment Center, California State University, 1978. 110p. ED 168910.
    Legends can be incorporated into elementary social studies curricula to help students understand how people transmitted history and culture from one generation to another before they learned to read and write. Taga the Great is a legend which helps explain the 16-feet high latte stones on the Mariana Islands, Tinian and Rota. According to legend, Taga was born on the island of Guam. Already

in childhood, he exhibited supernatural powers such as the ability to uproot large trees and leap from one Pacific island to another. When Taga grew up and became chief of Rota, he engaged in and won numerous contests of wit and strength with other chiefs. Taga's fame spread throughout the Mariana islands and caused him to be the envy of all people, including his own children. To build a house great enough to please him, Taga quarried and carved very big stones and formed large pillars which he covered with wood and thatch. The house was very fine and admired by all who saw it. Taga's downfall began, however, as soon as his house was completed. His pride in his own superior strength prompted him to murder his little son, and his other children died soon afterwards out of remorse. As each child died, a pillar of Taga's home fell down. Soon only one pillar remained as a witness to Taga's glory. From the legend of Taga, students can gain insight into human strengths and weaknesses as well as into how the big latte stones of Rota and Tinian came into existence.

491. Why people don't listen to warnings; with discussion of implications for futurists, by Fran Koster. April 1978. 88p. ED 152674.
The document reviews recent literature on warning processes, evaluates the effectiveness of warnings in changing public policy and personal behavior, and applies warning literature to specific problem areas. Warning is interpreted to include a statement of the problem and a proposed course of action. The document is presented in six parts. Part one identifies the three major groups for which warning literature has been reviewed: (1) shortages of basic supplies, including food and fuel; (2) calamities and accidents related to toxins, chemicals, and radioactivity; and (3) failure of society to provide basic services. Part two presents case studies of responses to air raid alarms, floods, alcohol abuse, and panic by public officials. Responses to warning differed according to the extent to which the event was unfamiliar, sudden, unexpected, and localized. Part three outlines a strategy for effective warnings. Part four lists 44 findings from warning literature, and presents two disaster scenarios. Part five forecasts circumstances which will probably require warnings in the future. These include diminishing oil supplies, water shortages, nuclear explosion, petroleum-related accidents, insecticide poisoning, and the collapse of the social security system. Part six suggests that futurists should concentrate on educating leaders in urban areas on matters related to toxic and nuclear plants and on centralizing collection and analysis of forecasts pertaining to stressful circumstances.

492. Barriers to school breakfast. Washington, DC, Children's Foundation, November 1978. 107p. ED 164112.
The School Breakfast Program described in this booklet was legislated by Congress and implemented nationwide in public and non-profit private schools by the U.S. Department of Agriculture. The first chapter of the booklet presents a narrative summary of research data that support the need for school breakfasts. The second chapter discusses the historical background of the program

and describes the program's administration and funding procedures. The third chapter details problems in implementing the program, such as costs of teacher supervision, lack of adequate eating facilities, lack of student participation, and other problems. Prejudices and arguments raised against the program are outlined in Chapter 4. Chapter 5 presents summaries of selected school breakfast programs in 10 states: Arizona, Connecticut, Maine, Massachusetts, Montana, Nebraska, Ohio, Oregon, South Carolina, and Wisconsin. The final chapter provides recommendations for fostering school breakfast programs at the national, state and local levels. Appendices describe one successful breakfast program in Great Falls, Montana, and present tabular statistics on student participation in selected lunch and breakfast programs.

493. Popular images of America, edited by Hidetoshi Kato. Honolulu, East-West Center, University of Hawaii, September 1977. 123p. ED 163538.
    Drawn from papers presented at the East-West Communication Institute Seminars on popular culture held yearly from 1974 to 1976, the essays in this report focus on popular images of America held in four countries. Essay topics are: images of the American woman in Japan, the changing images of America in Korean literature, images of America in Malay poetry and short stories, and images of America in Tagalog short stories.

494. Essays in comparative popular culture; coffee, comics, and communication, by Hidetoshi Kato. Honolulu, East-West Center, University of Hawaii, December 1975. 41p. ED 162385.
    Based on papers presented at the East-West Communication Institute conferences and seminars in Hawaii between 1973 and 1975, these five essays focus on intercultural communication, emphasizing that popular culture existed with great diversity for centuries before modern media and that popular cultures have importance and impact on the everyday life of the common people in all cultures. The essays discuss the effects of global communication, particularly through radio and television, on the popular cultures of developing countries; the factors involved in popular culture research that distinguish it from communication research; an illustrated analysis of a revolutionary Japanese comic strip; the role of stimulants (tea, coffee, and tobacco) in effecting self-change and their use in the communication process of various cultures; and the place of stereotypical images in intercultural communication.

495. The Routes not taken; a look at the long term impact of "Roots", by Walter Gantz. Paper presented at the annual meeting of the Association for Education in Journalism, August 1978. 20p. ED 163487.
    Of 219 people interviewed within a week of the broadcast of the miniseries "Roots," 104 people were reinterviewed one year later to determine the program's long-term effects, including its perceived and experienced impact on race relations in the United States and its stimulation of viewers to search for their own roots/

heritage and to read the book "Roots." Results indicated that respondents tended to attribute long-term positive interracial outcomes to "Roots," feeling that the program improved race relations by providing a keener sense of understanding, knowledge of, and respect for blacks in the United States; few respondents felt that "Roots" worsened race relations. These perceptual and cognitive shifts, however, were not matched by behavioral changes in any of the investigated areas; despite initial expectations, few respondents in the followup had detected any changes in their own behaviors with people of other races, had actively sought to discover their own roots, or had read the book version of "Roots." One explanation for the lack of long-term behavioral changes is that anticipated changes may have been minimized by a communication environment that returned to "normal" after heightened interest in "Roots" waned and that no longer placed a premium on altering one's interactions with people of other races, reading the book, or searching for one's roots.

496. County by county in Ohio genealogy, revised edition, by Petta Khouw. Columbus, Ohio State Library, 1978. 158p. ED 160094.
The State Library of Ohio's genealogy collection of over 8,000 items is listed by county. Within each county listing the sources are designated as atlases, cemetery and death records, census records (the majority from the 1800's), family-church-Bible records, marriage records, or county and township histories. Vital records consist of material copied from original records in county courthouses and elsewhere, as well as materials copied by the Ohio Society, Daughters of the American Revolution since the Library is the state depository for Ohio DAR materials.

497. Writing a successful research grant proposal, by E. Patricia Orlich and Donald C. Orlich. Olympia, Washington Research Coordinating Unit for Vocational Education, July 1975. 64p. ED 112016.
The guide provides suggestions for vocational educators who desire to write proposals for research, demonstration, or development. The guide's first chapter, Organizing Your Ideas, outlines procedures for communicating one's intentions and for preparing a prospectus or abstract, and offers models of abstracts. The second chapter, Writing the Proposal, covers the following areas: statement of the problem, review of the related research and literature, objectives, procedures or methodology, preparing a project time line, project evaluation, dissemination procedures, staffing, budget requirements, and appendixes. The final chapter, Submitting a Proposal, covers planning for the details and evaluating the proposal. The guide also includes an index.

498. Institute on writing grants, by Harris K. Goldstein. New Orleans, Delgado College, 1973. 103p. ED 111477.
The proceedings of this institute cover sources for grant proposal ideas, grant proposal writing procedures, the content of a grant request, procedures of granting agencies, and problems in carrying out granted projects, including report writing.

The relationship of the granting agency to the grant recipient is
viewed throughout as a partnership, rather than an adversary connection. Types of grants include: planning, research, training,
demonstration, equipment, facilities, and program development and/
or expansion. Federal funding agencies are listed in material published by the Government Printing Office; private agencies, in the
Taft Information System. For a grant proposal to be funded, it
must be feasible, specific, have a competent and experienced research director or principal investigator, and fit the funding agency's
policies. These proceedings discuss budgeting, the handling of grant
money, and the hiring of personnel, focusing on probable problem
areas. Examples are cited from the experience of the institutional
research team at Delgado Junior College (Louisiana). References
to printed matter and studies which might help in writing grant proposals or in carrying out granted projects are given throughout.

499. Local history; a handbook for the collection, preservation,
        and use of local history materials, by Enid T. Thomp-
        son. Englewood, CO, Englewood Public Library, 1975.
        61p. ED 110055.
        A manual, designed to define the materials of local
history and to tell how to deal with them, provides step-by-step
instructions for setting up such collections. The collecting and
selecting process is described, as are the organizational problems
and possibilities in handling books, pamphlets, newspapers, periodicals, photographs, pictures, tape recordings, ephemera, clippings,
manuscript materials, memorabilia, maps, drawings, and private
collections. Additional advice is given for obtaining ownership or
use of nonpublished materials, physical preservation of materials,
cataloging and indexing, and providing services to the public and to
local and national organizations. Information is also provided for
training staff and volunteers as well as for developing special projects in the areas of oral history, community records, community
resources, current history collections, and resource persons. A
bibliography and a list of addresses and sources are included.

500. Teaching local history; trends, tips, and resources, by Fay
        D. Metcalf and Matthew T. Downey. Boulder, CO,
        Social Science Education Consortium, Inc., 1977. 110p.
        ED 151237.
        Trends, tips, and resources for teaching local and family
history are identified in this state-of-the-art paper. Using the local
community as a historical resource can make American history more
relevant and meaningful to students and aids in the development of
a wide range of skills, including library use skills, writing skills,
and skills used in evaluating historical data. A study of a community will yield information about its social history, economic
history, family history, architecture and public art, and folklores
and cultural journalism. Suggestions about how to retrieve a community's history and teaching activities and techniques for using the
information are provided in each chapter. Many of the suggestions
describe projects and activities that teachers currently use in their
own classes. A final chapter contains a list of local history resources,
including books, photographs, and materials on how to use local sources.

501. The Building of a populist impulse, by Hazel Heiman. Address given at the annual faculty lecture series, University of North Dakota, November 1973. 22p. ED
088114.
During the late nineteenth century, political rhetoric
in some regions of the United States was affected by the philosophy
of "populism," based on the belief that government exists to serve
all the people, not just special interests. The Populist Party thrived
in isolated rural areas, particularly the Dakota territories, at a time
when residents were seeking political force to organize for statehood. The party also served as a platform for farmers to express
their dissatisfaction with the distant industrial, business, and economic interests that they felt controlled them. Persuasive appeals
were based on political and economic discontent, a fear of natural
conditions and failure, and the isolated farmers' needs for social
interaction. As community centers were established, there were
increasing occasions for face-to-face communication. Persuasive
dialogues occurred during such meetings as summer encampments
and conventions, chautauquas, lyceums, and particularly political
rallies. As a reform movement, populism reached its climax in
South Dakota in 1896 when the party slate was elected.

502. Reusing railroad stations; a report. New York, Educational
Facilities Laboratories, Inc., May 1974. 155p. ED
093047.
Railroad stations are a unique American resource that
should continue to serve public and private interests even though
their original purpose may have passed. Large stations should be
considered as prominent civic structures whose redevelopment could
offer significant opportunities to influence the future character, economy, and operation of urban centers. This report tells the story
of rehabilitating sturdy, often handsome structures, ideally combining in one building several uses including public transit as a component of multiple use. Ten examples of the successful reuse of
stations have been selected, representing different sized stations,
uses, and ways in which reuse has been accomplished. Despite
these and other encouraging examples of reuse, many architecturally
resplendent stations remain in jeopardy. Five examples are given
of endangered stations sited on highly valuable urban land. An analysis of the economic routes open to those interested in acquiring and
reusing railroad stations points out the limited money available and
the necessity of the private sector joining with government if the
larger stations are to be saved.

503. Official master register of bicentennial activities, 4th edition.
Washington, DC, American Revolution Bicentennial Administration, January 1975. 653p. ED 102981.
The Congress of the United States directed the American
Revolution Bicentennial Administration (ARBA) to "prepare the master calendar of events of local, State, National and international
significance which will take place between March 1975 and December
1976." This book, which is divided into six sections, contains the
indexes and details of these Bicentennial activities. Sections 3, 4,
and 5 comprise the bulk of the book: Section 3 includes five cross-

referenced indexes; Section 4 is a concordance, or key word index; Section 5 contains details on all of the cataloged projects and events. ARBA gathers, organizes, disseminates, and archives Bicentennial data with the help of a computerized Bicentennial Information Network-- BINET, through which subscribers have access to on-line, up-to-the minute information. Information in this edition is from BINET files, and updates and replaces all previous editions. Information is current as of January 2, 1975, and catalogs 4,619 projects (described as a significant effort or program which results in a particular Bicentennial activity) and 1,512 events (described as a specific occurrence which takes place as part of a project).

504. The Population Reference Bureau's population handbook, by Arthur Haupt and Thomas T. Kane. Washington, DC, Population Reference Bureau, Inc., 1978. 65p. ED 171597.

This handbook offers information on population dynamics. The population data resource is intended for use by journalists, policymakers, teachers, high school and college students, libraries, advertising agencies, and family planning groups. The document is presented in 12 sections. Section I introduces demography, explains the purpose and scope of the handbook, and details population growth's impact on every facet of life. Section II identifies and describes measures and tools used by demographers to describe population. Sections III through X focus on age and sex composition, fertility, mortality, morbidity, nuptiality, migration, urbanization and distribution, and population change. For each of these topics, the handbook includes background information; a glossary of population and demographic terms; illustrations, maps, graphs, and charts; and statistical analysis of selected country and state population figures. Section XI provides a glossary of 113 population terms. The final section offers a directory of population information sources.

505. Rescue skills and techniques. Washington, DC, Defense Civil Preparedness Agency, Department of Defense, July 1972. 86p. ED 106488.

The guide has been prepared for use as a textbook in rescue training courses at DCPA (Defense Civil Preparedness Agency) approved training schools and is to be used in rescue training programs of State and local governments. The document explains the various types of rescue missions, command structure, the personnel of the operating unit, personnel training, and standard operational procedures. Rescue skills and techniques are explained to those who are training for rescue service in peacetime or attack-caused emergency. The guide describes in detail the rescue squad's tools and equipment and gives instructions for their use. The wide range of operations that squadmen perform; such as, rope and ladder work, lashing and rigging, shoring, tunneling, trenching, and casualty handling, are covered in detail. The guide also contains information on basic types of building construction and the ways in which buildings may collapse as result of blast or other causes.

506. Modern Japanese novels in English; a selected bibliography,

by Nancy J. Beauchamp. Columbus, Service Center for Teachers of Asian Studies, Ohio State University, May 1974. 44p. ED 109045.

Selected contemporary Japanese novels translated into English are compiled in this bibliography as a guide for teachers interested in the possibilities offered by Japanese fiction. The bibliography acquaints teachers with available Japanese fiction that can be incorporated into social sciences or humanities courses to introduce Japan to students or to provide a comparative perspective. The selection, beginning with the first modern novel "Ukigumo," 1887-89, is limited to accessible full-length novels with post-1945 translations, excluding short stories and fugitive works. The entries are arranged alphabetically by author, with his literary awards given first followed by an alphabetical listing of English titles of his works. The entry information for each title includes the romanized Japanese title and original publication date, publications of the work, a short abstract, and major reviews. Included in the prefatory section are an overview of the milieu from which Japanese fiction has emerged; the scope of the contemporary period; and guides to new publications, abstracts, reviews, and criticisms and literary essays.

507. A Report of the Commission on Federal Paperwork; final summary report. Washington, DC, Commission on Federal Paperwork, October 1977. 85p. ED 149426.

The Commission on Federal Paperwork was charged by Congress and the President with the task of making recommendations to eliminate needless paperwork while assuring that the federal government has the information necessary to meet the mandate of law and operate effectively. The 36 reports of the commission (summarized in the appendixes) examined 18 major program areas such as tax, occupational safety and health, education, health, and housing; 13 government processes, including rulemaking, information resources management, forms clearance, and the role of Congress; and the cost and other burdens of paperwork for five segments of the economy. Almost 50 percent of the 770 recommendations of the committee are summarized in the report.

508. Lake Tahoe; a bibliography; its history, natural history and travel guides, by Maureen Trimm. Sponsored by Office of Education, DHEW. Washington, DC, November 1977. 46p. ED 149787.

The Lake Tahoe region of California and Nevada is an area that is under intensive federal, state, regional, and local study. This bibliography is a selective listing of 258 monographs and 58 maps which will assist scholars in obtaining a historical perspective of the region. The monographs are arranged alphabetically by author, followed by title, imprint, and date of publication. Maps are arranged alphabetically by region, followed by locale, scale, and size. Holdings symbols which refer to libraries in the Sierra Libraries Information Consortium, a bi-state cooperative of 25 California and Nevada academic, public, and special libraries are included for both types of materials.

509.   Pelly Bay, NWT; profile of a cooperative community, by
        Kenneth D. Jensen.   April 1974.   32p.   ED 149900.
        The development of Arctic Canada's resources has his-
torically been guided by two contrasting administrative approaches:
one favoring the free play of profit motives in a laissez-faire market economy and the other the coordination of development through
formalized government planning.   In both approaches, Eurocanadians
are the dominant figures, while Eskimos are depressed and subservient.   Against this background, a third approach to development is
emerging--the Arctic cooperative movement.   This movement aims
to encourage Eskimos to participate directly in the development of
their communities.   Pelly Bay, an isolated Eskimo community on
Simpson Peninsula, joined the Arctic cooperative movement in 1966.
The coop's first priority is to satisfy the immediate, basic needs of
the community for an Eskimo-owned retail store and for a producers'
coop to encourage local industry.   Today, its program is one of the
most ambitious of the Arctic coops involving tourism, large-scale
commercial fishing, and air transport.   At present, every family is
a member of the coop, and all decisions are made through the elected board of directors and executed by the coop manager and his
staff.   To date, coop ventures have been successful; community
morale is high and coop revenues continue to increase.   Yet, local
initiative is often curtailed by poor communication between the vil-
lage and the myriad of government agencies regulating Northern development.

510.   Garner Ted Armstrong; the guile that begets, by Richard L.
        Weaver, II.   1978.   27p.   ED 150652.
        This article analyzes the rhetorical message of Garner
Ted Armstrong, leader of the World Church of God, and attempts
to explain his church's financial success and audience appeal in terms
of this broadcast message.   Each message is specifically organized
to deceive the audience through the following strategy: (1) gain attention by using shock statements or by arousing guilt; (2) create
an image of suspense or intrigue; (3) hold audience interest by appearing knowledgeable; (4) convince the listener that the answers for
all questions can be found in the Bible; (5) move the listener to action by offering specific literature that has these Biblical answers.
The article states that Armstrong's overt and purposeful declaration
of an objective and rational approach, while actually engaging in a
subjective and emotional address, is unethical, but responsible for
his overwhelming success.   Quotations from Armstrong's broadcasts
and annotated footnotes are included.

511.   Consciousness raising and Christian worship as small group
        communication, by Gary Burns.   Paper presented at the
        Annual Meeting of the Central States Speech Association,
        April 1978.   29p.   ED 153280.
        Consciousness raising movements and charismatic Chris-
tian worship display an extraordinary degree of rhetorical similar-
ity.   This four-part paper outlines the likenesses of the two groups, indicates where they differ, and focuses on the social and political

dimensions of consciousness raising. The first section lists the following similarities between the charismatic movement and consciousness raising: use of some of the same specialized words or labels, standardized responses to questions, rationalization of persuasion as good for the target person, concentration on disclosure of feelings, and polarization, which involves constant exposure to group doctrine. The section on the social dimensions of consciousness raising asserts that the process developed as a response to widespread needs for satisfying interpersonal communication and has become the exclusive property of the radicals. This response, according to the final section of the paper, involves confrontation as an extension of communication. The resulting radicalization displays a rhetoric of self-persuasion and a group-centered nature that is characterized by the prevalence of fantasies and myths, frustrated attitudes, and the search for relationships.

512.   Public relations in the 1980's, by Richard E. Wiegand. January 1976.   33p.   ED 153225.
       Approximately 70,000 to 100,000 people work in public relations today in the United States. This document discusses the field of public relations at present and the view for 1980 as seen by practitioners and educators. The thesis is advanced that practitioners, educators, and students must raise the field to greater professional heights in order to improve its quality and gain acceptance in more organizations. The following topics are discussed, among others: definitions of public relations, the background of current practitioners, new roles, the issue of professionalism, the educational base, the need of businesses for public relations, accreditation and professional improvement, and the future of public relations. A bibliography is appended.

513.   Citizen participation. Washington, DC, Community Services Administration, DHEW, January 1978.   147p.   ED 151295.
       This booklet identifies citizen participation requirements for more than 300 federally assisted programs administered by 18 departments, agencies, and commissions. It has been published in response to the government's desire to assist citizens in learning how, when, and where to go to participate in and influence the governmental decisions which affect their lives, as well as to improve government efficiency at all levels. The booklet is also designed to assist state and local officials in understanding the mandated requirements for citizen participation by providing a summary of those requirements. Each federal program is listed by its authorizing agency; is designated by title and number assigned to it in the Catalog of Federal Domestic Assistance; contains a program description and describes the requirements for citizen participation. Agencies listed include: ACTION; Departments of Agriculture, Commerce, HEW, Housing and Urban Development, Interior, Justice, Transportation, and Labor; Environmental Protection Agency; National Science Foundation, and others. Use of the Federal Register and consultation with the responsible agency are recommended. Also included are samples of frequently occurring problems and possible solutions for

bringing about effective citizen participation, techniques and tools to enhance citizen involvement, plus suggestions for evaluating the process. A glossary and bibliography conclude the booklet.

514. Citizen participation in the public schools, by Robert H. Salisbury. Sponsored by the National Institute of Education. May 1977. 305p. ED 153161.

This report analyzes data resulting from a survey of school participants in six St. Louis area districts. It attempts to discover what motivates people to participate in the public schools, and what effect such participation has on them. Findings include: (1) the more people participate, the greater the impact of that participation will be on them; (2) the greater the impact, the more likely it is to be in the realm of personal self-development; (3) people who participate in one kind of activity do not necessarily participate in another; (4) the type of participation can be substantially independent of the amount (e.g., a supportive activist may spend as much time as a purposive activist, but he spends it doing different things for different reasons); and (5) citizen participation in its usual forms has relatively little direct effect on educational policy.

515. Ancient Greek and Roman rhetoricians; a biographical dictionary, edited by Donald C. Bryant. New York, Speech Association of America, 1968. 113p. ED 114889.

This biographical dictionary contains over 200 entries on Greek and Roman rhetoricians. The compilation omits persons who were exclusively performers or composers unless they were also theorists, critics, authors of treatises or textbooks, or teachers of speech. Bibliographical notes are attached to particular biographies rarely and only for special purposes. Generally, the standard biographical compendia and the particular sources relevant to each rhetorician have been drawn upon for the entries. Included in this dictionary are such people as Acylas, Adrian, Antipater, Ariston, Aristophanes, Aristotle, Blandus, Celsus, Chrysippus, Cicero, Cleanthes, Corvus, Crates, Dion, Epicurus, Favorinus, Glycon, Hyperides, Isocrates, Lycon, Lysias, Menecles, Philo, Plato, Sedatus, Theophrastus, and Verginius Flavus.

516. Ancient Rome; the Latin teacher and life in the big city, by Edwin S. Ramage. 1976. 28p. ED 145724.

This paper attempts to answer the question of what life was really like in ancient Rome, with a view to using this kind of information as cultural background for teaching Latin language and literature. There were many problems associated with daily living in ancient Rome. Writings of some inhabitants of ancient Rome attest to the fact that these problems were very similar to those of most large cities today: overcrowding; poor urban planning; unemployment; housing shortage; traffic problems; noise and air pollution; sewage problems and danger from fire, flood, and falling buildings. Solutions to these problems and the resulting frustration of living in Rome included moving to the suburbs for the wealthy, welfare for the poor, and attempts at urban planning and decentralization by the government.

AUTHOR INDEX

SUBJECT INDEX